Making
Business Location
Decisions

Roger W. Schmenner

Fuqua School of Business
Duke University

Prentice-Hall, Inc., *Englewood Cliffs, New Jersey 07632*

Library of Congress Cataloging in Publication

```
Schmenner, Roger W., 1947-
    Making business location decisions.

    Bibliography: p.
    Includes index.
    1. Industries, Location of.  2. Factories--Location.
3. Industries, Location of--United States.  I. Title.
HD58.S347      658.2'1        81-22657
ISBN 0-13-545863-3            AACR2
```

Editorial production/interior design: Margaret McAbee
Manufacturing buyer: Ed O'Dougherty

Printed in the United States of America

10 9 8 7 6 5 4 3 2 1

PRENTICE-HALL INTERNATIONAL, INC., *LONDON*
PRENTICE-HALL OF AUSTRALIA PTY. LIMITED, *SYDNEY*
PRENTICE-HALL OF CANADA, LTD., *TORONTO*
PRENTICE-HALL OF INDIA PRIVATE LIMITED, *NEW DELHI*
PRENTICE-HALL OF JAPAN, INC., *TOKYO*
PRENTICE-HALL OF SOUTHEAST ASIA PTE. LTD., *SINGAPORE*
WHITEHALL BOOKS LIMITED, *WELLINGTON, NEW ZEALAND*

for Will and Andy

Contents

Preface

For many executives the choice of where to place their company's next increment of capacity is a step into the unknown. Indeed, for all but the very largest corporations the location decision is an infrequent occurrence, perhaps a once-in-a-career experience for the managers involved. It is no wonder, then, that location decisions are approached with as much trepidation as they are.

This volume is a guide for executives charged with evaluating the placement of a company's productive capacity. By calling on the experiences and thinking of managers, most from among the most important corporations in the nation, and by analyzing the characteristics of hundreds of actual location decisions taken within the last 10 years, this book seeks to guide and reassure those executives burdened with plant location decisions. It relates how many of America's leading corporations have tackled such decisions and assesses the character of the decisions they have made.

This book is more than a checklist of things to think about when choosing a new plant site. While the factors that can influence a site choice are discussed in detail, this book takes a broader view of location decision-making. Before any new site can be selected, the company must determine whether space is really needed and whether that space ought to be constructed as an expansion of an already existing plant, as a new stand-alone facility, or as a relocation of existing capacity. These, in themselves, are important considerations that are inexorably intertwined with the more specialized selection of a suitable site. They, too, merit analysis, and the arguments that advocate one over the other are scrutinized in these pages.

More than this, the book investigates how different kinds of corporations have organized themselves for deciding capacity and location questions. After all, for many managers, the anxiety of the decision rests as much with organizational issues as it does with the criteria that should be used to evaluate capacity and sites.

The book also examines how companies have altered the location of their productive capacity over the course of the 1970s. Using information from two painstaking private "censuses"—one that covered 410 of the Fortune 500 companies nationwide and the other of all manufacturing within the Cincinnati metropolitan area—recent trends in location are documented and reviewed. These private censuses permit the separate identification of on-site expansion and contraction, plant openings and closings, plant acquisitions and divestitures, and relocations—which is simply not possible with Census of Manufactures or other government-collected data. For example, this book is able to discuss the mechanisms by which Sunbelt manufacturing has grown or that of older central cities has declined. Industry breakdowns are accomplished as well.

Although fundamentally a guide for business executives, this volume also has a good deal to say to representatives of the public sector. Business location decisions cannot help but be intertwined with government at every level. The attraction and retention of jobs in a state or locality is a high priority for many government officials, and the mechanisms by which such attraction and retention can be accomplished are eagerly sought. By documenting the use of public policies of various kinds, this book substantiates the importance—or unimportance—of key government policies and makes suggestions that are better attuned to actual business location decision-making.

I am deeply grateful to the scores of company managers who spent hours educating me about industry location and to those hundreds of managers who diligently completed the questionnaires I mailed to them. Without such generous cooperation this book could not have been written. I wish I could acknowledge by name all those who contributed, but the list is simply too long. I can acknowledge my debt to the funding sources which have unwritten my research: The Associates of the Harvard Business School; the Office of Economic Research, Economic Development Administration, U. S. Department of Commerce; the Office of Policy Development and Research, U. S. Department of Housing and Urban Development; and the Center for Law and Economic Studies of the School of Law at Columbia University. Of course, the findings and conclusions of the research sponsored by these groups are my responsibility and do not purport to reflect their views. Two of these research grants were administered through the Joint Center for Urban Studies of MIT and Harvard University, which proved to be an ideal research haven.

Special friends and colleagues have influenced me in profound ways over the years and their impact on me colors many of the pages of this volume. Robert A. Leone, Robert H. Hayes, and Wickham Skinner have all played important roles in my intellectual development in these matters. John R. Meyer merits particular recognition for he helped steer me to this topic years ago, has counseled me on it countless times, and has monitored my progress over the years.

I have been aided as well by a research staff that took great pains with the huge task of managing, entering, checking, and adjusting the data that lie at the heart of this book. Principal research assistance was provided by Betty Forsythe, Lou Loustalot, Richard Saltman, Hope Schlorholtz, Holly Snyder-Ra'anan, and Marian Stevens. Diana Koricke and Denise Saltman also devoted hours of their time to the research. Marilyn Shesko helped me countless times witn computer snafus, and Karen Atkins and Elaine Ciccarelli Mossmann provided top-notch secretarial support.

ROGER W. SCHMENNER

Introduction: some perspective on the location decision

This book addresses the domestic plant location decisions of American manufacturing companies. It is fundamentally concerned with how and why change occurs in the geographic deployment of manufacturing plant and equipment. The book views the location decision from the business executive's perspective. Its objectives include business policy: helping executives cope with a costly, non-standard decision that occurs irregularly during a career—and public policy: how governments aid, and perhaps influence, manufacturing location decisions and start-ups.

It is important to recognize at the outset that the location decision involves more than selecting a particular site. Industry location should not be studied in isolation because it is merely one segment in a series of decisions which, taken together, determine the composition, character, and change of a company's manufacturing capacity. To my mind, one must first have a firm grasp of *why* a company may need new capacity, and *what* that new capacity should do for it, before plunging into the selection of an appropriate site. This book addresses itself to the larger decision process of planning new capacity.

Elements in the Location Decision Process

In broad terms, the four main elements that comprise this larger decision process include:

(1) *Recognizing future capacity shortfalls or surpluses*

Naturally, the first step that management must take before changes to capacity are made requires evaluation of the adequacy of a company's existing capacity over time. Such evaluation must bring together estimates of (a) future sales of existing and planned products, usually by year and often by geographic area, and (b) future production capacities, given plausible ranges of the product mix that will be demanded and assignments of production responsibilities to each plant. Incorporated into these capacity estimates should be any previously decided capacity adjustments which may still be in the process of design or execution.

(2) *Considering all of the short-term and long-term options for remedying any recognized capacity shortfall or surplus*

There are generally a host of short-term and long-term means of adjusting capacity given company agreement on the size and time pattern of anticipated capacity shortfalls or surpluses. Most commonly a company must deal with capacity shortfalls, but surplus capacity arises in almost all companies from time to time. Coping with surpluses is difficult and can involve agonizing decisions about closing down established plants.

Plant closings are the topic of Chapter 5. Most discussion in Chapters 1-4 deals with expansion. This section restricts its attention to the expansion of capacity.

In coping with a time pattern of increasing capacity shortfalls, the menu of remedies may include the following items.

Possible short-term capacity measures

(a) Changes in production control and scheduling that are often undertaken to increase capacity:

- Scheduling overtime for the existing workforce.
- Scheduling second- or third-shift production, or bringing in temporary workers.
- Resequencing production runs or narrowing the product line so as to group "like products" together, eliminating time-consuming machine or organizational setups, improving productivity, and reducing confusion on the factory floor.
- Evening out the production rate and holding more finished goods inventory (a "level" production strategy) rather than producing to "chase" demand and holding little or no inventory.
- Reducing the incidence of parts shortages and their resulting inefficiencies by adding inventories (raw materials and/or work-in-process) or by trying to manage suppliers better.
- Rebalancing an assembly line by adding more workers and narrowing the job content of each worker on the line.

(b) Subcontracting

Possible longer-term capacity measures

(a) Adding more or newer equipment to existing space to break any existing bottleneck.
(b) Expanding on-site to enlarge existing buildings to accommodate more equipment, personnel, or warehousing.
(c) Changing the process technology, often making it more capital-intensive and smoother flowing from raw materials through to finished goods.
(d) Sharing underutilized space at another company plant, perhaps not even in the same division.
(e) Purchasing or leasing an existing building at another site.
(f) Constructing a new plant at another site to supplement existing capacity.
(g) Relocating an existing plant to a new site and improving its operation by so doing.
(h) Acquiring an existing company in the industry, possibly one with excess capacity.

Given a particular capacity shortfall, some of these possible remedies may be more attractive than others. However, it usually takes a good deal of study to isolate and support that option, or more probably, that mix of options which best satisfies the time pattern of anticipated capacity shortfalls at a reasonable cost.

(3) *If a new site is desired, deciding where, in general, it should be*

The evaluation of the remedies to combat a capacity shortfall may result in recommendation and approval for a completely new plant site. In most multiplant companies, particularly the largest, the search for a suitable site nearly always commences with a decision about a general region or area of the country that is most appropriate. Often, this decision is implicit in the study and evaluation of the capacity options themselves, but many times, the company is extraordinarily free to roam multi-state areas of the U.S. searching for good plant locations.

(4) *Actual site selection*

Once a general area for any new plant location is decided upon, the particular town and then site that best meet the company's needs are sought, closely analyzed, and the decision ultimately made and enacted.

Much of the rest of this book deals in greater detail with the four elements that constitute the location decision and illustrates how typical manufacturing companies attack each stage.

This Book's Background

This work is the culmination of three related research projects which spanned the last five or six years. These research projects are described in greater detail in the appendix to this book. Suffice it here to mention the sources of the insights and data that are presented in the chapters which follow. The research projects undertaken concentrated on successively larger geographic areas and successively larger companies. The first project investigated industry location around the Cincinnati metropolitan area during the first half of the 1970s. While a number of large companies were interviewed, and several large plants were surveyed, much of any examination of a metropolitan area must necessarily address small plants. The second project eliminated the examination of the smallest plants (those under 20 in employment) and widened its geographic scope to encompass most of New England. The third, and by far the most ambitious, project addressed the domestic location decisions of 410 of the nation's largest manufacturers, drawn almost exclusively from the Fortune 500 list.

The information and data analyzed by these projects were developed in three distinct ways:

(1) *Interviews.* In the course of my research, I interviewed 85 companies about their plant location decision-making (18 in Cincinnati, 7 in New England, and 60 other very large corporations in major cities across the country). These company interviews were supplemented with about 15 others, involving industrial realtors, developers, public officials, and location consultants.

(2) *Privately accomplished plant "censuses."* Using data from various sources, and employing as much cross-checking and company confirmation as possible, plant lists for certain geographic areas or for selected companies were compiled both for an early 1970s year and a later 1970s year. Each year's entry included information on location, employment, the product manufactured, and company and division affiliation. By matching entries across years, the status of each plant as new, closed, stayed-put, relocated, and the like was established. These data represent the best source of plant location information publicly available. Moreover, the across-years match provides special information which lies beyond the capabilities of the Census of Manufactures, even if its confidentiality restrictions were lifted.

(3) *Plant-specific survey returns.* Using the plant census as an address list, detailed surveys were sent to thousands of plants around Cincinnati, New England, and nationally within the Fortune 500 group. In some instances plants of all types were surveyed, while in others only plants that demonstrated certain characteristics were surveyed. In all, about 1,600 plants returned usable survey responses which provide statistical support for many of the insights gleaned from the interviews.

This book, then, can be viewed as a melding of these distinct, but related, research projects and data sources.

This Book's Organization

The first two chapters present the implications of this succession of research both for business and for public policy. Chapter 1 concentrates on business decision-making conclusions and offers some advice to manufacturers who are considering plant siting or relocation. Chapter 2 performs the analogous function for state and local officials, who sit on the other side of the plant site decision process. The analysis behind these conclusions, along with further recommendations, occupies the book's remaining chapters. The third chapter offers numerous examples of location decisions, drawn mostly from the Fortune 500, and scrutinizes the decision processes of some of the nation's largest manufacturers. Chapter 4 documents what manufacturers have actually decided about the pattern of their production capacity. The fifth, and final, chapter focuses on the vexing decisions associated with the closing of established plants. The appendices include a detailed description of the study designs for the underlying research.

1

Making Better Capacity and Location Decisions: advice to manufacturers

As the introduction suggests, a manufacturing location decision should be viewed as a series of three smaller but interrelated judgments: (1) recognizing when a projected capacity shortfall is serious enough to merit the construction of additional manufacturing space; (2) considering whether new space ought to be erected on an existing site, an entirely new facility developed, or an existing plant relocated to a new site; and (3) deciding where any new facility ought to be located.

These judgments are interrelated in two major ways: (i) the managers making them can be and frequently are the same and must work within an established organizational structure, and (ii) the issues that argue for one course of action over another can and do overlap these three judgments. Accordingly, business policy can be improved both by better organizational structures for the location decision process and by a firmer grip on the issues which should control the choice.

Ad Hoc Versus Formal Capacity Planning

The manner in which potential capacity shortfalls or surpluses are officially recognized differs significantly across corporations. Within the past decade or two, most large corporations in the United States have adopted some formal planning system, which, among other things, is established for the purpose of recognizing potential shortfalls or surpluses. To understand how formal business planning and the business location decision are connected, it is helpful to review what most corporations did prior to formal planning and what many, particularly smaller, corporations still do.

Ad hoc recognition of future shortfalls and surpluses

The responsibility for recognizing potential shortages or excess capacity has rested traditionally with the senior operating managers of a business unit. These plant managers or, more often, division general managers or presidents of subsidiary companies, are generally aware of current capacity utilization in the plant or plants for which they are responsible. They are usually well-informed about sales trends and marketing innovations, especially if their division/plant/company is evaluated as a profit center (which includes revenue plus cost responsibility) rather than as a cost center only. Frequently they can supply a fountain of ideas for remedying shortfall situations.

Under this traditional approach, the initiative for proposing capacity expansion rests almost exclusively with these senior managers, who can propose projects at any time. Those managers sitting over profit centers (particularly, division general managers), then champion their proposals through even more senior levels of corporate management, to the Board of Directors, which has final approval of all capacity adjustments of any long-term consequence. This traditional ad hoc procedure relies heavily on informal communication among senior division and corporate managers. Differences of opinion on any proposal tend to be voiced informally and early; if differences persist, any "battles" over a proposal are usually waged over the formal request for capital appropriation when it is submitted to the Management Committee (the most senior policy-making group of the corporation) or to the Board of Directors itself.

While this ad hoc procedure of managing capacity change has served a host of companies well, its smooth working depends on attentive, well-informed, far-sighted division management; a well-oiled network of corporate communication; and an adaptable staff, usually at the division level, to prepare and follow through on project proposals. If any of these factors is missing, an ad hoc procedure is likely to falter. Moreover, the informality of this approach places heavy weight on the track record of any proposal champion. Here the ability of a division head to guide his own capacity proposal through to final approval by the Board of Directors is often determined by his past history with similar projects, and not necessarily by the merits of the project proposed.

Formal business planning systems

Partly in response to the potential pitfalls of ad hoc techniques, many large corporations have instituted formal business planning procedures which are explicitly designed to make tasks like the recognition of future capacity shortfalls as systematic as possible. While there exists great diversity in the actual systems these corporations have adopted, most share these six features:

- The corporate plan is targeted for a multiyear period, usually 5 years, although many capital-intensive companies use a 10-year horizon, whereas companies which are dependent on consumer tastes or fashion use a 3-year horizon.
- The planning exercise forces the marketing and production functions to confront each other on strategic issues. Typically the marketing group is required to project market share, sales by product for each year, and to forecast the impact of new products, new market development projects, and competitive reactions. The production group is typically required to specify how and when capacity and/or new process technology can be developed to support marketing's plan. Competitive market forces and company strengths/weaknesses are also reviewed as part of a formal plan.
- Not only are marketing and production forced to confront one another, but it is also expected that they will strike some balance in their positions where both can feel comfortable.
- The production data sought usually include plant-specific information, and, in the best plans, capacity shortfalls are considered in terms of square footage, workforce, and equipment needs.
- While the business plan for the fifth year out is understandably sketchy, the plan for the forthcoming year serves as the basis for the next budget and can be viewed as a performance contract between the corporation and its divisions. The plans for years 2–4 usually show graduated levels of detail.
- The planning exercise itself, as well as its review and approval by upper management, frequently serves as the arena for any battles over controversial proposals. Sometimes this early skirmishing clears the field of problems and renders the capital appropriations request procedure even more of a rubber stamp than it would be under the informal ad hoc approach.

Comparison of ad hoc and formal planning

A typical ad hoc scenario might have division management preparing and championing a specific proposal to remedy a perceived shortage of capacity. The shortage may have been recognized after repeated increases in sales or because it completes a move toward more vertical integration. The proposal may have been simmering with division management for some time or it may have been a recent perception. Senior corporate management would have been told informally of the proposal-in-process beforehand, but frequently not all that much beforehand.

In contrast, a typical formal planning scenario would be rather more deliberate. The division production management's initial suspicion of a potential capacity shortage, triggered perhaps by a review of marketing's forecast over the 5-year planning horizon, would be written into the plan for the fourth or fifth year out. Some rough estimate of the shortfall expected and the necessary investment in plant space and capital to cover it would be included. In successive years, as the marketing function's forecast is confirmed and adjusted, the operating division would add increasing detail and accuracy to its capacity shortfall and would suggest ways to remedy it. These remedies would be costed out with increasing detail and

care over time but usually under the assumption that the corporation as
a whole has enough capital, or access to capital, to assure that the investment
project would be funded. Frequently, the incentive in a formal planning
process is to introduce a project early so that its "inevitability" is built up
over the years of review. In some companies approval comes easier that
way.

These typical scenarios can be characterized as "bottom-up" recognition of production capacity shortfalls. Most new investment projects begin
when plant and division managers begin to register some discontent about
the extent or nature of their present capacities; however, some such projects
are initiated by the uppermost layers of corporate management. These
projects, while fewer in number, are significant in themselves for they usually represent major changes in manufacturing. A substantially different
product line, a new manufacturing complex, the closing of a major facility,
as well as acquisitions and divestitures are all likely to be suggested by the
highest levels of corporate authority. Studies of such top-down suggestions
are generally made by the corporate staff, and not by division managers
who become involved almost exclusively in division-sponsored proposals.

Of course, the corporate staff may become involved in the "bottom-
up" proposals as well. The extent to which the corporate staff does become
active in such situations depends on several things: the detail and certainty
with which division operating managers broach their proposals, the
strength of their arguments, the degree to which the initial proposals could
affect other corporate operations, and the degree to which the initial proposal could benefit from outside and/or expert advice.

Ad hoc and formal business planning systems have been described
here as mutually exclusive alternatives for recognizing future capacity shortfalls or surpluses. While most large companies follow either one or the
other, many other companies allow both to coexist. In such companies, the
nominal system is formal business planning, but exceptional cases can be
brought up outside of the formal plan without provoking too many raised
eyebrows from senior corporate management or pointed questions as to
why such proposals had not been incorporated into the division's business
plan. In most instances, permitting both ad hoc and formal planning to
coexist provides more flexibility within the company and enables it to react
to fast-moving or unpredictable circumstances. Frequently, marketing can
grossly underestimate sales which puts production in a situation where
speedy capacity adjustments must be made. In other instances, an ad hoc
approach outside of the maintrack formal plan, if not abused, can serve
to spotlight particular proposals which, so their champions reason, might
not get the attention they deserve had they been buried in the formal
business plan.

Companies which adopt ad hoc versus formal planning systems

My interviewing of 60 Fortune 500 companies in diverse industries and locations, while not exhaustive, does permit some generalizations about the types of companies which recognize their capacity shortfalls through ad hoc procedures and those which employ formal business planning.

Of the companies interviewed, nearly three-fifths rely predominately on formal business planning to isolate shortfalls in capacity. About one-sixth rely exclusively on the ad hoc procedure. The remaining one-quarter of the interviewed companies mix ad hoc and formal planning, usually by letting some proposals be considered outside of an established formal plan. A sizable number of the companies that allow combination planning do so in order to expedite responses to fast-breaking opportunities. These opportunities may surface as unexpectedly rapid sales increases, as newly feasible products, or as acquisitions. In many of these same companies, top-down suggestions that involve additional capacity are likely to trigger an ad hoc corporate analysis rather than a divisional review and modification of an existing business plan.

While any distinctions are not completely clear cut, there appear to be discernible trends between companies that use formal planning predominantly and those that use ad hoc procedures predominantly. In general, the more capital-intensive the industry, the more likely that future capacity shortfalls are recognized through a formal business planning system, often with a horizon of 10 rather than 5 years. Among the industries characteristic of this approach are petroleum refining, primary metals, transportation equipment, and much of the chemicals industry (especially industrial chemicals). In addition, some heavy machinery manufacturers and many food processing companies with national distribution channels employ formal business planning exclusively. The speed and flexibility of an ad hoc system are simply not required by such firms, primarily because the lead times necessary for acting on opportunities are so long for such capital-intensive companies that no opportunity can be fast-breaking; all must be deliberate. There are some apparent exceptions to this classification of course: pulp and paper companies, other chemicals companies, and other, notably regionally-strong, food processors. These companies are more apt to identify and analyze capacity shortages on an ad hoc basis, although they may have a nominal formal planning process.

At the other extreme, the kinds of companies that tend to employ predominantly ad hoc procedures include:

1. Conglomerate Corporations—These are composed of basically autonomous companies, divisions and subsidiaries, often in radically different industries.

The control these conglomerates exercise over their independent component companies is limited largely to financial controls. Within a conglomerate, member companies may have formal business plans of their own, but the major corporate control over capacity is often exercised through the capital appropriation request's chain of approval and not through a formal business plan review.

2. Agribusiness Cooperatives—These companies, owned by farmers who sell their products to the company and who buy the company's feeds, fertilizers, and other farm goods, are constantly on the alert for new business opportunities. The analysis of these opportunities and of the present operation's capacity shortcomings is thus often best left to an ad hoc approach.

3. Founder/Family-Controlled Companies—In these companies, control is generally so concentrated at the top that the more informal ad hoc system is likely to prevail.

Other companies follow an ad hoc approach to forecasting capacity shortfalls but they share no general characteristics. Likewise, companies that permit a combination of ad hoc and formal planning do not share common traits.

Table 1-1 categorizes the companies interviewed into the three major procedures employed in recognizing potential capacity shortfalls or surpluses: formal business planning systems, ad hoc procedures, and combination systems. The companies listed have approved their names for inclusion in this table. I should note, however, that this table is not intended to be a definitive classification, merely suggestive. Different managers in some of these companies would no doubt dispute this classification, disagreeing with the executive(s) with whom I met. Also the dynamics of the individual corporations may have led to recent changes not included here. This table is designed to provide some background and food-for-thought as to the advantages certain types of companies see for themselves in recognizing their potential capacity needs in different ways.

Should A New Plant Be Established?

As noted previously, capacity shortfalls can be made up in a variety of ways. The short-term measures—overtime, second or third shifts, inventory policies, modifications in production control, and subcontracting—are remedies usually taken by the division itself and do not require corporate clearance. Long-term measures—additional floor space, fundamental changes in production technology and the like—are the concern of corporate managers as well as division managers. In all of the companies that were interviewed, no matter how the need for a capacity change was recognized and regardless of how fomal the planning and study of alternatives, the final decision to expand on-site, to seek a new location, or to close an established facility was mutually agreed to by both the division and the

Table 1-1

Companies Representative of Various Procedures

for Identifying Capacity Shortfalls

Ad Hoc Procedures
American Standard
Crown Zellerbach
Oxford Industries
Perkin Elmer
RCA
(4 other companies)

Formal Business Planning

Alcoa	Lockheed
Anheuser-Busch	Motorola
Black & Decker	Pet
Brown Group	Phillips Petroleum
Burlington Industries	Pillsbury
Cities Service	Ralston Purina
Cluett, Peabody	Reliance Electric
Dart	Rockwell International
Del Monte	Texas Instruments
Du Pont	TRW
FMC	Union Carbide
General Foods	U.S. Steel
IBM	Westinghouse
Indian Head	Whittaker
Inland Steel	(7 other companies)

Combination of Formal Business Planning and Ad Hoc Procedures

Agrico Chemical Company (of the Williams Companies)
Beatrice Foods
Burroughs
Diamond Shamrock   Simmons USA
Gold Kist   Union Camp
Honeywell   United Technologies
Land O' Lakes   (2 other companies)
Levi Strauss
Martin Marietta

corporate managements. These companies recognized that both sets of executives must be satisfied with any decision of this magnitude.

This is not to say that there are not some fundamental differences of opinion in these matters. The points of view of division managers, especially plant managers, and of corporate managers, can be very different. Frequently, plant and division management lean toward on-site expansion more heavily than does higher level corporate management. The nature of the usual management evaluation systems helps to explain this. A typical plant manager is acutely conscious of the advantage of spreading plant and corporate overhead allocations over a sizable number of units of output. A plant manager is favorably evaluated for low overhead absorption rates and so lobbies for on-site expansion rather than a new location because this would yield more units of production for his plant and, in the short-run, less overhead allocation per unit produced. In like fashion, some division general managers tend to resist the establishment of new locations because their division's overhead is increased by so doing. Moreover, many managers believe that they can manage ever larger plant size effectively. Corporate level executives, from their experience and vantage point, know that increasing plant size is frequently an invitation to managerial chaos, and thus are more amenable to establishing new plant locations. Older managers are sometimes painfully aware of plants which in the past grew too large and complex and simply went out of control.

Whatever the final decision—on-site expansion or seeking a new site— the collaboration between senior division and senior corporate managers is generally informal, even when the study of the options has been a formal one. The decision may take years to reach but it is one that relatively few individuals are privy to and one that is informally accomplished.

Issues in the decision to expand on-site or off-site

Despite the informality of its resolution, the decision whether to expand on-site or whether to open a new plant is influenced by a host of factors. The decision process usually commences by giving first consideration to on-site expansion. Only if compelling problems with on-site expansion exist do manufacturers typically turn to opening a new plant or to relocating an existing one.

On-site expansion has some inherently attractive features; it is frequently the least costly way to add space. The land is already owned and construction costs are often lower if expansion merely entails knocking out a wall and building around an existing structure. This is especially true for facilities which have been planned, graded, and built with expansion in mind. Speed is another benefit of on-site expansion; a site search can be foregone and, more important in many instances, environmental permits can be secured more rapidly. Overhead expenses can be spread over more units of output, thus lowering unit costs, particularly when overhead services such as plant maintenance, utilities, personnel, engineering, accounting, purchasing, and so on can be extended to the added space with little or no expansion of the services themselves.

Also arguing for on-site expansion are the complications that companies foresee in splitting operations to accommodate a new plant. Often there are no easy product line divisions along which to separate operations, nor is there a ready separation of the stages of the production process itself. In many instances, as well, management ranks are deemed so thin as not to be able to supply the managers necessary to start up and sustain a new, separate plant.

While it is undeniably attractive in many respects, on-site expansion, particularly repeated on-site expansion, is fraught with some very real problems. For example, as more space is added on-site, the plant's layout usually makes less and less sense, primarily because such expansion is generally accomplished by shifting around only a portion of the plant at any one time. As a result, departments which were once side by side, and for good reason, become separated. This complicates materials handling and storage and is apt to foster more errors and delays than need be. Managers become isolated from one another and/or from the workers they oversee which weakens management effectiveness. In short, on-site expansion can frequently strain intra-plant transportation and communications, with negative consequences for product delivery and quality.

Inadvertently, staying at the same site often postpones the introduction of production process modifications. Old equipment is kept in use, old methods are followed, and the advantages of newer equipment and improved techniques are foregone with consequences for future costs and product innovation. This tendency can be exacerbated by inflexible labor-management relations, especially over time, which can erode productivity and flexibility by creating and sustaining work rules (usually special manning requirements). Debilitating restrictions sometimes occur as a result of past concessions to labor, thought to be unimportant, which later return to haunt a management that needs to alter its operations for greater effectiveness.

On-site expansion usually requires that more workers, and, often, more products, be managed. Such an expansion of responsibilities can frustrate smooth operations. The existing cadre of managers may be asked to supervise more than they are capable of, thus lessening the attention certain problems should receive. With more products and output from the same plant, decisions about the levels, composition, and uses of inventories become more difficult. Decisions about production control—what to produce and when, and how to sequence it through the plant—become vastly more complex as well, just when the cost accounting system, for the same reasons, is becoming more arbitrary and less helpful. With more products in the plant, management runs the risk of complicating supervision, inventory, and production control systems, and of placing demands on managers, workers, and systems which are incompatible. A plant previously focused on particular tasks and responsibilities may become unfocused and lose some competitive advantages. If the plant is not already organized, it becomes a more likely target for unionization and its complications.

Decision rules

The kinds of problems spawned by on-site expansion have not gone unnoticed by manufacturers. To guard against the traps they represent, companies have developed some informal decision rules to accompany their management senses about such situations.

The most prevalent of these informal decision rules involve plant size, usually stated in terms of employment. The decision rule, usually unwritten but nevertheless discussed and communicated within the corporation, generally states a maximum, or ceiling, for employment at any one plant, or at least, a level above which corporate authority is apt to feel increasingly uncomfortable. The ceilings themselves vary considerably, from about 300 on the low side to about 6000 on the high side, with most figures running between 500 and 1000 employees. The low-range figures are often those of companies in highly competitive, labor-intensive industries—apparel, shoes, many metal-working operations, and standard product assembly operations. The larger employment ceilings prevail in processing industries which are capital-intensive, some transportation equipment plants, and in electronics. Certain industries, like aerospace, have no ceilings at all on employment at any one site.

Most employment ceilings are stimulated by management's concern for possible confusion, lack of control, inflexibility, and unionization. Some, however, are related to community size. Many companies dislike being too big a presence in an area and having to shoulder much of the responsibility for its economic well-being. To avoid becoming too dominant in a community, several companies place informal employment ceilings on their plants at something like 3% or 4% of the population within commuting distance (for example, 20 miles). Other companies impose this constraint in reverse: realizing that a suitable new plant must be of a certain large size, they consider only areas of sufficient size to supply the required labor and yet constitute only 3%–4% of the area's population. For a few manufacturers, primarily those seeking lower wage workforces in out-of-the-way places, it is hard to escape being the dominant economic force in a community, although even then, plant size may be constrained by community size and the availability of labor.

A second informal decision rule that some corporations follow is that no plant which is unionized will be expanded on-site. This dictum is grounded in management's concern for maintaining productivity and flexibility at its facilities. There may be instances where unionized plants have been expanded modestly for some over-riding reason, but major expansions are not often permitted at unionized facilities. In these cases, new plant openings are more prevalent; often new locations in right-to-work states are sought. The unionization of existing facilities in right-to-work states is less than in other states, and new plants are even less frequently unionized in right-to-work states. However, the margins (44% to 57%, and 14% to 29%, respectively) by which these facts are true are not as great as may be commonly believed. Companies can expect to open and maintain non-union plants in other than right-to-work states and they may unnecessarily constrain themselves by insisting on plant sites in right-to-work states.

Still other informal decision rules concern themselves with how product lines at existing facilities should be separated to guard against some of the traps of repeated on-site expansion. For companies with well-established production processes, the newer plants are typically assigned mature products, with relatively few engineering changes contemplated and little need for sustained engineering or management troubleshooting. Such an assignment of product responsibility often eases plant start-up and permits the design and dedication of the process to the high volumes which characterize mature products. In other companies, generally those enjoying rapid growth and/or a high level of research and development, there may be no mature or high volume product. In such cases, the new plant is assigned some new, volume-expanding products, and becomes a focal point for the research and engineering innovation that so often leads to success in such markets.

Multiplant strategies

Another important class of informal decision rules deals with the "charters" of a company's plants and how a proposed remedy for a capacity shortfall fits into the established pattern of plant charters, or what might be called the multiplant manufacturing strategy of the company. Most multiplant manufacturing strategies are consistent within a corporation's operating divisions and are designed to delineate plant responsibilities clearly. Most manufacturers have found over time that a clean separation of responsibilities and a set of consistent and stable demands on each plant leads to smoother, more effective operations. Within any operating division, one of four multiplant manufacturing strategies is likely to prevail.

PRODUCT PLANT STRATEGY   Under this multiplant strategy, the division's array of product responsibilities are divided among plants, so that one, or a few plants produce a designated product for distribution everywhere within the division's domestic market area. This involves high volume items which are anchored to a particular location because of natural resource constraints—food packaging (canning, frozen foods). It relates to products that can be separated by model (size, features, raw materials) where no single model is so high volume relative to the industry that it can be considered a commodity—measuring and scientific equipment; industrial and farm equipment; appliances; some electronics; most apparel; textiles; some metal fabrication.

MARKET AREA PLANT STRATEGY   Under this multiplant strategy, the division's domestic market area is divided among plants, so that a single plant produces most, or all, of the division's product line but only for distribution to a specified region surrounding it. This strategy involves those commodity and near-commodity items that are widely distributed and because of competition are sensitive to transportation costs—beverages, staple foods, some steel, many paper products, glass, glass and metal containers, oil refining, some chemicals, some furniture.

PROCESS PLANT STRATEGY   Under this multiplant strategy, segments of the full production process are assigned to separate plants. This may keep certain technologies "pure" and may enable economies of scale or more efficient loading of special equipment. A process plant strategy often has some plants acting as "feeders" of components to a final assembly facility. This affects complex products—automobiles and other transportation equipment, many computers, machine tools. It applies to vertically integrated industries one leg of which may be tied to natural resources or energy—aluminum, some forest products. It involves specialized operations, one or more parts of which are susceptible to significant scale economies—shoes, some apparel, some chemicals.

GENERAL-PURPOSE PLANT STRATEGY   Under this multiplant strategy, it is deliberate policy to maintain plants which can be assigned any number of responsibilities—product, market area, process, or a combination—for varying lengths of time. These plants are valued for their flexibility rather than for their stability of products, markets, or production process segments. This strategy affects Department of Defense suppliers—aerospace, shipbuilding. It also applies to consumer package goods companies which market products that have short lives or those that are highly sensitive to advertising or consumer tastes.

Further insight into the variations in plant charters by industry and industrial characteristics can be gained by referring to Table 1-2, which displays the percentages of selected industry groups that fall within the four multiplant strategies mentioned. This table also gives a sense of the prevalence of each strategy, at least for those plants which are altering capacities through on-site expansion, new plant opening, or relocation.

Table 1-2 supports many of the industry examples given above. For example, the product plant strategy is most common among labor rate sensitive industries (textiles, apparel, furniture, leather, consumer electronics), general machinery/transportation equipment industries, and high technology industries. These industries typically are not commodity pro-

Table 1-2

Plant Charters by Industry Group
(Entries are percentage of plants with that charter)

Industry Group

Plant Charter	Agriculture Tied	Market Sensitive	Forest Tied	Labor Rate Sensitive	Heavy Chemicals /Oil/ Rubber	Specialty Chemicals/ Metal	Heavy Metals	Industrial Machinery/ Transportation Equipment	High Technology	All Industry
Product Plant	30	25	43	83	65	54	58	80	73	58
Market Area Plant	65	70	50	11	21	38	33	8	3	31
Process Plant	5	4	0	6	9	8	8	8	19	9
General Purpose Plant	0	1	7	0	5	0	0	4	5	3
Plants Responding in each industry group	20	77	14	18	43	13	12	74	63	334

NOTE: Definitions of each industry group—

•Agriculture-Tied = Some food processing (e.g., meat), tobacco.

•Market-Sensitive = some food processing (e.g., dairy), paper converting, printing, asphalt making, plastics fabrication, can making, miscellaneous manufacturing.

•Forest-Tied = Lumber, pulp and paper mills.

•Labor Rate-Sensitive = Textiles, apparel, furniture, leather, consumer electrical goods.

•Heavy Chemicals/Oil/Rubber/Glass = High volume chemicals, oil refining, rubber, stone/clay/glass/concrete.

•Specialty Chemicals/Metals = Specialty chemicals and drugs, some metal fabrication.

•Heavy Metals = Primary metals, some metal fabrication (e.g., structural).

•Industrial Machinery/Transportation Equipment = Most machinery, most transportation equipment.

•High Technology = Office equipment, computers, electronics, space vehicles, instruments.

13

ducers and can often identify particular products for separate production. The market area plant strategy is overwhelmingly popular with market sensitive industries [some food processing, paper converting, printing, asphalt making, plastics fabrication, can making, and miscellaneous manufacturing (Standard Industrial Classification code 39)]. It is popular also with most agriculture-tied and forest-tied plants in the sample, many of whose products are commodity or near-commodity items.

Process plant and general purpose plant strategies are much less popular among the plants sampled. The process plant is most popular with high technology companies, as expected, and with companies in industries like chemicals, metals, and equipment where the degree of vertical integration and scale economies can be substantial. The data offer little generalization about the general purpose plant strategy.

As this enumeration of the kinds of strategies suggests, there are a number of influences on plant charters which may, on their own, trigger new plant openings as opposed to on-site expansions. In a division which follows a market area plant strategy, for example, concern for transportation costs as the market area for the products grows can be persuasive evidence for a new plant opening. Since transportation is an important and controllable cost it is no surprise to find these companies monitoring such expenses diligently and using sophisticated, mathematical techniques to determine whether a new plant is the best way to add needed capacity and, if so, where it should be located. A variant of this theme is the company whose plant locations can be influenced by the demands of particularly large customers, as is the case sometimes with glass, metal, paper container or furniture manufacturers. In these companies, a geographic shift in the market may be reason enough to forsake on-site expansion in favor of the establishment of a new plant.

For the division pursuing a process plant strategy, influences on the desirability of vertical integration can affect the decision to build additional capacity on-site or off. As an example, a vendor (supplier) base around a particular facility that is consistently saturated with orders can be a persuasive reason for that facility to seek additional expansion elsewhere. Changing production technologies and/or changing production economics can also influence a choice of on-site expansion versus opening a new facility; the greater the attractiveness of increased vertical integration for those companies adopting a process plant strategy the greater the likelihood of a new plant being established.

And, for a number of divisions operating under a product plant strategy and anchored to locations because natural resources are there, any shift in resource availability is likely to induce more new plant openings than on-site expansions. Already mentioned is the opening of a new plant to produce either a mature or a new product line, thereby reducing the possibility of confusion at an existing facility.

In the general purpose plant strategy, what is frequently noteworthy is the abandonment of that strategy whenever the division need no longer cater to the whims of particular customers (for example, the Department of Defense). As a company diversifies away from particular customers, or as its product line becomes more standard and long-lived, determinedly single purpose facilities are often established to concentrate on cost reduction or some other competitive priority.

When opening a new plant or relocating the existing one is preferred

The foregoing pages have portrayed on-site expansion as the capacity increasing option that is considered first, is ordinarily preferred, but is fraught with some stubborn problems, particularly if expansion on-site has been a repeated practice. Remedies for these problems often take the form of new plant openings or plant relocations. Opening a new plant and relocating an existing one, however, are not substitutes for one another. One is a better remedy for certain of the problems with on-site expansion than is the other.

In general, opening a new plant is preferable if problems apparent at the existing plant involve product proliferation, workforce size, and meeting anticipated growth. The company that wishes to avoid chaos in the factory due to too many products in process, or to side-step possible workforce unionization, job bumping, depersonalization in the quality of work life, and so on, or to get a grip on rapid growth through careful management of multiplant strategy, generally favors opening a new plant. A new plant can exploit the latest production technology and the most sensible plant design. Its operating policies can be meshed carefully with the product(s) chosen for manufacture and the competitive priorities of cost, delivery, craftsmanship, which are attached to them, enabling a "focused" operation.

However, plant relocation is generally preferable if problems at the existing plant involve basic issues of production itself (poor plant layout, expensive/faulty materials handling, blocked adoption of new process technology, labor costs and/or work rules, the need to overhaul production and inventory control) and/or a lack of management depth. By relocating, the company can make a completely fresh start with the production layout, equipment, and systems required, while scrapping the old factory and much that went with it. A longer distance relocation may also save labor costs and related expenses.[1]

---

[1]An alternative to a longer distance relocation is the opening of a new plant coupled at about the same time with a significant reduction in the workforce level at the existing plant. This is sometimes done to avoid pension and other costs incurred when plants are closed. This compensating capacity adjustment is discussed further in Chapter 4.

Table 1-3 summarizes the relative advantages of new plant openings and relocations vis-a-vis expansion on-site.

Conducting a Business Location Search and Selection

Once the issue of on-site expansion versus new plant establishment has been resolved in favor of a new plant, a suitable new site must be sought. This section begins with a brief, stereotypical overview of the chief phases in location search procedures that most companies follow. Chapter 3 refines and details the different organizational forms which large companies have adopted for the search itself. The remainder of this section comments on organizational issues with the location decision process and offers some suggestions.

Phases of the location search

The chief phases of a typical location search involve these eight steps and in roughly this sequence:

1. The decision to seek a new site having been made, the division affected notifies those corporate staff members who may be involved in the selection of a new site and informs them of any desires the division has about a new plant location. The division personnel involved typically include the division general manager; the division's chief manufacturing manager, the chief engineer, the personnel manager; and a facilities coordinator (if one exists). The corporate staff executives contacted generally include the director of facilities planning (if one exists), director of manufacturing, director of central engineering, and/or director of real estate.

Often this notification of the corporate staff is more courtesy than necessary since the interested parties may already know of the new location from the formal business planning exercise as well as what was approved for inclusion in the plan. In some companies, a corporate staff member is the one who initiates contact with the division. In many companies, division/corporate staff contact is formally mandated by top management directive, and in still others, contact is expected and, if not pursued, may slow down the approval procedures for any recommendation made later.

2. A joint division-corporate staff team is assembled to study the matter (variations on this phase are discussed below) and basic information about the prospective plant is developed. The basic information about the plant may include the following estimates:

• Size (acreage of the site and square feet under roof)

• Product line(s) to be manufactured and production technology to be employed

• Labor force requirements (number of employees when plant operating at full capacity, skills, union/non-union desired, wage rates desired, shifts, number in office versus number in factory, manning plan for start-up)

Table 1-3

Relative Advantages of Branches and Relocations Vis-a-Vis Expansion On-Site

Problem Area	New Plant Opening	Plant Relocation
Plant layout and materials handling	Radical improvements possible. Some possibilities of improving old base plant as operations are placed in new one.	Radical improvements possible.
New process technology	New technology for plant opening possible; likely that base plant will keep same technology.	Scrapping of old plant, equipment, and methods possible; new technology can supplant it readily.
Production and/or inventory control	Can mean radical change to production control procedures and policies in new plant, though not much change to be expected for old plant. Inventories can build up.	Can mean radical changes in production and inventory control. Inventory levels more likely to be unaffected.
Managerial impact	Additional managers required to open and run plant opening. Staff demands increased to co-ordinate plant-to-plant interactions.	Old set of managers can generally run new plant without spreading themselves too thin.
Production proliferation	Can easily manage new products, especially if new plants are organized as product plants.	New products less easily managed.
Size of work force	Keeps work force levels at all plants under desired ceilings.	Little or no effect.
Financial burdens	Extra overhead demanded to cover more than one location, new plant start-up expenses.	Moving costs, new plant start-up expenses.
Ease of meeting future growth	Relatively easy. Geographic growth met best with new market area plants; product introductions with product plants; vertical integration with process plants.	Not easy. Shares many future capacity problems with on-site expansion alternative.

- Transportation needs (modes required, location of major customers and major supplies and the shipment sizes to/from each [so that the sensitivity of transport costs to location can be quantified])
  - Utilities needs (power, water, sewerage, natural gas, etc. requirements)
  - Environmental consideration (expected levels of air and water pollutants)
  - Nature of interaction with other company plants (Is new plant to be a satellite of an existing operation or not?)
  - Division views about desirable plant sites, especially whether metropolitan or rural areas should be sought

Likely candidates for the division-corporate staff team include:

From the division: director of manufacturing, chief plant engineer, personnel director, plant manager designate, and/or key staff people for each of these managers.

From the Corporate Staff: director of facilities planning, director of real estate, staff aide to the industrial relations director, staff aide to the director of engineering, staff member from the transportation/logistics department, staff member from the environmental affairs department, staff member from the tax department.

3. If it has not already been done, the engineering program for the new plant is split apart at this point from the location search itself, and both are pursued simultaneously. Informal communication exists between the two study groups of course, and when the actual site is chosen, engineering is brought in to analyze the effects of site topography, geology, and other local features on the design and engineering of the plant.

4. As its first task, the location study team generates a list of key criteria for the new plant's location. Critical influences for the business location decision may include markets, labor, supplies and resources, logistics, environmental features and regulations, and competitive presence and reaction. This leads to the adoption of an, often informal, "musts" list of conditions which have to be met at any new location and a "wants" list of desirable, but not necessary conditions which can be traded off against one another.

The "musts" list for a new location is likely to be highly individual to the corporation as well as to its industry. While many factors are apt to be considered, one or a few controlling concerns usually stand apart as absolutely essential to the new plant's ability to compete successfully and they may be very different from those pertaining to other rival corporations. The remaining factors are then relegated to a "wants" list with some rough priorities assigned to them.

5. The "musts" list generated is then used as the standard against which major regions of the U.S.A. are evaluated. By comparing the known attributes of particular regions against this list, those regions which make sense for the location of the proposed plant can be identified and supported.

For example, if market access is critical, and 50% of the market growth is expected on the East Coast with the remaining 50% scattered throughout the country, it makes sense for the corporation to seek a new location east of the Mississippi River. Similarly, if maintaining a non-union operation is viewed as essential, the right-to-work states in the South and in the plains states from North Dakota to Texas become very attractive.[2]

Frequently regions cannot be categorized so neatly. For instance, while the South has had lower wages traditionally than the Northeast, this is no longer as true as it was. Moreover, within any region there are pockets of lower wages and underemployment and these subregional, generally rural areas can be readily tapped by companies seeking lower wage rates as a key criterion.

6. Having developed a list of candidate regions, on either clear-cut or more arbitrary grounds, the location team begins to identify particular sites within those regions on which to locate the plant. Usually, time, expense, and inclination restrict the number of sites that are scrutinized rigorously by the location team and the corporate specialties such as environmental affairs or tax that are called in. A typical upper bound would be 25 sites thoroughly investigated; more likely, fewer than 10 would be subject to full scrutiny. Thus, the location team must identify and screen a potential region full of sites to select a more manageable number.

Two general means of identifying and screening sites are popular. One thrusts the burden of initial site search on entities outside of the corporation: state development agencies, railroads, electric power companies, location consultants, and various informal contacts. Discreet, sometimes anonymous contact at one or more of these entities is made and an outline of the particular needs for the plant is communicated. These entities are expected to return with a list of, typically, 5 to 15 candidate sites which might satisfy the company's criteria. It is then up to the location team to sort through the list of preferred sites to identify those most worthy of intensive investigation.

The other popular means of identifying sites is for the location team itself to screen the promising ones. In most cases, this means resolving to examine only a few metropolitan or rural areas, generally chosen on the basis of some particular criteria, such as metropolitan areas of more than 1.5 million population, or college towns of less than 50,000 population served by a particular railroad, or a non-union town of 50,000–100,000 population within a 2-hour radius of corporate headquarters by air with 3 or more flights a day between the two. Once a list of qualifying towns is developed, the list of particular sites is then refined through contacts with local development agencies, industrial realtors, developers, or similar people. The location team then sorts through this information for the sites they consider most promising.

7. Having screened the most promising sites, the location team is then charged with investigating them thoroughly. This ordinarily means compiling even more data about these sites, verifying it, and combining it into a form which can be used to compare one site against another.

At this point in the process, site visits are usually made. A good deal is known already about each contemplated location, so that the site visit is primarily a means to gather qualitative and subjective information and impressions about each location and to verify the information already gathered, much of it quantitative.

---

[2]The 20 "right-to-work" states are Alabama, Arizona, Arkansas, Florida, Georgia, Iowa, Kansas, Louisiana, Mississippi, Nebraska, Nevada, North Carolina, North Dakota, South Carolina, South Dakota, Tennessee, Texas, Utah, Virginia, and Wyoming.

The site visit provides:

• Information about the community and its government—the attractiveness of the area as a place to live and raise a family (especially important as a means of attracting managers and engineers) gleaned from riding around and talking to people about housing, schools, medical facilities, universities, cultural and recreational activities, and civic pride; and the attitude of local government entities toward industry and the means which it uses to assist local business operations.

• Information about the labor force—what area manufacturers and others say about prevailing wage rates, unionization in the area, worker attitudes, absenteeism, turnover, availability, and training.

• Information about the plant site itself—topography, geology, parking, area traffic, quality of roads in area, local public services (e.g., bus lines, fire protection ratings), utilities available, and the condition of any structures already on-site.

The information gathered earlier but verified by a site visit ordinarily includes:

- site price, option availability, and terms
- labor force statistics (population, unemployment, commuting patterns, wage rates)
- local and state tax rates and financing opportunities (industrial revenue bonds)
- state and federal environmental requirements
- transportation rates and service quality.

With all of this objective and subjective information in hand, the location team usually ranks the sites that remain in contention and may recommend that options be taken on the top one or two properties.

8. At this point the location decision almost invariably reverts to the division for which the additional capacity is being sought. That group must live with the new site, so it is the division general manager who ordinarily chooses the site from the team's recommended list, or who exercises a veto on the matter.

SITE APPROVAL   A site choice having been made, an option is taken on the land, and the division turns to supporting its choice formally through the upper tiers of management. This means completing the documentation of a formal capital appropriation request, much of the data for which has been accumulating over the course of the location search. Because the capital appropriation request deals with funds for building construction or purchase, as well as for the site itself, it is here where the engineering cost analysis joins with the location decision process to form a cohesive package to set before the company's Management Committee and its Board of Directors.

The typical capital appropriations request includes the following features:

• As formal a statement of the rationale for the plant as possible, which may have changed in subtle ways since the plant was first proposed.

- Marketing's sales projections for the product(s) the plant will produce.
- Cost estimates for one-time costs such as site acquisition and preparation, building construction or remodelling, equipment, labor recruitment and training, and manager/engineer relocations.
- Estimates of a construction schedule, a manning plan, and a start-up schedule and costs.
- Estimates of the cash flow of the plant for, say, the next 3 to 5 years and beyond, incorporating both one-time costs (mentioned above) plus ongoing revenues and costs, including labor costs and fringe benefits, transportation and materials costs, overhead expenses, inventories and other working capital needs, taxes, and maintenance.
- A net present value analysis of the proposal using the above figures.
- A discussion of the relative merits of the proposed plant and its site versus other capacity proposals and other plant sites seriously considered.

During the time it takes to argue for, amend, and approve the capital appropriations request, the site itself is verified to assure management that there are no "snakes under the rocks." A typical option length of several months (6 months is common) permits soil tests and other site-specific investigations to proceed, including any environmental impact statements and approvals needed. Any required detailed plant engineering that depends on the site's character can also be started at this time.

Once the project is approved by the Board of Directors and funds released, the option on the land is exercised, more detailed engineering is done, construction or remodelling is accomplished, and the plant is started up. Occasionally, start-up is preceded by some special labor force training (often in leased space) or by actual pilot plant operations (again, often in leased space) so that plant start-up can be as smooth as possible and the needed capacity brought on as soon as possible.

These steps, then, represent a basic description of the location search and decision. As mentioned, the numerous deviations from and refinements to this process are discussed in detail in Chapter 3. This description is meant as a touchstone for that discussion and for the analysis and suggestions that follow.

Organizing the location search

While most companies pass through location search and decision phases in more or less the same sequence, the ways in which they organize their searches vary markedly. The organizational schemes employed range from highly centralized, corporate analyses to very decentralized, division-based analyses with a number of different schemes in which division management and the corporate staff interact. Table 1-4 summarizes these different schemes; they are discussed more fully and with various company examples in Chapter 3.

Table 1-4

Anatomy of Company Location Search Organizations

Type of Organization	Key Characteristics
Centralized Organization Schemes	Location search initiated by corporate level managers and studied by corporate staff. Any affected division brought in to approve/concur.
(1) Large Corporate Group Study	Location search initiated by a senior management committee and studied by a staff group drawn from a variety of functions (e.g., real estate, planning, industrial relations, logistics, plant engineering, environmental affairs, energy management, corporate tax, governmental affairs). Study usually chaired by real estate or planning function. Studies generally frequent; study group may be a semi-permanent body. Studies can be very detailed and quite sophisticated in analysis. The division for which new location is sought usually has final selection rights, or at least veto power, over choice. Division responsible for supplying data on size, product, process technology, and other needs for the study. Final site selection, as against town choice, may be left to real estate function.
(2) Small Corporate Group Study	Location search initiated by the chief executive officer or by a small group of very senior managers. Study done by a small staff group usually tied to the business planning function and with CEO as the "client in mind." Analysis can be more informal than large group study and is more likely to reflect CEO's own views about desirable locations.
Joint Division/Corporate Interaction	Location search typically initiated by division and, at the least, championed by the division through the approval process. Study involves both corporate staff and division managers, although to widely varying extents.
(3) Staff-controlled	Division, after specifying needs of the new plant, more or less relinquishes location choice to a corporate staff executive who is then solely responsible for presenting a menu of location choices to division management for approval. Division often only has veto power over corporate staff ranking of potential sites.

22

Table 1-4 (continued)

(3) Staff-controlled (continued)	Corporate staff executive (the "chooser") generally very experienced and well-connected. Analysis can be markedly quantitative, almost always exhaustive in scope and geographic coverage. Analysis can include completion of the capital appropriations request itself.
(4) Staff-led	A team is assembled to study and recommend sites to the affected division. Majority of team comprised of corporate staff people but some on team (1 or 2 of 4 or 5 total) reside in division. Team chaired by corporate staff function, such as real estate, which makes all key contacts both inside and outside the corporation and controls pace of the study. Corporate staff often views itself as a "missionary" to the division, to lead the division through the uncertainties and complexities of the location decision. Analysis is generally quantitative and well-supported and may include significant portions of the capital appropriations request.
(5) Division Led	A team is assembled to study and recommend sites to the affected division, but the majority of the team is comprised of division people. Corporate staff representatives on team view themselves more as "technocrats." Division representative chairs team and arranges all key contacts inside and outside the corporation and sets pace of the study. Division alone responsible for capital appropriations request. Corporate staff usually called in as a matter of course or may have corporate mandate to participate.
(6) Division-controlled	Division totally responsible for site selection and plant start-up. The team assembled is a division one, which invites selected corporate staff people to participate to a very limited degree or which must provide certain information or check out certain matters with the corporate staff. The team's responsibilities often include more than site selection, often including engineering and construction oversight, workforce training, and plant start-up. A plant

Table 1-4 (continued)

(6) Division-controlled (continued)	manager-designate may be named early on to direct the team and lead it through the plant start-up phase.
<u>Decentralized Organizational Scheme</u>	Location search entirely the responsibility of the division.
(7) Division Only Study	Operates much like the Division-Controlled study ((6) above) except that there is no available corporate staff to invite into the study. Any expertise must either be "home-grown" within the division or must be brought in from the outside. Thus, this organizational scheme is the most likely to purchase the services of specialized location consultants. An informal network of discussion and approvals predominates. Divisions must "sell" their ideas to upper management. Previous "track record" becomes an important factor in evaluating the proposal and the division general manager who champions it through the approval process.

Aside on small companies

It should be noted that this anatomy of the decision-making process is more true of larger, multiplant companies. The location decision process at smaller companies, though sharing many of the same traits, has some generally distinguishing characteristics of its own. Among such characteristics:

• Informal, top down decision-making—The "team of specialists" decision-making that prevails in the majority of large corporations is less apt to apply to smaller businesses. There, instead, the decision to locate a new plant originates most often at the top of the company and involves only a handful of top level managers. More than in large companies, personal preference is likely to intrude on the decision process.[3]

• Local Search—in most instances, a small but growing company's second or third plant is likely to be located within comparatively short range of its first plant. Most small companies' early growth is not compromised by transportation expenses to distant markets, so geographic spread of manufacturing capacity is only infrequently required. Moreover, management development is a chronic deficiency of small, growing companies and lack of management depth usually argues for keeping plants within close proximity of one another.

Local search also complements the informality of the site decision process at smaller companies. By staying within the local area, the company management restricts itself to locations it either knows about first-hand or which it can easily scout. In so doing, it lessens the trauma of having to deal with the tremendous uncertainties the establishment of a second or third plant can bring.

The choice of organizational scheme

No one set of the organizational schemes discussed seems to dominate, either in theory or in practice. The test of any such scheme is whether it is conducive to good but timely decision-making. Are all issues aired thoroughly? Are particular capacity plans or locations rejected needlessly? Are some plans or locations considered to the exclusion of others? For many managers I have talked with, the most dangerous deterrent to good location decisions is the intrusion of personal preference and emotion into the process. It is my view, then, that the organization schemes which should be favored are those which are least subject to personal whim.

Under this rubric, the division-only study and the centralized, small group study of locations, particularly if coupled with an ad hoc procedure for identifying capacity shortfalls, are the least attractive organizational structures. In the former, division line managers, buffeted by the day-to-day responsibilities for operations and unfamiliar with the non-standard and strategic features of new plant location and start-up, may tend to skimp on planning and shoot from the hip with location suggestions. In the latter,

[3]For example, data derived from Cincinnati and New England indicate that smaller companies are more likely to be located so as to reduce the commute to work of the chief executive officer. This is discussed more in Chapter 3.

too much reverence for the chief executive officer's stated—or supposed—opinion on location may needlessly confine the decision process.

Trends in the adoption of organizational schemes over time support this view. More of the companies interviewed indicating a change in their organizational approach to location decisions have shifted toward greater staff domination of the decision process. And, a few companies noted that their decision-making had evolved from a centralized, small group study of location as they had grown larger.

Despite the susceptibility of these two organizational schemes to personal preference, companies that operate with those schemes routinely avoid their perils for the location decision. One effective means of keeping personal preference at bay is to have a strong, controlling concern to guide the site generation and evaluation procedures. If what constitutes or constrains an acceptable site is well known, even lack of familiarity with location decision-making is not apt to lead to poor choices based on personal preference. If the decision is straightforward enough, a company is not likely to be penalized by having an inexperienced division line management team tackle it.

If no single consideration is so important that it can be promoted as a controlling concern, then, it seems to me, the organizational framework guiding the location decision should demand a *set procedure* for generating and analyzing potential locations. The more well established the routine of the location decision process, the less likely that personal preference will take control of the decision.

One way to assure that both the procedures and the issues surrounding plant location are well established is to support the analysis of the need for any new capacity with (1) as formal a statement of the plant's charter responsibilities (products produced or developed, processes undertaken, technological innovation encouraged) as possible, and (2) thoughtful consideration of how the plant's charter could change over time (added responsibilities, pattern of growth, size limit, changes in products produced, increased or decreased vertical integration, degree of new product or process innovation). A firmly grounded notion of any new plant's expected charter and life cycle provides much of the background information for developing the criteria which are useful in controlling the location decision process. The more the plant's charter and life cycle are left to evolution within the company, the greater the chance for a mismatch in subsequent years between the corporation's needs and desires and the capabilities of its manufacturing plants.

---

[4]Robert A. Leone and John R. Meyer, "Capacity Strategies for the 1980's", *Harvard Business Review*, Vol. 58, No. 6 (Nov.–Dec. 1980), pp. 133–140.

Planning the plant's life cycle

Many marketing managers have found it useful to view their products as progressing through some kind of life cycle of birth; slow initial acceptance; rapid growth in sales; stable, mature sales; and then a tapering off, leading perhaps to obsolescence and death in the marketplace.

Production managers may find an analogous notion useful, that of a plant's life cycle. Plants, too, are born, progress through start-up, fill up with more and more workers, are frequently expanded with additional bricks and mortar, manufacture product in a more or less steady state for years, and then taper off into obsolescence and death, perhaps from a terminally ill cost structure. By explicitly recognizing this kind of life cycle, and the factors which lead to the transition between stages, managers can expect both longer and healthier plant lives.

Explicit recognition of a plant's life cycle does not come a moment too soon. Several factors, some of recent origin, are converging now to render a new plant decision an even more uncertain and difficult one than before. An enumeration of six factors makes the point.

● Inflation—As an excellent article has spelled out[4], one discomfitting implication of inflation is its effect on the cost of plant and equipment. In a growing number of industries the total cost per unit produced is actually higher in new plants than in old. This has resulted in a U-shaped, cost-over-time curve in industries like steel, pulp and paper, electric utilities, and others where capacity now lags rather than leads market demand. In this reversal of past history in these industries, new capacity must now be considered more soberly and extensively than ever before if it is to be justified economically.

● Advanced technology—While technology is often the key source of methods and equipment that help to combat inflation, it can also create a proliferation of products. This is not in itself bad, except that, to take liberties with a famous phrase, "old products never die, they just clog up the factory." If new capacity is not to fall victim to this syndrome, careful planning must be done.

● Increasing international competition—As any number of firms can now attest, U.S. manufacturers can no longer be sloppy about quality, product design, delivery or much else, if they are to remain successful over the long haul; international competition is simply too keen to permit such sloppiness anymore. The implication is that capacity, like any other manufacturing decision, must be deliberated carefully.

● Government regulation—Environmental and safety regulations, however well intentioned, have complicated the planning horizon, location choices, and economics of starting up new plants, especially those in heavy industries.

● Energy costs—By the same token, government manipulations and rising energy costs complicate the engineering and planning for any new plant. In addition, higher cost transportation may offset the size and location choice for the new capacity contemplated.

● Increasing geographic spread of domestic industry—The increasing industrialization of previously non-industrial areas of the nation (Sunbelt, rural) implies that it will be less and less possible to select low-cost domestic sites for new manufacturing plants. Over the long term, costs are likely to equalize across regions, which will have an impact on the capacity decision.

The upshot of this enumeration of influences on capacity decision-making is that managers must now think smarter—and longer term—about plant charters, capacities, and new locations than ever before. Many well managed companies are adjusting their thinking about capacity. A number have initiated special staff positions to concentrate on facilities planning, and some are even using, de facto, the implications of a plant's life cycle.

The utility of the life cycle concept lies in its ability to force the corporation to evaluate the long term use of that plant. The more a company considers how a new facility will be used and changed over the years in response to various contingencies, the better able it will be to design the plant and its manufacturing systems expressly for such contingencies. The plant then will be better attuned to the company's requirements at every point in its useful life.

It is advantageous to think of the plant's life cycle in three parts which correspond to the "charters" the company would like to ascribe to each.

EARLY CHARTER   This defines what the plant is intended to do. It should include features that should be planned for in start-up, such as:

- products manufactured and output goals for the initial start-up period and beyond
- plant size and configuration
- equipment to be used and flow pattern of product within the plant
- number of workers, sex and age, and skill levels required, in the initial months and as the plant is broken in during the first few years
- labor training that is required to meet the workforce goals
- stance toward the adoption of quality of worklife programs, from cross-training to job enlargement to team concepts
- production scheduling and control systems to be employed
- how the plant must interact with other plants and/or warehouses, including supplies or products shipped, modes used, personnel borrowed for troubleshooting, and the like
- overhead functions such as new product engineering, major raw materials purchasing, direct receipt of customer orders, industrial engineering. Which of these will the plant be responsible for, and which functions it can and cannot expect to take over as it grows. (Most new plants do not have the independence of existing facilities and, in fact, view themselves as "spin offs" from particular plants elsewhere.)
- how the new plant will be expanded subsequently and what will trigger that expansion (sales goals met, new products introduced)
- what products and technology are inconsistent with the plant as designed and thus must not be forced on its management
- what it would take to close the plant (division-wide sales drops, new product failures, cost problems or the like).

MATURE CHARTER   This defines the plant and its role in the long term and governs how its managers should react to change. It includes:

- employment ceiling above which no more growth will be permitted on-site
- how "focused" manufacturing can be maintained, such as restriction of product line expansion and restriction of process technologies undertaken
- what kinds of change will be permitted and not resisted (which types of product variations; which new products; which changes in equipment, flow, vertical integration; which changes to interplant logistics and communication)
- what it would take for this plant to spin off a new plant of its own, and what role this plant would take in aiding or directing the new one
- whether this plant will be part of a cluster of plants, sited in the same general area of the nation, and whether the "mission" product line of the cluster could be expected to change
- whether this plant will be expanded into a complex of more than one plant on the same site, and how the overhead will be absorbed and managed so that potential tenant-landlord relationships among plants in the complex are minimized
- how various workforce issues will be handled, such as worker advancement, quality of worklife programs, age and sex composition of the workforce, labor union organization and any contract negotiations, job hopping, and wage effects on the plant's competitiveness.

PLANT CLOSING   This distasteful consideration deals dispassionately with characteristics of the plant or its environment that would make it a candidate for closing. Among the issues to ponder in this regard would be:

- obsolescence reflected in technology-deterring plant layout, materials handling, or other physical aspects of the plant
- severe and unremitting sales declines (How much of a drop and how fast?)
- substantial cost increases in labor, transportation, raw materials
- militant union or personnel problems

Using the plant life cycle concept

Although it is difficult to envision that a company could thoroughly forecast all three stages of this early charter, mature charter, plant closing life cycle, these considerations form a useful checklist for a company in the planning stage for a new plant. Depending on the responses, plant life cycle considerations may make a significant impact on the initial choice of plant size, character, or location.

The usefulness of a well-defined plant charter coupled with a plant life cycle forecast becomes apparent in some of the statistical results reported in Chapter 3. The most important characteristic between plants which "spun off" new branches and those which did not was whether the management had perceived the flow of the original plant's production process becoming less rigid and more flexible. I interpret this result to mean that some spin offs were forced on certain plants because they had lost focus over time, becoming more flexible than they really should have.

A spin off to a new plant is one way to regain some of the rigidity or focus it once had. This implies that the more clearly management can foresee the loss of focus in an operation, the better able it will be to adjust capacity and responsibilities before much valued factory effectiveness is lost. In a similar vein, the survey results show clearly that the new plant opening has a better defined focus to its operations. Although it is more dependent on other company facilities than already existing plants, it is more likely to manufacture a narrower range of products and to be more stable in its product mix.

The better a company anticipates changes in its product mix, growth rates, and process changes, the more attuned to competitive priorities the new plant is likely to stay. In this regard, it is important to be wary of the lure of sites already owned by the corporation. Under the guise of low-cost, easily occupied space, companies can be sucked into locations that are not suitable for other reasons, and the plant's focus can be compromised. Companies like IBM are extremely cautious about managing their land banks; sites are not pushed on their divisions; the divisions maintain control of the location process, and new sites in the land bank are guided from the start by the companies' management committees. Such care is commendable, especially because high technology companies like IBM are typically footloose.

Other organizational issues

Several other observations regarding organizational structure and the location decision are applicable. The concepts of formal business planning have been spreading through more and more large companies in the last decade or two. As one might imagine, the fervor and comprehensiveness accompanying formal business planning vary considerably from company to company. Some formal business planning procedures fail to incorporate facilities planning into the planning process and this failing, in my opinion, should be avoided. Specifically, addressing the anticipated physical characteristics of any proposed capacity should be encouraged. Some business plans deal strictly in dollar sales and units of production, and do not translate any sales or unit shortfalls into manufacturing square footage required, machinery and personnel required, or process technologies contemplated. The more information like this incorporated into the planning process as a matter of course, the more smooth-running the entire location decision process can be expected to be.

Another useful tension to maintain is the corporate staff-line management tension which must resolve any difference of opinion regarding on-site expansion versus new site development. As noted earlier, division line management often pushes for expansion of their existing facilities, while corporate staff members or senior line managers within the corporation, frequently with histories of coping with the difficulties inherent in continued on-site expansions, resist such policies in favor of establishing new plants. There is usually merit to both sides of this argument, which suggests that a company is well served if it can stimulate diverse points of view on the matter.

The corporate staff can become increasingly important for another important reason, decision complexity. Government regulations, particularly on air and water pollution control, are now important and difficult to understand constraints on location decisions. Companies are larger, with operations farther flung; coordinating operations across plants and across divisions is often necessary. This complicates planning for new facilities. Constructing a new plant demands more specialized expertise in a company (environmental affairs, logistics/transportation, plant engineering and construction) then ever before. This expertise is usually most efficiently housed within the corporate staff.

The increasing complexity of the location decision requires caution however. For most companies, the location decision process involves relatively few people in the detailed study of needs and options. This small scale fosters speed and decisiveness. If increasing complexity demands that more than, say, a dozen managers become actively engaged in the decision process, managing that many potentially opposing views may become too difficult. Considerable care should be given then to the organization and direction of any location decision team. Some companies have more or less permanent team members, used to working together. This permanence and experience is important, because the team studying the location proposal need not be concerned about the procedures of the selection process but can devote itself to the issues. With more of a "pick-up team" for the decision, the probability of process-related problems bogging down the decision is heightened.

Factors Affecting The Choice of Location

For almost all sizable corporations, the evaluation of a proposed business site includes a systematic consideration of its costs and benefits. The capital appropriations request for the site, and the documentation that stands behind it, typically include a raft of figures and qualitative considerations. As much as can be quantified is—site and site preparation costs, construction or purchase/renovation costs, equipment costs, labor and fringe benefit costs, start-up costs (training, inefficiencies), working capital requirements such as inventories, materials, and accounts receivable, freight in and freight out expenses, taxes, workmen's and unemployment compensation payments, relocation expenses for managers and engineers, and a forecast of the revenues expected to be generated by the plant. Often both costs and benefits are combined in net present value (or internal rate of return) calculations which summarize the projected financial attractiveness of the location. The qualitative considerations then serve to support or to temper the financial analysis.

While the sophistication of the financial and qualitative aspects of the capital appropriations request and its supporting documents can vary markedly among corporations, and while assembling the data usually requires repeated iterations before it is accomplished satisfactorily, management generally feels comfortable with its review and evaluation. What makes the location decision uncomfortable for many companies is not the final steps of evaluation but the beginning steps of the process where potential sites must be generated to satisfy acknowledged capacity needs. It is in the initial stages of the location search where the non-standard, unfamiliar nature of the location search process and the complexity of the elements that need to be considered combine to create hesitancy in many managers. To overcome this hesitancy, most firms try to simplify and systematize the process by resorting to a checklist.

A site selection checklist is a useful device for it suggests many factors which could have a bearing on the location decision. A variety of such checklists are available, and their originators pride themselves on their comprehensiveness, which often translates into length.[5] Often their very length defeats their usefulness, especially in the early stages of the decision process. Such comprehensive checklists can be useful in later stages of the decision process because many items listed on them are site-specific and reveal problems associated with the site itself, such as potential engineering/ construction difficulties.

The lengthy checklists fail to simplify what is inherently a complex decision. For many companies, the first task of the individual or team that guides the location search is the development of priorities, so any checklist should be pared down to manageable size.

Making the checklist work

A checklist of my devising is shown as Table 1-5. This list is deliberately shorter than most one can obtain; it is limited to the early stages of the location search, when suitable sites are identified. It contains almost all of the factors which my research indicates are important, possibly controlling, concerns of manufacturing location decision-makers.

The most common way to simplify the multitude of influences documented in checklists like Table 1-5 is to designate certain factors as "musts"—particular elements which must be present at the new location if

[5]A *Site Selection Handbook* (a quarterly and a companion to Industrial Development Magazine) can be obtained from the Industrial Development Research Council, Conway Publications, Inc., 1954 Airport Road, Peachtree Air Terminal, Atlanta, GA 30341.

A *Guide to Industrial Site Selection* is available from the Society of Industrial Realtors and National Association of Office Parks, Society of Industrial Realtors, 925 15th Street NW, Washington, DC 20005.

Table 1-5

Major Factors That Shape Plant Location Searches

Item	Quantifiable?	Data typically developed from	Company unit typically responsible
Access to Markets/Distribution Centers			
Cost of serving present markets/distribution centers	Estimate possible	Location of markets/distribution centers, quantities of each product shipped to each market/distribution center, shipping mode, freight rates, handling charges	Logistics
Trends in sales by area, ability to generate sales by company presence in area	Somewhat	Estimates of same data listed above	Marketing
Access to Supplies, Resources			
Cost of transporting supplies	Estimate possible	Location of suppliers for which transport expenses will be incurred by plant, quantities shipped from each location, by which mode, freight rates, handling charges	Purchasing, Logistics
Trends in supplier by area	Somewhat	Estimates of same data listed above	Purchasing
Community, Government Aspects			
Ambience, charisma of community	No	Site visit, hearsay, polls of people's preferences	Location team
Cost of living	Yes	Bureau of Labor Statistics area figures	Location team
Cooperation with established local industry	No	Site visit	Location team
Community price (appearance, activity, citizen views)	No	Site visit	Location team

Table 1-5 (continued)

Item	Quantifiable?	Data typically developed from	Company unit typically responsible
Housing (availability, prices)	Somewhat	Site visit, discussions with realtors	Location team
Schools, cultural attractions, recreation	Somewhat	Site visit, program offerings from state/local sources, % going to college, etc.	Location team
Colleges nearby, graduate programs	Somewhat	State/local sources	Location team
Churches, civic groups	Somewhat	Site visit	Location team
Competitive Considerations			
Competition's location	Yes	Industry sources	Division
Likely competition reaction to this new site	No	Industry sources, own knowledge	Division
Environmental Considerations			
Government "attainment" area or not?	Yes	Federal/state environmental protection agencies	Environmental Affairs
Are pollution rights of other companies available for purchase?	Yes	State EPA development agencies, companies in area	Staff, Location team
Ease and speed of compliance	No	Federal/state EPA, militancy of local conservation efforts	Staff
Interaction with Rest of Corporation			
Is new plant to be a satellite of another plant or not?	Yes	Own knowledge	Division
Is plant to be supplied by or to supply other company plants?	Yes	Own knowledge	Division
Extent of expected engineering/management troubleshooting from headquarters	No	Own knowledge	Division

34

Table 1-5 (continued)

Item	Quantifiable?	Data typically developed from	Company unit typically responsible
Labor			
Prevailing wage rates	Somewhat	Bureau of Labor Statistics, State/local publications, poll of manufacturers in the area	Personnel, Location team
Extent and militancy of labor unions in area	Somewhat	Does state have "right-to-work" law?, BLS data on union workers, work stoppages, NLRB certification/decertification elections, poll of area manufacturers	Personnel, Location team
Productivity (absenteeism, turnover, worker attitudes)	Somewhat	Poll of area manufacturers	Personnel, Location team
Availability (population, area unemployment, commuting distances)	Somewhat	BLS data, Census data	Personnel, Location team
Skill levels available	Somewhat	Poll of manufacturers in area, local training programs	Personnel, Location team
Site Itself			
Area of site, sq. ft. and layout of each structure	Yes	State/local development agencies, railroads, power companies, developers, realtors, site visit	Location team, especially real estate function
Price of site and any structures	Yes	Seller	Location team
Ability to option site, length, cost	Yes	Seller	Location team, especially real estate function
Condition of site and any structures (including structural assessment, topography, geology, and other concerns for construction and improvement)	Yes	Site visit, especially once option is taken	Location team, especially real estate and engineering functions
Area parking and traffic	Somewhat	Site visit	Location team
Construction, remodeling costs, insurance	Yes	Site inspections, engineering plans	Project Engineering team

Table 1-5 (continued)

Item	Quantifiable?	Data typically developed from	Company unit typically responsible
Taxes and Financing			
State income tax (corporate, personal)	Yes	State government office	Tax department, Location team
Local property and local income tax (if any)	Yes	Local government office	
Unemployment and workmen's compensation	Yes	State government office	
Other state/local business taxes	Yes	State/local offices	
Tax incentives and/or concessions (holidays, abatements, exemptions, credits, accelerated depreciation, and the like)	Yes	State/local offices	
Industrial and/or pollution control revenue bonds	Yes	State/local offices	
Transportation			
Trucking service (number and reputation of truckers, rates charged, quality of service)	Somewhat	Area trucking companies, other manufacturers in area	Location team, Logistics
Rail service (number and reputation of railroads serving site, frequency of service, rates)	Somewhat	Railroads, other manufacturers in area	Location team, Logistics
Utilities, Services			
Availability, quality, and price of water, sewerage, electric power, natural gas	Somewhat	Utility companies, poll of manufacturers in area	Location team
Quality of roads, police, fire, medical, other services	Somewhat	Site visit, poll of manufacturers in area	Location team

36

the company is to be competitive there. Other factors may then be designated as "wants"—desirable elements which are conscientiously sought in a new location but which could be foregone if other influences, including the "musts", are too severely compromised.

The "musts" required and, to a lesser extent, the "wants" desired, are derived from the company's prevailing multiplant manufacturing strategies and from the dominant operational costs which location can influence. The first task of the location search team is to understand thoroughly the reasons for any new plant, how it is expected to fulfill the company's goals, how it fits together with other company plants, and which costs (or revenues, for that matter) could be expected to vary with different choices of location. From this understanding, the search team can usually agree on one or more criteria which are absolutely critical to the plant's effectiveness. These essential criteria are often common to the industry, springing from its economics, which include the breadth and vigor of competition, supply and distribution cost, production technologies, new product development, value added expenses, production seasonality or cyclicality, and pace and character of its growth. Sometimes these criteria are also particular to the company and how it views its competitive position within the industry.

The point here is that a location team can agree on a primary concern which becomes the controlling influence throughout the location search. Selecting the controlling concern can cut through the complexity of the decision and simplify the work and the discussions considerably. From interview and survey data, the following six requirements proved dominant; Chapter 3 discusses these in much greater detail:

- *Primary concern for labor costs*—The cost of labor is a major constraint on highly competitive industries such as apparel, leather, furniture, and consumer electronics. It is of minor concern to many capital-intensive operations.
- *Primary concern for labor unionization*—A new workforce that is nearly impossible to organize is perhaps the most prized side benefit of a new plant site, and it is the controlling consideration for many companies. This ranks high with labor cost sensitive companies, many specialty products companies, and makers of industrial equipment.
- *Primary concern for proximity to markets*—A site near established markets is absolutely essential for commodity or near-commodity items with a low value to weight. Paper converting, printing, plastics fabrication, can making, and a number of other industries are constrained by transportation costs.
- *Primary concern for proximity to supplies/resources*—Several industries are tied to certain suppliers or resources: paper mills must be near trees and water, fruit and vegetable processing near farms, petrochemical complexes near oil pipelines, and so on.
- *Primary concern for proximity to other company facilities*—Some manufacturing plants cannot live alone; they operate as satellites to a base or main plant. Without a steady stream of supplies, work-in-process inventories, management knowhow, engineering talent, and the like, from a main plant, such plants would wilt. Satellite

plants cannot be located too far from the main plant without stretching the lines of support too taut.

● *Primary concern for the quality of life in an area*—The most fearsome competitive advantage the high technology industry can wield is a happy, productive staff of engineers. Since proximity to markets or supplies is not essential in such companies, such firms can be extraordinarily free to locate in attractive places for their engineers and managers to live.

Other considerations may become primary concerns of the team charged with the location decision, but these are the major ones which research of mine and others supports. What is important to remember about these controlling concerns for the location decision is that they are outgrowths of the economics of the industry or of the company's particular manufacturing priorities. They are unique to individual situations; they are not widely applicable across industries or companies.

Second to these are other constraints pertaining to the site itself (must have railroad siding, must be on water, must have certain utilities like natural gas), but these are fairly low level requirements which can often be met within a fairly short radius.

Usually it is not too difficult to isolate one controlling concern for a location choice, but if there is no controlling concern, if no one factor stands out before all others, the task becomes more difficult. When no controlling concerns are evident, it is my recommendation that the company's site search procedures be rigid and well-established so that the generation of cost and logistics data and the analytical evaluation of sites be careful and orderly so that the final decision does not fall prey to the vagaries of casual personal preference. (Chapter 3 offers some procedures which companies use to assure this rigidity.)

Of course the location decision does involve subjective judgments; the issues are too complex, measurement of some factors impossible, and some data too imprecise. What can be quantified should be, but managers should not be cowed by hard numbers when reasoned, hard-to-quantify considerations argue for a different choice.

Sometimes neglected considerations

Responsible search teams seldom ignore location influences which can be quantified easily. More often ignored are the hard-to-quantify influences, particularly those which might represent hidden costs. During my conversations with location decision-makers two considerations have struck me as being neglected sometimes. These were brought to my attention as "things we should have looked into" or "things we are glad we looked into."

Attracting and Retaining Engineers and Managers

It nearly goes without saying that a company wants a new plant location in a town or area that is an attractive place for its managers and engineers and their families to live. Yet, with primary concerns for costs, labor availability, unionization, and the like, sometimes the livability of an area is taken for granted. What sometimes happens in such a case is that the plant is started up, but after a while the company finds it increasingly difficult to persuade managers or engineers to transfer there. Time spent at the plant is viewed as "hardship duty", and special inducements may have to be offered. This problem is most often faced by companies moving into small towns; it is most acute among northern-based companies moving into small southern communities. It is an interesting irony that several southern-based companies I spoke with still view themselves as having a competitive advantage over northern-based companies that have only recently opened facilities in the South. In this view, the southern-based company feels more comfortable siting plants in the smallest southern communities, because it is more likely to attract managers who have grown up in the South—many in small towns—and who feel happy to return to that style of life.

An intriguing variant of this situation is the problem encountered when a company has some manufacturing plants in locations that are viewed as particularly attractive. In these cases, getting managers and engineers to transfer out is difficult and can frustrate the smooth rotation of these managers and engineers through various positions of responsibility in the company.

The Movement of People and Materials Between Facilities

The subtle costs of moving materials, managers, and engineers have been recognized by a number of companies. This cost consideration accounts for clustering facilities in the same general area and is popular with those companies following a process plant multiplant manufacturing strategy.

Although recognized as important to some firms, the cost of interplant movement is sometimes neglected by others. The result may be higher logistics costs than expected or more time spent shuttling between plants. This has the consequence of reducing the amount or frequency of travel made to an inconveniently located facility, leaving it to operate without proper support more than it should. Some companies are so conscious of executive/engineer travel time that they insist that new plants be located close to an airport capable of holding the corporate jet, or an airport with non-stop (or one stop) service between the cities or with frequent scheduled flights each day between the cities.

Coping with Government Regulation

Government regulation of business operations has had its effect on the location decision process. As one might expect, the impact of regulation, particularly environmental regulation, varies between widely divergent extremes. On one hand, many companies loosely classed as light manufacturers are unaffected by government regulations and seem able to proceed with site selection as before. On the other hand, some heavy manufacturers' site choices are so at the mercy of government regulatory judgments that they can honestly say that their next plant will be located "when and where they let us". Between these extremes lie many companies for which regulation has been an inconvenience of lesser or greater cost.

What kinds of inconveniences and costs has government regulation imposed on the plant location decision process? Three major costs apply:

1. Cost of compliance—This includes expenses for pollution control equipment, production process changes, land for lagoons and clarifiers, test facilities, and the personnel to manage the pollution control activities of the company. These are direct, out-of-pocket expenditures incurred in complying with environmental, OSHA, or local government regulations.

2. Capital gains and losses—Some companies are better able to comply at low cost with government regulations than others, due primarily to providential decisions made years ago. In the course of their competitive struggles, then, these companies have reaped capital gains relative to those companies more poorly positioned to comply. Location can be one reason for a capital gain of this type, because some locations are more suitable for pollution control activities, or their expansion, than others. Indeed, there are attainment and non-attainment areas for air pollution, and impacted and non-impacted areas for water pollution which underline this fact. An advantageous location is more apt to be successfully expanded on-site and for lower cost than less advantageous sites.

3. Time delays—Strictly from the standpoint of the location decision process, the largest single cost of government regulation is perhaps the time delay it imposes. Many companies are now compelled to seek longer options on industrial property than was formerly the case, so that the information necessary for compliance with government regulations can be assembled. Delays in the approval process for environmental rulings must also be factored into the time frame of the decision. For some companies, these delays can be measured in years, not weeks or months, and the impact of these delays on the economics of a manufacturing project can be enormous.

The imposition of these costs has driven many firms to make at least some changes in the way they approach the location decision process. Among the most common adjustments are the following five:

1. More on-site expansion—If the cost of establishing a new plant is increased, as it is with the introduction of more government regulation, it is not surprising that new plant construction is eschewed in favor of lower cost alternatives like on-site expansion. On-site expansion is lower cost, in this instance, because the land is already available, some overhead services can be shared, and any new permits which are needed are likely to be secured with greater dispatch than with a completely new plant.

2. Multiple divisions sharing a site—A number of companies, notably those in the chemicals and food processing industries, have broadened the concept of on-site expansion to include the placement of more than one division at a single site. In such capital-intensive industries, there tend to be few diseconomies of scale, and some overhead functions at the site, notably those involving compliance with environmental regulations, can be readily shared. When new capacity is called for in these companies the initial response is to search among existing sites, occupied by no matter which division, for space in which the new capacity can be erected. Like on-site expansion, this tactic is likely to save both time and out-of-pocket expenses.

3. Land banking—An even more popular method of telescoping the time and cost of erecting new capacity is to procure sites in advance of need and hold them in a land bank, so that the time spent searching, checking out, and improving a site can be avoided. In this way, the delays due to environmental issues are worked out ahead of time. Fully one in six of the companies interviewed engage in land banking, at least occasionally. A division that requests new capacity is first directed to the available sites in the land bank before it is permitted to search on its own for new sites. While land banking can be a useful device, the cautions cited above still hold.

Less dramatic but still important modifications to the location decision process have been the following two policies:

4. Site-survey library—Some companies, notably the largest, have sought to shorten search time for new locations by establishing and maintaining their own libraries of information on sites scattered over wide expanses of geography. Companies, using this library, can be in the final evaluation stages of the site selection process within a couple weeks of the decision to open a new plant. This can reduce search time substantially and mitigate any regulatory delay.

5. Parallel search and engineering projects—Site selection has traditionally preceded the detailed engineering for a new plant. Although some facilities planning may have been done which provided the location team with the basic information and constraints, the two projects were basically accomplished in serial fashion. More recently some companies have begun the detailed engineering of a new plant at the same time the location search is underway; thus a parallel, rather than serial, effort is undertaken. Parallel pursuit of site selection and engineering can reduce the lead times for plant start-up, although it may lead to some over-design of a facility or to special constraints for the site search (e.g., looking for particularly flat pieces of land, etc.).

2

Helping Industry

Locate New Capacity:

advice to states

and localities

Despite manufacturing's declining share of total employment, industrial development remains a visible and often controversial portion of the public policies of states and localities. Yet, the role of government in the manufacturing location decision has been very difficult to assess. Is government policy a significant influence on location? If so, how? Should industrial development be the "second war between the states" as *Business Week* dubbed it a few years ago? This chapter assesses the impact of government policies on the manufacturing plant location decisions of companies and offers some suggestions to the officers of government who are charged with further policy development.

What The Trends Say About Regions, States, and Cities

Significant trends are apparent in the changes evident from the geographic pattern of industrial location during the 1970s. These trends, which are largely secular in nature and seemingly inexorable in direction, have important implications for public policies addressed to economic development in the states. Before investigating the evidence on particular public policies, it is useful to review these key facts and trends, so that the manufacturing location decisions that have been realized can be put into perspective.

A major trend running through the data, which is developed in close detail in Chapter 4, is that industry of all types is becoming more geographically heterogeneous in the United States. The North, while still industry-rich, is no longer so dominant as it once was. The central cities, while still bastions of industry, have steadily ceded employment to the suburbs and rural areas. Regions once the sole centers for specific manufacturing industries are no longer so dependent on the fortunes of that manufacturing.

Each region's business mix now looks more like the national industry mix than it did 10 or 20 years ago. For example, textiles are no longer so dominant in the South Atlantic states. Food processing is no longer so dominant in the West North Central region, nor is apparel in the East South Central, nor transportation equipment (chiefly aircraft) in the Pacific states. And, industries that were under-represented in each region have grown larger and more representative of that industry's importance to the economy as a whole.

Conversely, the distribution of particular industries across regions looks more like the national distribution of all industry. Although selected regions remain as important to some industries as they have historically been, in most cases the variance of the distribution of industry across regions is lower now than it was in the past.

This increasing geographic heterogeneity occurs in four ways: new plants are started up, existing plants closed, plants are relocated, and established plants are expanded or contracted on-site. As one might expect, the economic importance of these "components of change" differ from one geographic region to another.

For some time the incidence of plant closings across regions has been much the same, however the incidence of new plant openings across regions has been varying markedly. The so-called Sunbelt has been doing very much better, in a relative sense, at attracting new plants than the so-called Frostbelt. The Southwest is an especially active area for new plants whereas the Mid-Atlantic region lags noticeably. This divergence between new plant start-ups and plant closings is a key determinant of the increasing geographic heterogeneity that has been observed. The other key determinant is the employment growth at existing plants. Established plants in the Frostbelt are not being expanded at a rate concomitant with established plants in the Sunbelt. In contrast, the relocation of plants inter-regionally that is, the nearly simultaneous closing of a facility in one region and the opening of new plant in another region to do fundamentally the same task—often with the same management and/or equipment—is of nearly negligible importance in explaining the employment gains in the Sunbelt and contractions in the Frostbelt.

These regional trends suggest that the Frostbelt states are probably better off trying to promote industrial growth from within—a strategy of tending one's own garden—rather than trying to attract development from the outside. The benefit to the Sunbelt states of advertising their attractions to companies headquartered elsewhere, on the other hand, is very much greater. Even in the Sunbelt, certain kinds of companies with specific kinds of multiplant manufacturing strategies are better suited to some states than to others. For example, the East South Central region (Kentucky, Tennessee, Alabama and Mississippi) can expect to continue attracting plants for which transportation costs to predominantly national markets are critical concerns. In this sense, the East South Central is becoming a "Lower Midwest." Florida, on the other hand, is a lot like New England, cut off by distance from an ability to house transport-sensitive plants. Florida's development, like New England's, thus rests with transport-insensitive companies, like most high technology ones; these companies are more apt to be influenced by quality of life considerations. To cite still another example, rural areas of the South Atlantic and West South Central regions are most attractive to companies seeking lower labor costs and no unionization to help maintain their positions in highly competitive industries.

Attention to the "components of change"—expansion and contraction, openings and closings, relocations—is of considerable importance to metropolitan areas. Many central cities, especially those traditional manufacturing centers in the Northeast, have been losing employment, in absolute as well as relative terms, to suburbs and rural areas. How these losses have occurred is of considerable significance to officials who must formulate policies designed to retain, develop, or aid in stabilizing central city manufacturing. The data, taken from major companies and from the Cincinnati metropolitan area, suggest that the future of manufacturing employment in most cities, especially the older industrial cities of the nation, lies not with America's largest manufacturers, but with the smaller, generally single plant companies that inhabit cities. While major manufacturers are typically a substantial presence in a city, the changes in employment at their plants are usually modest. The major manufacturers' plants do not account for much change in city employment, especially in older cities; their rates of birth and death are very low. And, while there are several notable "company towns," in most metropolitan areas, few plants are operated by the same company.

Not only is city employment often dictated by the actions of small company plants, but the net decentralization of industry from city to suburb is due not so much to the immigration of growing plants—such movement has probably occurred all along—but rather to more plant closings in the city than plant openings.

Judging from the Cincinnati data, the central city has lost some of the powers formerly ascribed to it as an incubator of new firms. Though many new companies locate in the city because of proximity to suppliers, customers, and special business services, the central city does not spawn a disproportionate share of new companies. Indeed, all surveyed plants located in central areas place a higher value on proximity to customers, financial, and special business services than do plants in other locations. Centrally located plants are more likely to sell locally and direct to customers. Yet relative to the existing stock of plants, many suburbs and fringe areas do better in attracting new enterprises. Plants are no longer so tied to city transportation modes such as railroad marshalling yards and may in fact be better served by truck, with less congestion, in the suburbs. Labor and space for manufacturing and storage are now readily available in most suburbs as well. Most plants pay few, if any, penalties by locating in the suburbs.

It should be noted that in the swiftest growing areas of the country— predominantly the Sunbelt—the actions of large manufacturers in starting up new plants or expanding existing ones are of vastly greater significance, even for central cities. There is often still plenty of room in these central cities, so that they "look" more like suburbs than do the central cities of America's traditional belt of manufacturing.

From this over-view of the current significant trends in industry location, we turn to evaluations of the particular types of public policies that are designed to stimulate economic development.

To Tax Or Not To Tax

The influence of tax rates on state and local economic development has long been a hotly debated issue. Anecdotes fly on both sides of the question, and statistical tests of the effects of taxes have never been as precise as both proponents and critics would like.[1] While I cannot pretend that my own data about tax and financial effects on industrial development are thoroughly persuasive and definitive, they do add weight to the general view that the taxation and financing schemes developed by government entities have only a minimal effect on the selection of new plant locations. The evidence for this comes in a variety of forms.

---

[1]A kind of Heisenberg Uncertainty Principle prevails in many of the statistical tests which try to sort out the effects of taxes from other influences on location choice. The Heisenberg Uncertainty Principle of modern physics, loosely interpreted, suggests that the researcher's attempt to measure one aspect of the phenomenon in question may actually impede his ability to measure, at the same time, another aspect of the phenomenon. So it goes in isolating tax effects from other effects on industry location. Trying to control for variations in tax levels and tax incidence across wide expanses of geography leads the researcher to area-based economic models—where the observations are parcels of land—that necessarily aggregate individual company decisions and thus submerge much of the complexity of the location decision and ruin the precision of many of the independent variables one could hope to include. On the other hand, trying to control for variations in plant-specific influences on the choice leads the researcher to plant-based economic models—where the observations are individual plants—that necessarily ignore much of the geographic variation in taxes that a company sorts through in evaluating regions, communities, and sites. Other models, which look at special situations where only taxes are alleged to have changed, also suffer from aggregations of companies or industries and the real possibilities that things other than tax changes are occurring in systematic fashion.

Interview evidence

In none of the more than 80 interviews I have had with key location decision makers in, mainly, large companies have I heard that state or local levels of taxation have been the most significant determinant of a plant's location. Almost every company takes a look at taxes; indeed, tax costs are one of the costs of a new site which can be quantified and presented in the documentation that supports the project's formal capital appropriation request. Nevertheless, taxes themselves are merely a minor consideration, capable of altering the decision in favor of a particular site only if almost all other factors are equal. The level of taxation on the plant itself is often so insignificant a concern that what importance taxation may have in site selection is due largely to the level of taxes on personal income and home real estate. Thus personal taxation figures into the subjective evaluation of the quality of life in an area.

Judging from my interviews with company executives, taxes (including workmen's and unemployment compensation) are more likely to dissuade a corporation from siting a new plant somewhere than they are likely to attract a corporation to a particular place. In descriptive terms, high taxes are more apt to "push" corporations away from potential sites than low taxes are likely to "pull" corporations in from other sites. Further, it is the particularly visible taxes which seem to incur the wrath of corporate decision-makers: for example, one state's hike in workmen's and unemployment compensation rates, or another state's high inventory tax. Apparently, the more invisible a tax on a corporation can be, the less likely it will influence a location search negatively. Another way of making this point is to observe that making tax comparisons of prospective plant sites, while done all the time, is not an easy task to do in anything other than generalized terms. The problems are numerous, beginning with the sheer number of taxes a corporation (not to mention its employees) must pay at the various levels: state income taxes, real property taxes, personal property taxes, workmen's compensation, unemployment compensation, inventory taxes, corporate franchise taxes, state sales taxes, intangible taxes, local income taxes, among others. Layered on top of this are a variety of possible exemptions, rate changes, and different assessment practices. All this makes comparing the tax burdens of particular sites a more imprecise activity than one might imagine.

Company executives have given me other justifications for the relative unimportance of taxes in making the location decision.

● Remaining a good neighbor—When a large corporation locates a new plant in a town, it is acutely aware that it is making a long-term investment. Among the last things it wants to do is aggravate the population that will make up its workforce. Many companies reason that winning sizable tax concessions from a town is not the most advantageous way to announce a company's arrival to a new labor market. In the long run both the company and the town will benefit, it is thought, if the company makes a point of paying its fair share.

• "What they give with one hand, they can take with the other"—According to this line of thinking, having a location decided by tax policy can haunt a company later if the town decides to reverse that policy. Most companies plan to stay in a community decades longer than any set of state or local government administrators could hope to stay in power; thus they view tax policy as a short-term phenomenon. Companies sensitive to this argument often look at the variability in past tax policy, rather than at current taxation levels as a more significant indication of the long-term viability of a site.

Evidence from relocating plants

Although, it is difficult to design and implement a definitive test of whether taxes really do play a significant role in plant location, a persuasive, direct indication may be achieved by examining the actions of relocating plants. Relocating plants offer a "before and after" measure of effective tax rates, and are plausibly the type of plant most sensitive to tax rate differentials.

Table 2-1 reports on comparisons of present site tax rates against previous site tax rates for selected plant relocations drawn from Cincinnati, New England, and the Fortune 500 companies nationally. A perusal of these data quickly suggests that there are two kinds of relocating plant, and other non-tax evidence substantiates this. Most relocating plants are small single-plant companies which are growing rapidly, are in desperate need of space, desire to revamp their production processes, wish to retain their workforces, and thus do not move more than 20 miles from their former plants. The survey results suggest that tax rate differentials matter little to these plants; they are as likely to move to higher tax rate jurisdictions as lower.[2] This evidence on the prevalent, short-distance plant relocation is buttressed by the results displayed in Table 2-2. There it is seen that the average effective tax rates for mover plants within the Cincinnati area are not dramatically different pre- and post-move, and that they are very much in line with other types of plants. Moreover, plants with high capital-labor ratios (which one might expect to be sensitive to high property tax rates if some of the incidence of that tax rests with the plant and is not completely shifted backward onto landowners or forward to customers) do not relocate in jurisdictions that tax property lower. Similarly, plants with low capital-labor ratios (which one might expect to be sensitive to high municipal income tax rates if they bear some of the incidence of that tax themselves) are no more likely to settle in low income tax levying towns.

[2]The income tax rate results for Cincinnati should be interpreted carefully. Many towns in the Cincinnati area levy municipal income taxes and these rates tend to decline with distance from the City of Cincinnati itself. Because within-metropolitan area plant relocations, in any city, are generally decentralizing, one would expect relocating plants to have lower post-move income tax rates in Cincinnati, even if tax rates made no difference to the choice of location.

Table 2-1

A Summary of Tax Rate Results for Relocating Plants

Tax	Cincinnati			New England		Fortune 500 Nationally	
	Single Plant Companies	Plants of Multiplant Companies	Short Distance (< 20 miles)	Long Distance (> 20 miles)	Movers into New England	Short Distance (< 20 miles)	Long Distance (> 20 miles)
Property tax rate							
Same as previous location	51%	18%	48%	25%	47%	58%	13%
Higher than previous location	28%	27%	34%	9%	20%	21%	44%
Lower than previous location	21%	55%	18%	66%	33%	21%	44%
Income tax rate							
Same as previous location	63%	9%	90%	56%	21%	95%	69%
Higher than previous location	8%	18%	7%	0	36%	0	6%
Lower than previous location	29%	73%	2%	44%	43%	5%	25%
Number of plants	53	11	84	35	16	19	16

Source: Schmenner studies 1978 and 1980.

Table 2-2

Average Effective Tax Rates - Cincinnati Data

Panel A. Average Effective Property and Local Income Tax Rates by Category

	Property Tax Rate		Local Income Tax Rate	
Single Plant Companies	Average	Standard Deviation	Average	Standard Deviation
Stay-Put Plants	1.532	0.015	1.681	0.038
Mover Plants - Before Move	1.527	0.024	1.753	0.077
Mover Plants - After Move	1.543	0.025	1.522	0.088
Plant Openings	1.438	0.047	1.600	0.099
Branch Plants				
Stay-Put Plants	1.448	0.022	1.526	0.065
Mover Plants - Before Move	1.459	0.035	1.700	0.138
Mover Plants - After Move	1.436	0.042	1.068	0.127
Plant Openings	1.459	0.050	1.136	0.200
Plants with less than 40 Employees				
Stay-Put Plants	1.535	0.017	1.629	0.050
Mover Plants - After Move	1.526	0.027	1.464	0.094
Plant Openings	1.471	0.040	1.523	0.103
Plants with 40 or more Employees				
Stay-Put Plants	1.479	0.019	1.648	0.044
Mover Plants - After Move	1.521	0.036	1.321	0.145
Plant Openings	1.334	0.059	1.000	0.000

Panel B. Average Effective Tax Rates for Mover Plants,
by Capital-Labor Ratio Category

	Property Tax Rate Post Move		Local Income Tax Rate Post Move	
Mover Plants	Average	Standard Deviation	Average	Standard Deviation
High Capital-Labor Ratio ($\geq$ 2.27)	1.539	0.022	1.448	0.106
Low Capital-Labor Ratio ($<$ 2.27)	1.527	0.042	1.465	0.122

	Property Tax Pre Move		Local Income Tax Pre Move	
	Average	Standard Deviation	Average	Standard Deviation
High Capital-Labor Ratio ($\geq$ 2.27)	1.510	0.022	1.698	0.109
Low Capital-Labor Ratio ($<$ 2.27)	1.524	0.040	1.776	0.095

NOTE: Tax rates are given as percentages of estimated market values.

Source: Schmenner study, 1978.

This evidence strongly suggests that tax rates play next to no role in the location choice of the most prevalent form of relocating plant, the short distance mover. Indeed, if taxes do matter to such plants, they must act in very peculiar ways to effect the results they do. And surely the margins on which they act are very thin ones.

The long-distance mover is an entirely different breed. The evidence here reveals the long-distance mover to be highly cost conscious, moving not only to lower tax locations but to lower wage and land cost locations as well. This is understandable, since the long-distance mover is most likely to be enduring profitability problems, least likely to be growing rapidly, and most likely to be consolidating operations from two or more facilities which are then closed.

Table 2-1 shows that the long-distance mover (and in the Cincinnati area, the branch plant of a multiplant company) is the most likely to move to lower tax rate jurisdictions, although this is much less true among plants in the Fortune 500 survey. A conclusion that taxes do influence the locations of these very special and rare plants seems warranted. My best estimate is that about 20% of relocating plants move more than 20 miles, thus influencing about ½ of 1% of the manufacturing employment in any area in any one year.

Evidence from plant openings

What of taxes and the plant opening? The evidence on this point is less direct. Table 2-2 displays some average effective tax rates for new branch plants in the Cincinnati area. These rates are no lower than for other types of branch plants, suggesting that the impact of taxes on new site selection around a metropolitan area is not keen. Tables 2-3 and 2-4, derived from the study of the Fortune 500 companies, display the frequencies with which a number of factors were cited by newly opened plants, not as "musts" or constraints but as factors perceived as "desirable, if available" and which "helped to tip the scales in favor of this site." This survey question was designed to elicit the *marginal* effect some options had on a location decision already constrained by other factors. Low taxes are mentioned as important influences by 35% of the new plants, a not insignificant fraction, although similar fractions obtain for a number of possible location influences. Moreover, there seems to be some tendency for low taxes to be valued more by the high technology, industrial machinery/transportation equipment, specialty chemicals/metals, labor cost sensitive and market sensitive industry groups), which would be entirely natural to expect since these industries are more footloose and thus less subject to many other influences on location choice.

Desiring low taxes was cited by about the same fraction of long-distance mover plants (31%), suggesting that the long distance mover and the new plant opening may be rough equivalents in their desires to lower

Table 2-3

Influences on Site Selection: Factors Viewed as "Desirable, if Available"
—All Industries

Factor	Percent of Those Plant Openings Citing at Least 1 Factor Which Check This Factor	Percent of Those Movers Citing at Least 1 Factor Which Check This Factor
Favorable labor climate	74	44
Low land costs	60	50
Near markets	42	22
Low taxes	35	19
On expressway	35	28
Rail service	30	22
Low construction costs	29	33
Low wage rates	28	25
College nearby	26	14
Low energy costs	25	14
Government help with roads, sewerage, water, labor training	25	3
Near suppliers	23	25
Government financing	13	6
Available land/buildings	3	11
Near other division facilities	3	3
Air transportation	1	0
Quality of life	1	0
Retain labor force	0	3
Number of plants citing at least one factor	159	36

Source: Schmenner study, 1980.

tax rates. It should be reiterated, however, that the long-distance mover in the Fortune 500 sample was as likely to move to a higher property tax rate area as to a lower one, and that a similar comparison of income tax rates reveals much the same thing. If the analogy is possible, it appears that taxes for newly opening plants may play a role in some decisions, but these decisions are not likely to be numerous. It seems reasonable to assert that low taxes, taken by themselves, are no guarantee of better than average industrial development. The number of location decisions swayed by taxes appears to be too few to ensure such a result.

Tax and financing policy and business climate

The foregoing results demonstrate fairly convincingly that tax and financial incentives have little influence on almost all plant location decisions. Taxes and financial inducements seem to be, at best, tie-breakers acting between otherwise equal towns or sites. These traditional linchpins of state and local industrial development efforts simply cannot be relied on, by themselves, to attract new plants that would otherwise locate somewhere else. In fact, that the tax and financial results introduced above are

Table 2-4

Percent of Site Location Influences "Perceived as 'Desirable, If Available' and Helped to Tip the Scales in Favor of This Site," by Industry Group (Plant Openings Only)

Industry Group

Influence	Agriculture Tied	Market Sensitive	Forest Tied	Labor Cost Sensitive	Heavy Chemicals/Oils/Rubber/Glass	Specialty Chemicals/Metals	Heavy Metals	Industrial Machinery/Transport Equipment	High Technology
Low Land Costs	66.7	55.0	50.0	81.8	57.1	42.9	75.0	66.7	41.4
Low Construction Costs	33.3	17.5	12.5	54.5	28.6	28.6	0	31.0	27.6
Low Energy Costs	22.2	17.5	12.5	18.2	28.6	57.1	75.0	23.8	20.7
On Expressway	11.1	42.5	25.0	36.4	28.6	42.9	50.0	38.1	17.2
Rail Service	44.4	45.0	75.0	27.3	50.0	57.1	100.0	9.5	0
Near Markets	55.6	60.0	62.5	36.4	64.3	42.9	50.0	28.6	3.4
Near Suppliers	22.2	15.0	50.0	27.3	50.0	28.6	25.0	16.7	10.3
Low Wage Rates	22.2	25.0	0	36.4	14.3	42.9	25.0	26.2	41.4
Favorable Labor Climate	100.0	65.0	62.5	81.8	64.3	85.7	100.0	61.9	79.3
College Nearby	11.1	15.0	0	27.3	21.4	14.3	25.0	26.2	51.7
Low Taxes	11.1	35.0	25.0	45.5	28.6	71.4	25.0	35.7	31.0
Government Help with Roads, Sewerage, Water	22.2	32.5	0	9.1	14.3	28.6	0	31.0	13.8
Government Financing	0	15.0	12.5	0	0	14.3	0	11.9	10.3
Number of Plants in Group	9	40	8	11	14	7	4	42	29

Source: Schmenner study, 1980.

so weak suggests that the traditional tax and financial incentives—tax reductions, moratoriums, rollbacks, assessment breaks, industrial revenue bonding, et. al.—may not be worth the cost. That is, the increased revenue brought into a state or locality by the siting of new plants that would have located elsewhere were it not for various incentives may not exceed the revenue foregone from new plants that would have located there without incentives. While this contention cannot be proved one way or another, the insignificance of tax and financial incentives in the reported results seriously brings into question the appropriateness of such policies.

Nevertheless, the relative unimportance of tax and financial incentives does not give states and localities free rein to peg tax rates at any level without fear of deterring future plant locations. I am persuaded that personal preference and "business climate" still play a role in at least some location decisions. "Business climate" constantly eludes precise definition because it means different things to different people, yet for all it remains a rough metric of a location's expected ability to maintain a productive environment over the foreseeable future. Attitudes are important to the business climate: the attitude of working people to hard work, to quality work, to unionization; the attitude of government to business, as reflected in government aid in solving joint problems, and in regulations, tax rates, and financing; the attitude of government in managing itself, its services, its schools. A location's perceived business climate is markedly self-perpetuating and hence difficult to turn around, but there is no doubt that it does exert influence on new plant location decisions.

Low tax levels, the availability of industrial revenue bonds, and other fiscal policies, are sometimes representative to the search team of a state or community's desire to host new industry and to reflect a willingness to work with industry on the physical concerns that enable smooth handling of site preparation, plant construction or renovation, and start-up. To be safe, a state or locality may also find it helpful to avoid being "fiscally conspicuous." The fiscally conservative city or state government tends to blend its tax rates into the backgrounds of its neighbors. What is to be avoided is the single tax that stands out from the others. Here, a state or locality may find it more useful to levy a variety of smaller taxes rather than a single, conspicuous tax.[3] Evaluating all the tax differences among sites is not a trivial exercise, so if a city or state can avoid being discarded early by a search team's possibly irrational look at a conspicuous tax, that area stands a better chance of favorable review.

---

[3]To be sure, this fiscal policy may thwart worthwhile movements to simplify taxation. Its intent is not to proliferate taxes but to eliminate highly visible tax rates which seems to gather as much criticism as revenue and may put off the growth of business in the area. If the states and localities within a region simplify their tax structures in concert, this effect of the fiscally conspicuous tax could be greatly muted.

Government Programs That Are Used and Valued

Table 2-5 summarizes the use of public policies by plants that have been surveyed in Cincinnati, New England, and nationally (the latter as part of a study of the Fortune 500 companies). Although these results may surprise some people it is clear from all three sources that, on average, specific public policies are used comparatively little even by large companies. Not even the ubiquitous industrial revenue bond is used as much as some believe.

Corporations use government policies very selectively. Of the Fortune 500 sample, 71% received some government assistance. This figure is supported by the New England data which show that 40% of the new plants in that region had no dealings with state or local governments. It is important to note that physical help with the location decision is used more often than financial help. Again, Table 2-5 shows that 61% of the Fortune 500 survey sample have used at least one physical aid the government offered, whereas only 31% of the new plants have used financial assistance. Only a mover plant is more apt to use financial rather than physical help from the government.

Table 2-6 displays how various public policies differ in their use by Fortune 500 companies across regions of the country. Note the differences in the intensity of use among regions. There seems to be a case here for "supply creating its own demand" in the use of selected public policies. For example, industrial revenue bonding began in the East South Central region and state and local officials there have considerable experience with it. It is not surprising to see companies in that region using such financial assistance to a much greater degree. Similarly, the labor training assistance pioneered in the South Atlantic states seems to have created its own demand also. Its use is far more intensive there than elsewhere in the nation.

One public policy does appear to be an effective inducement to industrial development, namely, the state right-to-work law banning the union shop. As Table 2-3 shows, a favorable labor climate is broadly held to be advantageous, and right-to-work states are frequently preferred for new plant sites for just that reason. How do the right-to-work states fare? Of the Fortune 500 plants which stayed put in the 1970s, 34% were located in right-to-work states. Of that group, 44% have been unionized, as opposed to 57% of the plants in non-right-to-work states. Of newly sited plants in the 1970s, only 14% of those in right-to-work states have been unionized as opposed to 29% of the new plants in non-right-to-work states. Apparently, locating in a right-to-work state does help a plant stay non-union, but it is clear that plants can remain non-union almost anywhere in the country. (The least favorable area is the East North Central region).

Table 2-5

The Use of Government Aid by New Plants: Frequencies
By Which Different Kinds of Plants Used Specific Government Assistance

Item	Cincinnati Data Mover Plants		New England Mover Plants			Fortune 500 Data Nationally	
	Single Plant Companies	Plants of Multiplant Companies	Single Plant Companies	Plants of Multiplant Companies	Newly Opened Plants	Mover Plants	Newly Opened Plants
Number of Plants	53	11	74	38	82	36	161
Financial Help							
Industrial revenue bonds	4%	18%	7%	8%	29%	14%	21%
Industrial revenue bonds for pollution control	NA	NA	NA	NA	NA	3%	5%
Tax concessions of any sort	NA	NA	14%	16%	11%	28%	14%
Physical Help							
Roads, sewers, water	NA	NA	NA	NA	NA	3%	38%
Labor training	NA	NA	NA	NA	NA	6%	30%
Help with environmental permits	NA	NA	NA	NA	NA	6%	22%
Zoning changes	2%	0	3%	2%	3%	8%	12%
Expansion of sewage treatment	NA	NA	NA	NA	NA	0	10%
Traffic, parking adjustment	NA	NA	NA	NA	NA	3%	6%
Character of Dealings							
Highly attentive and helpful	NA	NA	31%	42%	46%	NA	NA
Only modestly helpful	NA	NA	29%	19%	12%	NA	NA
No dealings	NA	NA	38%	40%	40%	56%	29%

Source: Schmenner studies, 1978 and 1980.

55

Table 2-6

Percentage of Plant Openings By Major Manufacturers Using Various Public Policies, By Region

Regions

Public Policy	New England	Mid-Atlantic	South Atlantic	East North Central	East South Central	West North Central	West South Central	Mountain	Pacific
Physical Help									
Roads, sewerage lines, water mains, etc.	56	29	56	20	18	21	44	80	22
Labor training	0	21	61	13	36	21	35	0	0
Environmental permits	22	29	31	20	5	7	17	40	26
Zoning changes	0	7	11	13	14	0	9	60	17
Expansion of sewage treatment	22	14	11	7	5	7	9	20	9
Traffic, parking adjustments	22	0	8	13	0	0	0	20	4
Financial Help									
Industrial revenue bonds	0	21	14	13	50	21	13	20	13
Industrial revenues bonds for pollution control	0	0	8	7	0	0	13	0	0
Tax abatements, holidays, or other tax concessions	0	14	8	7	32	14	22	0	4
Number of plant openings from region	9	14	36	15	22	14	23	5	23

Source: Schmenner study, 1980.

There is no question that right-to-work states are booming. While only 34% of all stay-put plants in the sample are located in right-to-work states, one half of all the new plants have been sited in them. The data suggest that the edge of non-unionism in right-to-work states has triggered a more-than-proportional number of plant openings there.

Of course, many right-to-work states are located in the Sunbelt. Having the majority of right-to-work states is a key element in the Sunbelt's attractiveness. In the analysis in Chapter 3, which characterizes the differences between both new and old Sunbelt and Frostbelt plants, being non-union was the most important discriminating factor. A public policy of being a right-to-work state clearly is an important one.

Labor training

It was noted that while labor training programs are widely available throughout the nation, they are heavily used only in the South Atlantic states. Why are they used so much there and not elsewhere? To explore this point, the labor training assistance offered by the South Atlantic states has been compared against that offered by other states. While this comparison is by no means exhaustive, certain characteristics of the programs of the South Atlantic states (and selected others) stand out. These characteristics fit well with what manufacturers have told me they value, and thus the type of program appears to be the explanation.

The characteristics of these programs which set them apart from others include:

1. Many South Atlantic states provide pre-employment training programs which are custom-designed for a specific company or plant. These pre-employment programs are not mere extensions of technical institutes or community colleges nor are they on-the-job training or CETA programs targeted specifically to the long-term unemployed. Rather, they are designed specifically for a company's new plant and are set up near the site of that plant.

2. The manufacturer is more likely to be made aware of the pre-employment training program by the state development agency, which views itself as the "one-stop shopping" center for a manufacturer's new plant needs. The program is not typically left to the manufacturer to be "applied for."

3. The company itself is involved in the program design and instruction. The company may use its own curriculum and instructors, at state expense. Thus, the training programs are extraordinarily flexible and comprehensive in design and are responsive to the particular needs of the company involved.

4. Final hiring decisions are made after training is complete. The company is not committed to hiring trainees prior to the start of training, as in CETA-OJT programs.

5. The state bears all costs of these labor training programs.

The labor assistance programs of most other states are not as customized as these, and are tied typically to existing educational structures. Often they are less comprehensive and flexible, less geographically accessible, and may cost the company some money.

Physical aid

The survey findings suggest, then, that states and localities should concentrate on helping their manufacturer's with the physical items which go into selecting a plant's location, constructing it, and starting it up. States and localities should stand ready to offer the interested manufacturer (i) speedy and accurate information about potential sites, (ii) help in securing necessary environmental or zoning permits, and (iii) timely help with the roads, sewerage, water, waste treatment, and labor training which can make a real difference to the smooth start-up of a new manufacturing facility. I remain convinced that the industrial growth of the South has had more to do with Southern hospitality than with Southern tax rates. The regional differences in the use of such assistance as labor training suggests that supply does seem to create at least some of its own demand in these matters.

Recently there has been a rise in expediting mechanisms to counter the stifling effect that large bureaucracies have on industrial decision making. Some cities and states have sponsored ombudsmen to guide businesses through the red-tape mazes. Such programs have received uniformly positive reactions. Such expediting is highly valued by many large companies, and explains, in part, the favorable opinions they have of the industrial development programs of North Carolina, South Carolina, Nebraska, and elsewhere. It is difficult for the average businessperson to know how to secure quick rulings on zoning variances, building permits, environmental standards and regulations, parking regulations, and tax assessments and abatements. The more government can cut the red tape, the more industry it can expect to retain. This exceedingly useful function could be promoted even more than it has been.

Cities and states can also improve their responses to business queries and requests by realigning authority. If all business-related issues cannot be consolidated into a single agency, at least business affairs within specific departments and agencies should be grouped together. Thus a public works department could have an office expressly focused on the concerns of business firms in the area. Such specialization would have the added advantage of speeding the work of any ombudsman.

This kind of assistance has to be timely if it is to matter. The actual site selection phase of the decision process lasts only about 6 months. To my mind, this implies that any governmental aid like a grant, which must be applied for, should be avoided. It is unlikely that a searching company could afford the time to apply. Furthermore, any governmental incentive for a plant to locate in a particular area should fall on the manufacturer like manna: Quick. Guaranteed. No tests to meet. No hurdles to overcome. Nothing to do but locate in the area and the savings are instantaneous. Tax credits or reductions, although operating on a very "thin" economic margin, at least offer this advantage.

Site development

If tax and financial incentives are the first prong of a traditional development effort, the second prong is typically the preparation of industrial parks and sites. This is an expensive undertaking, often too much for most localities to finance themselves given the other debts they usually accumulate, therefore federal help is usually sought. For states and localities the federal government and its grab bag of grants and programs is the next best thing to costless economic development. Before 1970, the urban renewal program was the wellspring of many local efforts to develop urban industrial parks. More recently the Economic Development Administration has funded similar efforts to purchase, renovate, and develop industrial sites mostly within city limits, many of them nearly abandoned anyway.

Yet these efforts to prepare sites are years in development and the end result very different from what was expected. Almost always, the industry hoped for does not appear, so the space is sold for distribution services or for some other nonindustrial use. The reasons for this state of affairs are vexing. The length of time required for development is one factor impeding the entry of initially targeted companies to these areas. Another is the restrictions companies face if locating on government-controlled sites. These range from local parking regulations, to building codes, to federal minimum levels of employees per acre (a restriction that works against company "land banking" for future expansion and increases the attractiveness of suburban sites that have more space available for growth). Most localities, unused to being land brokers and developers, are not very good at it. Private firms are usually more efficient at providing usable sites for industry. In fact, localities typically become adept at site development only after hiring talent away from the private sector.

3

How the Big

Boys Do It:

examples from

the Fortune 500

As mentioned in the Introduction, a location decision should be viewed as three decisions in one: whether to add capacity, the nature of the added capacity (on-site, new plant, relocation), and where to site any new plant. Chapter 1 noted that a decision on whether to add capacity involves recognizing future capacity shortfalls, either by traditional, informal, ad hoc means or by the newer, more widespread adoption of formal business planning. A third composite alternative was also mentioned.

Chapter 1 also included a discussion of the relative advantages and disadvantages of on-site expansion, new plant opening, or plant relocation, and analyzed different schemes for organizing and conducting a location search.

The aim of this chapter is to fill out that framework for the location decision process and the suggestions offered there. The examples and analysis found in this chapter derive, for the most part, from the Fortune 500 companies, although other data are called upon periodically. The chapter is organized into the following major segments:

- Organizational Structures Adopted for the Location Decision Process: Examples from Major Corporations
- The On-Site Expansion—Plant Opening—Relocation Choice: Survey Results
- Influences on the Location Search Itself: Company Examples
- Influences on Location Choice: Survey Evidence

Thus, the organizational attributes of the location decision are discussed first, and then the issues which mold the decision.

Organization Structures Adopted for the Location Decision Process: Examples from Major Corporations

The first chapter summarized seven distinct organizational schemes that my interviewing of major manufacturers uncovered. The seven—centralized, large group study; centralized, small group study; corporate staff controlled; corporate staff led; division led; division controlled; and division only study—are examined here in considerably more depth with various company examples used to illustrate them.

The centralized, large corporate group study

ANHEUSER-BUSCH, INC.

Brewing and packaging beer is a capital-intensive endeavor, and for that reason alone it is no wonder that a company like Anheuser-Busch devotes a great deal of study to any decision to expand its manufacturing space and equipment. Moreover, beer being mostly water, the cost of transporting it to market is a significant cost influenced by location. The network of locations for a national brewer like Anheuser-Busch is extraordinarily interdependent as well, since the siting of a new brewery alters the existing distribution patterns of other breweries and thus also alters the transportation costs incurred by the company as a whole. To keep the company's total transportation expenses low, the distribution patterns of all its breweries must be analyzed as a group.

At Anheuser-Busch, the need for additional capacity is uncovered by the formal 5-year business planning exercise that is updated and reviewed each year. The marketing forecast, including sales volume, product mix, and geographical patterns, serves as the basis for the business plan. At issue each year is how much new capacity should be added, as opposed to the on-going piecemeal breaking of specific bottlenecks at existing breweries. It is the responsibility of the top rank management committee of the corporation to debate and decide this issue. The committee's decision on this matter usually does not indicate whether capacity should be added at an existing brewery by expansion or whether a new brewery should be built. This decision is deferred until after a study has been made.

Once the management committee has decided to add capacity, responsibility passes to the engineering department, which must develop the formal capital appropriations request and ask for funds to study the location of the new capacity. Study funds are usually approved within a month of the management committee's decision.

While the study of, and action on, new capacity rest formally with the engineering department, a major piece of analysis on the location decision is accomplished by the corporate planning department, whose task it is to recommend a metropolitan area in which to locate the new capacity. The selection of the particular site within that area is left to a group of vice presidents. The corporate planning department is also responsible for the financial analysis within the capital appropriations request. Final approval of any site is a matter for the management committee and the board of directors.

Anheuser-Busch is a particularly clear example of a location decision process which is initiated by the top rank of management and studied by a number of corporate staff functions, each assigned some rather well-defined responsibilities.

This kind of centralized study and decision-making on location is evident also in the large projects considered by basic metals manufacturers such as U.S. Steel and Alcoa.

U.S. STEEL AND ALCOA

At basic metals companies, such as U.S. Steel and Alcoa, the decision to construct a large new facility (steel mill, aluminum smelter, or the like) involves a staggeringly huge price tag, lead times of 5 to 10 years or more, and a great deal of planning and debate. Any large new facility of this type represents a non-trivial percentage of total national capacity, and thus it is paramount that the decision include careful analysis of the expected "metal balance" (demand projections, analysis of competitive capacity moves, analysis of the company's own ability to break bottlenecks and squeeze more capacity out of existing facilities) so that the investment will not generate capacity that is likely to sit idle for some years. In these companies, production capacity adjustments reside at the heart of the business and are the responsibility of a group of the company's senior managers.

To deal with these decisions, U.S. Steel and Alcoa have evolved rather formal procedures and centralized organizations. Both companies adhere strictly to formal planning for both business and facilities plans, with a 10-year horizon. At U.S. Steel a strategic planning department within the corporate staff has the responsibility of overseeing and counseling the development of these plans and their underlying data. To complement this effort a facility plans department supports the approved strategic plans with the necessary investment proposals and the engineering and financial analyses to substantiate them. The facility plans department is charged with developing capacity proposals, shepherding them through approval-in-principle by the company's corporate policy committee and the board of directors, and then assembling the formal capital appropriations request for later review and approval by those two bodies.

As expected, the economics of on-site expansion (called "brownfield construction") versus new site establishment ("greenfield construction") are overwhelmingly in favor of brownfield development, if it is feasible. Any remedy of a shortfall in the "metal balance" involves an assessment of the ways in which the shortfall can be met without incurring the costs and agony of planning, constructing, and starting up a vast new complex. This on-site versus off-site decision is critical to the early development of a proposal and informal agreement to it by the corporate staff, the operating division involved, and the senior corporate management.

If a decision is made to undertake greenfield construction, it is corporate staff—U.S. Steel's Facility Plans Department, or Alcoa's standing Building Site Committee chaired by an Executive Vice President—which coordinates a substantial, in-depth analysis of possible locations. At both corporations, specialists are called in to evaluate aspects of the decision. The resulting corporate staff team to investigate locations ordinarily includes engineering, personnel, transportation-logistics, real estate, construction, environmental affairs, public relations, the controller's office (tax and financial matters), and representatives from the operating divisions directly affected. Most team members are responsible for collecting and interpreting data in their area of expertise and then merging it with data from the others to decide   1) the best region for a new site, if that had not already been decided, and   2) the area within that region. (Fabrication plants are located typically with the market in mind, while basic metals plants are located with raw materials in mind.) There is not a lot of latitude in choosing a particular site since the requirements for it (on water, rail service nearby, and vast acreage—say 5,000 to 10,000 acres) often dictate that choice. Site selection of fabricated products is related to that market; whereas, if raw materials such as minerals are the basis of the product, site selection depends on the location of the mineral supply rather than the market. Considering this, at both U.S. Steel and Alcoa, final site selection is generally delegated to the real estate department and is not something the team itself becomes engaged in actively.

Anheuser-Busch, U.S. Steel, and Alcoa share some important features, listed below, which I have grouped together under the category of Centralized, Large Group Study of the location decision.

• The location decision process is initiated by upper level corporate management apart from the specific request of a division. Any divisions involved are brought into the decision process more to facilitate intra-company communication and data-gathering than to lobby senior management for permission to seek a possible new site. The true initiative for the decision lies with senior management.

• Senior management initiative is frequently prompted by a formal business planning system which can give capacity shortfalls considerable visibility.

• The study of possible site locations rests with the corporate staff. A particular and permanent section of that staff assumes responsibility for coordinating the study effort, specifically Corporate Planning, Facility Plans, or a standing committee).

• A variety of corporate staff specialists analyze the key criteria of the decision—transportation/logistics, personnel, environmental affairs, plant engineering, real estate, tax, governmental affairs, and so on.

• This team of corporate staff specialists is often charged with deciding the metropolitan or rural area for a new plant but may leave the precise site selection to the real estate group.

These features are evident again in another example of Centralized, Large Group Study of the location decision, that of Company W.

COMPANY W

The initiative for a substantial increase in capacity at Company W derives from the chief corporate planning committee, which reports to an executive vice president. This corporate staff group is responsible for melding the requests and plans of the various divisions of the company. The need for such a centralized group to perform this melding and to take the initiative on the plant additions is implied by the exceptional interdependence of divisions within this company. A single division cannot act or plan alone and still serve the best interests of the company.

The chief corporate planning committee looks ahead at least three to four years, and at its monthly meetings, key decisions about product plans and the concomitant facility and technology needs are made. If it is decided that new capacity is required in a particular division, the affected division then approaches the facilities planning department of the corporate staff with its need. This need reflects the division's interpretation of its mandate from the planning committee and includes estimates of square feet, personnel, power, transportation, water, and other requirements. At this point, the division would not specify where it would want to put that capacity, although the division manager and the division vice president have decided whether to expand on-site or near an existing plant, or whether to seek a new location at some distance from existing sites.

Having been approached with a division's need, the facilities planning department initiates a new location search. Using the division's estimated requirements as a base, the department scans its catalog of available sites and may also develop new site leads that may be appropriate. Based upon an initial rough-cut analysis of these, a half dozen sites or so are brought to the attention of the division's management. The division then selects three sites or so for more detailed evaluation.

For this detailed evaluation, the facilities planning department convenes a semi-permanent team of corporate staff specialists. The facilities planning group directs this effort which typically includes representatives from industrial relations, logistics, energy management, environmental affairs, plant engineering, industry-government relations, and tax. The team's output is a report to the division which makes a specific site recommendation and supports it with analysis by each of the representatives. The decision whether to accept the team's recommendation is the division's to make. The division general manager and his group vice president generally visit the sites and compare their own observations to the report. Upon reaching a site decision, they initiate the capital appropriations request; meld on-going engineering, construction, and equipment estimates into the documentation; and champion the proposal through the upper levels of corporate approval. Once approval from the company's executive committee and Board of Directors is received, the planning department acts to purchase the site.

The specialization and formality of the location decision process in Centralized, Large Corporate Group Study firms like Company W, Anheuser-Busch, U.S. Steel, and Alcoa is in marked contrast to two other forms of location decision-making: the Division Only Study and the Centralized, Small Group Study. We now consider these two types of decision processes.

The division only study

BEATRICE FOODS COMPANY

Beatrice Foods is a classically decentralized company, operating about 400 separate profit centers. These 400 profit centers, for the most part individual plants, report upwards through an ever-narrowing pyramid of corporate authority, as shown in Figure 3-1.

Initiative for new capacity and a possible location decision emanates most frequently from the profit center affected. This initiative is formally registered in the annual business plan which each profit center must develop. Location preferences may be stated in the business plan as may specific attributes about a location: labor market definition, product affected, site purchase versus lease, transportation constraints, and the like.

Side-by-side the formality of the business plan at Beatrice Foods lies an important network of informal communication. Before anything is placed in a business plan, it is informally discussed with several layers of management — the immediate boss, the boss's boss, subordinates, and other interested parties. This process not only shapes the initial idea, but gains commitment for it from those who must champion it through higher corporate levels.

This informal communication also helps to attach priorities to capital expenditure projects advanced from the various profit centers. The sum of capital requests from its profit centers in any one year is invariably greater than the capital budget the corporation could reasonably hope to finance. Thus, the funds must be rationed among the many groups competing for them. The rationing process is an informal negotiation among layers of management. After these negotiations, some projects are placed in the corporation's capital budget and are likely to be approved; the others are set aside, perhaps until the next year.

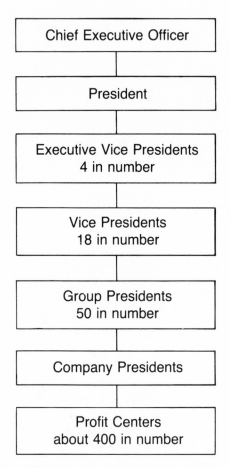

Figure 3-1. Hierarchy of corporate authority in Beatrice Foods

Note: Some profit centers report to so-called company presidents whereas others, mainly larger ones, report directly to group presidents.

This upward movement of project initiatives and plans, and the informal communication network that guides and accompanies them, characterize most of the location decisions made by Beatrice Foods. Two variations to this general procedure are worth noting, however.

1. Whereas most location proposals are triggered by the profit centers themselves, a few are attributable to higher management. Moreover, these latter proposals tend to be more strategic in concept than those advanced by the profit centers; perhaps these involve relocating an existing facility or a broader, faster expansion of geographic manufacturing and marketing for the strong, regional brands which abound at Beatrice Foods.

2. Another variation to the general procedure concerns the generation of initiatives from each profit center. Although most initiatives to add capacity are inserted into the plan, Beatrice Foods process permits some proposals to be considered outside of the business planning exercise. These proposals might represent responses to rapidly developing opportunities or an addition which is especially strategic in its implications.

Once a proposal for new capacity and a new location is approved as part of the capital budget, the profit center concerned develops the report recommending a particular location as well as the capital appropriations request that must go before the Board of Directors. In these endeavors the individual profit centers are essentially on their own. While the corporate staff is available for consultation, there are relatively few specialists on that staff on which to draw for engineering or site selection expertise. Thus, outside consultants are sometimes engaged to help the profit center management.

Muting this absence of corporate staff in location decision study are several facts about Beatrice Foods. For one, the demands of the consumer products industries in which Beatrice Foods competes differ markedly from the technological and environmental demands that affect U.S. Steel, Alcoa, or Company W. The operations are neither so technical nor so rapidly advancing that a profit center's own engineering staff cannot keep up with the industry's state-of-the-art. Secondly, much of Beatrice Foods' internal growth is generated by the geographic spread of its strong regional brands (Dannon Yogurt, Ekrich Meats, Tropicana Orange Juice). The location characteristics for expansions, and the layout of the new plants themselves, can be fairly readily modelled after existing plants. Thirdly, Beatrice Foods has been blessed by its ability to retain entrepreneurial managers, many from companies it has acquired through the years, who relish the kind of non-standard decision-making offered by a new location choice.

BROWN SHOE COMPANY

The Brown Shoe Company is a member of the Brown Group, Inc. About half of the Brown Group's sales are derived from manufacturing, and the largest single segment of manufacturing is the Brown Shoe Company. The shoe company is managed as a largely independent entity of the Brown Group, and its handling of location decision-making is no exception.

The decision on capacity change at Brown Shoe is initiated by a formal corporate business plan. Marketing forecasts guide the business plan and emanate from both the marketing department and the marketing research group on the company's staff. The time horizon for the business plan is set at three years because, in a fashion-sensitive business like shoes, forecasting beyond three years quickly becomes too speculative.

This fashion sensitivity and a traditional cyclicality of the shoe and apparel industries to fluctuations in gross national product contribute to a great reluctance at Brown Shoe to add "bricks and mortar" if some other means of adding capacity can be used instead. Such alternatives include increased overtime, juggling product lines among plants, increased subcontracting, altered production planning and the like. However, any persistent shortfall of capacity over the horizon of a year or two may signal the need for additional space. The issue is then assiduously debated within the company over many months.

Brown Shoe operates two clusters of plants, each cluster revolving around a mixing warehouse from which orders are filled. The plants in each cluster supply these two mixing warehouses with the specific shoe types (for example, welted shoes, cemented sole shoes, wood wedge shoes, high-fashion women's shoes) assigned to them. Each plant is responsible for one main type of shoe construction, which enables a purity of equipment, technique, and materials for each plant. If a genuine need for additional space is established, the next consideration is how that space ought to fit into the prevailing cluster of plants and plant charters. Thus, having established the need, Brown Shoe's senior management must decide whether the new capacity should be added by on-site expansion or new plant construction, and what changes should be made, if any, to the charters of existing plants.

If a new plant is decided upon, the search for its location devolves to the Senior Vice President for Manufacturing. The initial stages of the location search are largely a one-person effort, with the Senior Vice President for Manufacturing scouring maps, drawing on his own knowledge and on that of company personnel who have travelled widely in a region. The location search cannot be far-ranging as the cluster concept constrains these manufacturing plants to be within one day's truck drive from one or the other mixing warehouse in St. Louis or west Tennessee.

Having roughed-out the location search, the Senior Vice President for Manufacturing contacts state economic development agencies, specifies Brown Shoe's needs, and waits for those agencies to respond with a sheaf of community profiles which might be satisfactory. Once in hand, the most promising locations are sifted out. These always share excellent labor force characteristics, since shoe manufacturing is basically labor-intensive and fairly low-wage.

To assess the labor force better, plant managers from the nearest Brown Shoe facilities call on the communities' existing industry and report back to the Senior Vice President. If their reports are positive, personnel/industrial relations people from the Brown Shoe Company conduct a specific labor survey, and the Senior Vice President for Manufacturing visits the community to collect his own impressions and evaluate how Brown

Shoe would fit in there. The decision is his, although he must champion it before higher levels of management and the Board of Directors.

From these examples of Beatrice Foods and the Brown Shoe Company and from other company discussions, several distinguishing characteristics emerge to define the Decentralized, Division Only Study of a location decision:

• The location decision process is initiated by the division itself. A formal business plan may or may not have initiated the division's interest in a possible new location.

• Whether or not a formal business plan is involved, a division proposal is less visible than one initiated from the top of the company. Generally, some lobbying is required to convince senior corporate management to fund one division's proposal versus that of another.

• In contrast to a Centralized, Large Group Study, it is more likely in a Division Only Study that an informal network of discussion and approvals is invoked to clear a project through the Board of Directors or to place it within an approved business plan or capital budget. This is not to say that informal agreements never occur in a Centralized Large Group Study: merely, that the degree of informality seems greater in the Decentralized, Division Only location decision process.

• The Division itself is responsible for developing the report supporting a particular site and for drafting the capital appropriations request needed for final approval.

• While the initiative on location lies most frequently with the operating division, upper levels of management sometimes propose new or restructure initial proposals if they affect strategic matters. Pertinent strategic matters triggering such action might include the designation of a new plant complex or cluster, the relocation of a plant, or the geographic expansion of marketing and manufacturing responsibilities.

• Frequently the division team studying location is also responsible for coordinating the engineering and for planning, and even executing, the new plant start-up. The new plant manager-designate may be a member of, or leading, the team.

• In a Division Only decision process, the proposal advanced is more likely to be identified with an individual than is a Centralized, Large Group proposal. The track record of this individual becomes an important component in the evaluation of the project. By contrast, so many managers and so many resources are interrelated in a Centralized, Large Group process that the final decision seldom pivots on any one person's capabilities, not even the chief executive officer's.

• With a Division Only decision process it is more likely that the need for a new location comes up infrequently, perhaps only once in a division manager's "corporate lifetime." This situation, being so out of the ordinary, can cause some anxiety among division managers. It is not unusual for a division to call in consultants to assist the division in making its location decision. In fact, location consultants (The Fantus Company, A.T. Kearney, the Austin Company, and others) are most apt to be engaged by those major companies with a Division Only type of decision process.

Many of these key distinguishing characteristics are reinforced by the following example.

COMPANY X

Decision-making within Company X, a consumer products manufacturer, is decentralized. The recent decision of one of its operating divisions to open a new facility was initiated and studied by that division alone. Corporate level management was brought into the process only to approve the funds.

The need for a new facility for the division was not identified through the use of a formal business plan. Rather, the need had been a topic of repeated debate for twenty-five years, sparked whenever space became tight. On-site expansion at the main facility, the acquisition of another company, product rationalizations, and process/equipment modernizations kept postponing action on the construction of a new plant. Eventually, continued growth, a concern for the absolute size of the main plant, and a threat of federal government mandates on production processes in the industry convinced both division and corporate management that a new facility was desirable. A vice president at corporate headquarters, who early on supported the opening of a new plant, was instrumental in persuading other senior managers of the virtues of a new plant.

The Division Only study of a suitable plant location was assigned to a manufacturing staff person with long experience in the company. From division finance, transportation/logistics, and personnel managers, he organized a part-time site selection committee. Later the plant manager-designate joined this site selection committee. The committee was responsible for evaluating each of the prospective sites and for ensuring that all relevant aspects were examined carefully, so that their ultimate report to the corporate board did not commit any oversights. Most of the initial criteria, area screenings, and site visits were performed by the division manufacturing staff person and his assistant.

The site selection committee worked with an industrial realtor to contact state development officials, public utilities, railroads, and local chambers of commerce. The search and evaluation, however, was controlled throughout by the division's site selection committee.

Once a suitable site was chosen, the division's executive vice president and the previously mentioned vice president at corporate headquarters acted to champion the proposal through the top ranks of management and the Board of Directors.

The Centralized, Large Group Study of the location decision and the Decentralized, Division Only Study offer some rather sharp contrasts as we have seen. Some of these same contrasts in the processes of decision-making are evident in comparison of the Centralized, Small Group Study with the Centralized, Large Group Study.

Centralized, small group study

AGRICO CHEMICAL COMPANY (one of the Williams Companies)

The Agrico Chemical Company is a leading supplier of fertilizer. It was formed in 1971, as one of the Williams Companies of Tulsa, Oklahoma, when the fertilizer interests of the Gulf Oil Corporation were purchased. In 1972, the fertilizer business of the Continental Oil Company was acquired and revamped. By these actions, Agrico became a presence in both the nitrogen and phosphate fertilizer markets. Its recent sales and capacity have been growing rapidly, and it has earned a reputation for production innovation.

As its running start into the fertilizer field may have indicated, the Agrico Chemical Company is an extraordinarily entrepreneurial company, quick to seek new business opportunities and quick to act upon them. This mode of operation has several implications for the location decision process. For one, the company's chief executive officer is tremendously active in the determination of the need for a new location, in the initiation of the search, and in the choice of the site. However, the decision is based on an evaluation of alternative sites identified from a planning or other evaluation process. Much of the study for a location choice is undertaken by one, or at most a few, key staff people who take a very active role in recommending a particular location to the decision maker(s). At Agrico, the corporate staff remains the "nerve center" of the company. Most of the control of the company and initiatives for change rest in their centralized hands. Plants are evaluated as cost centers, with the manfacturing and the marketing line managers having very limited staffs of their own.

COMPANY Y

A similar structure exists at Company Y, a fast growing company which could be identified as "high technology". Like Agrico, Company Y is a remarkedly informal and entrepreneurial company. There is no formal business plan, although there are formal procedures for budgeting and capital appropriation. Control in the corporation is centralized and the chief executive officer is a very strong one.

A typical scenario at Company Y has the decision to seek a new location reached in discussions among the chief executive officer, the vice president for manufacturing, and the group vice president concerned with the project under scrutiny. These discussions are apt to be informal and range in duration from weeks to years. The outcome of the discussions would be a recommendation on plant size and charter and, perhaps, an indication of the general region in which the new plant ought to be placed. This recommendation, having earned the approval of the CEO, would be offered to the budget and executive committees for approval. If approved there, and by the Board of Directors, funds for the entire project would be appropriated.

Having launched the project in this way, potential locations are then studied. This responsibility falls to the corporate real estate manager, the key corporate staff person involved. Before 1976, there was no such officer in Company Y, providing further indication of the centralization of the location decision in such a company. (As it is, the real estate department has only recently grown from a one-person operation.) Communications between the corporate real estate manager and top management responsible for the project (the CEO or the group vice president) are close. The corporate real estate manager is actually working for the top rank of company management in these matters. The corporate real estate manager's report would include a ranked ordering of preferred sites. The final site decision would be made by the interested vice-president and by the CEO.

These two examples—Agrico Chemical and Company Y—provide us with some common features, listed below, which distinguish the Centralized, Small Group Study from both the Centralized, Large Group Study and the Decentralized, Division Only Study.

 • The location decision is approached as an integral aspect of the question "What business does this company really want to be in?" That is, the location decision is one that can be mentioned in the same breath, as it were, as potential acquisitions and divestitures.

 • For this reason, the location decision is very much the province of the company's chief executive officer, who is likely to be entrepreneurial, active, and exceedingly powerful.

 • Ad hoc capacity evaluation probably prevails. It is less likely that the need for a new location is identified by a formal business plan.

 • A few corporate staff people, often with considerable experience, are likely to conduct the study of particular candidate locations. These people are likely to consider top management as their client rather than the division that is to occupy the site chosen.

These distinguishing characteristics are reinforced by the following descriptions of the location decision process at two agribusiness cooperatives.

LAND O' LAKES AND GOLD KIST

Land O' Lakes and Gold Kist are both agribusiness cooperatives, Land O' Lakes serving the upper Midwest and Gold Kist serving the South. As cooperatives, they are owned by farmers in each area. They provide farm supplies, feed and fertilizers for their farmer-owners and, in turn, process and market what these farmer-owners grow. Land O' Lakes processes and markets principally dairy products, turkeys, beef, and soybeans; Gold Kist markets chiefly soybeans, feed grains, peanuts, pecans, poultry, and eggs.

Agribusiness cooperatives like Land O' Lakes and Gold Kist exist for the benefit of their farmer-owners. The cooperatives engage in constant dialogs with their membership to ascertain needs and capabilities. This kind of relationship places two special constraints on a location decision:

1. With the exception of product-specific cooperatives like Ocean Spray (cranberries), the membership of most agribusiness cooperatives is region-specific, which naturally constrains them to locate new processing facilities within their regions.

2. The character, and often the size, of a new facility is determined largely by the extent of the particular crops or livestock farming within a given radius of it. Sometimes the farmers can be induced to raise more of what is processed locally (for example, a soybean processing plant stimulating soybean farming in the area), but, new facilities more often are fitted into the prevailing farming patterns of the area.

The big decisions, then, are ones involving the choice of products to market and the extent of the cooperative's involvement in their raising, processing, marketing, and distribution. Location decisions derive from these larger business decisions, and examples of their importance abound. For instance, Gold Kist was a cotton cooperative originally, but it withdrew from cotton to market more profitable crops for its member-owners. One of Gold Kist's newer businesses is soybeans, which prior to the cooperative's involvement was not very important to southern agriculture. With Gold Kist's decision to encourage soybean farming and processing came the need to build soybean mills and develop the membership to sustain them. To cite another example, at Land O' Lakes the decision to acquire Spencer Foods and enter the beef business has had a significant impact on the cooperative's marketing, on its location decisions, and on its present and future strategy.

Given the close ties between product lines and location decisions in these situations, it is logical to expect that the initiative for new plants comes from the highest levels of management and that the study of potential locations is undertaken by top level staff people. Agribusiness cooperatives are more entrepreneurial than one might expect and are heavily dependent on quick, reliable communication among managers and between them and the farmer-owners to whom management is, in the end, responsible.

The initiative for a new plant is likely to come either from Board members, farmer patrons, the cooperative's president, group vice presidents, or the senior manager of a product line, such as poultry, dairy products or soybeans. Sometimes the initiative surfaces outside of any formal business plan but the need for added capacity is usually identified when long range plans are being developed by the cooperative and discussed at meetings of the corporate planning committee.

At Land O' Lakes, the study of a new plant site and the responsibility for the capital appropriation request lies with the group vice president. This officer usually calls in the corporate planning staff to join with in the study. Their report and its recommendations are reviewed by the cooperative's president and a special review committee of key managers before it is passed to the Board of Directors for final approval.

At Gold Kist, a new location study is performed by the corporate planning staff as part of overall economic feasibility studies prepared at the request of corporate group or division management. With assistance from engineering and real estate personnel the planning staff develops capital requirement estimates; the manager who initiated the project is responsible for the appropriation request. The study and its recommendations are reviewed by management at each level above the initiation level, and any additional information needed by management to make a decision is usually provided by the planning staff. Recommendations are then reviewed with the Board of Directors for final approval.

With these descriptions of the Centralized, Large and Small Group location decision studies, and of the Decentralized, Division Only Study, the poles of the search decision process have been staked out. In between lie the joint studies, which include a variety of division-staff interactions that companies have for making their location decisions.

Joint division-corporate staff interaction: the staff-controlled study

COMPANY Z

At Company Z the initiative for a new production location originates within the business divisions of the company, almost always as a result of formal planning which has taken hold in this corporation during the last few years. Division general managers are responsible for identifying prospective capacity shortfalls, analyzing them, and giving them visibility through the formal business planning exercise, and for lobbying for new facilities through the tiers of upper management.

Whereas the idea for a new plant is the division's, its managers do not actively participate in the study of potential new locations. Company Z policy places this responsibility exclusively with a corporate staff executive who makes all site selections. The division involved can veto a particular recommendation—after all, it must live with the decision—but its managers do not join with the corporate staff executive to study various sites. Rather, the division must call in this executive either prior to gaining the commitment of top management to authorize a new plant or after the management committee has reviewed the division's request for it. In either event, senior corporate management approval for the project usually occurs without the selection of a particular site, although there may be general agreement about the region into which the plant ought to be placed. The corporate staff executive may or may not have been a party to these discussions.

Once the decision to establish a new plant is made, the corporate staff executive begins the location search in earnest. The first task is to discuss with the division its requirements for the new plant, its size, the kinds of equipment that will be placed in it, where it will secure its supplies, where it will ship its output, what its labor and energy needs will be, and so forth. With these criteria known, he proceeds to identify suitable locations. This study is largely a one-person effort but three other groups, namely industrial relations/personnel, transportation/logistics, and tax typically provide data about the states and counties being seriously considered for the plant. The corporate staff executive couples this information to that gathered from his own research and from sources outside the company and develops an economic analysis of the potential locations.

From this, a set of preferred communities surfaces which are then visited by the corporate staff executive and some industrial relations staff people. The industrial relations people interview potential candidates for employment to gauge the labor climate as accurately as possible. The corporate staff executive visits potential sites, gets a "feel" for the vitality of the community, and talks to the town fathers. From such site visits, he ranks the sites and makes a recommendation to the division general manager and to his own boss, who is an officer of the corporation. The division general manager can veto the recommendation made, but usually accepts it. The division is responsible for authoring the capital appropriations request and shepherding it through the approval process.

OXFORD INDUSTRIES

Oxford Industries is an apparel manufacturer headquartered in Atlanta and has all of its plants in the Southeast. It is a divisional company, with eight separate divisions for shirts, men's sportwear, branded ladies sportswear, and other product lines. The operations of these divisions are decentralized; each division has a base plant which performs all production planning, order processing and handling, and which directs all manufacturing in the plants assigned to it.

At Oxford Industries the initiative for a new location originates with one of the division presidents. The company does not have a formal business plan but depends on the foresight of the division presidents to identify potential capacity shortfalls. Any need so identified is informally communicated to the management committee, consisting of half a dozen of the corporation's most senior managers. Informally, this committee and the division president debate the need for a new facility versus alternatives such as on-site expansion at existing plants or sub-contracting of the work to other companies. Some decision is reached then on how the corporation will cope with the anticipated capacity shortfall.

If a new plant is to be established, the vice president for manufacturing, a member of the management committee, assumes responsibility for the location decision. The management committee is kept informed of all developments, but the study of possible locations remains in his hands, although he is likely to draw information and support from the industrial relations staff and from a manager in the operating division. The division manager provides information about the physical characteristics of the proposed plant, and the industrial relations representative helps to assess the communities' labor force characteristics from published statistics, phone calls, and later, personnel interviews in the most promising communities. The vice president for manufacturing directs the information gathering, uses his contacts inside and outside the company to uncover potential locations, does most of the site visitation, and evaluates the communities considered. The evaluation of candidate sites completed, the vice president for manufacturing offers his recommendation to the division president who can veto it but usually does not. The division is responsible for the formal capital appropriations request.

From these two examples—Company Z and Oxford Industries—and from other corporations which organize their location decision processes along similar lines, the key distinguishing characteristics of a Staff-Controlled Study can be discerned.

- The operating division of the company initiates the request for a new plant location, but more or less relinquishes that decision to a member of the corporate staff. In some companies, it is formal corporate policy for the staff to control the decision; in other companies, the staff controls the decision more by force of its experience and proven competence.

- The division retains veto power over the recommendation and is generally responsible for the formal capital appropriations request, but the location search and study are conducted by the staff. Key elements of the appropriations request may be drafted by the corporate staff. The division acts only as a source of information. This kind of arrangement is frequently made in an effort to squeeze emotion and possible personal preferences out of the decision.

- The individual responsible for the location decision is usually a member of the corporate manufacturing staff or the real estate department. This staff member tends to have considerable experience. Although he may call in other staff people for their expertise only a handful of people generally become involved in the study.

The staff-led study

General Foods Corporation

General Foods Corporation is one of the nation's largest food processors; it manufactures and markets a kitchenful of such familiar products as Maxwell House Coffee, Birdseye frozen foods, Post breakfast cereals, Jello, Kool-Aid, and many more. These products are organized into divisions, which are overseen by division presidents. The plant managers of a division report directly to the operations manager for that division, who reports in turn to the president of the division. While the operations manager of any division is directly responsible to his own president, he has a heavy "dotted line" responsibility to the corporate vice president for operations, who reports in turn to an executive vice president.

The possible need for a new manufacturing facility surfaces during the annual, rolling 5-year strategic planning exercise of the company. These strategic plans flow up from the plants, through the divisions, to the top corporate management ranks. Capacity shortfalls are typically spotted there and potential remedies suggested. However, exceptional cases, such as unexpected growth, which demand new production facilities are sometimes considered outside the strategic planning process.

It is corporate policy at General Foods that all capital expenditures exceeding $200,000 are studied by central engineering and all studies of potential new sites must involve the industrial engineering section of central engineering. This team reports to the vice president for operations, through the director of central engineering. The involvement of industrial engineering personnel in the location decision is in General Foods' tradition of the past 25 years of increasingly centralized control over operations. Before, the company had been more decentralized.

Industrial engineering's review of the division's request for additional capital often triggers a debate between the two parties on the strategic manufacturing considerations embedded in the proposal. The corporate staff is more acutely aware of the advantages of grouping two or more product lines at a single location, both to lower overhead and to increase flexibility. Thus industrial engineering frequently steers the operating division to existing sites. Sometimes expansion at existing sites is not desirable, however, and a new site must be located.

Industrial engineering takes the leadership role in the location study. The study may be funded from division funds or from the central engineering budget. The first task in the study—identifying potential sites that could satisfy the division's needs—is carried out by industrial engineering itself using information from its discussions with the division. The industrial engineering staff also takes a first cut at the economics of the site, which, in General Foods' case, chiefly involves transportation but also includes labor rates, taxes, and environmental considerations. The list of potential sites is culled down further through site visits by a representative from industrial engineering and one from traffic, another corporate staff function called into the decision by industrial engineering.

Final evaluation of sites is not done by industrial engineering, however, but by a team of about 12 members drawn from traffic, personnel, purchasing, legal affairs, quality assurance (regulatory matters), construction engineering, distribution, real estate, public relations, and the operating division itself and chaired by industrial engineering. This team does the detailed analysis of the sites that industrial engineering has identified, and reaches the decision to select a particular site.

The capital appropriations request is developed and championed by the division through the necessary levels of upper management approvals.

FMC CORPORATION

FMC Corporation, a diversified manufacturer, markets products in six broad Groups—food and agricultural machinery and chemicals; industrial chemicals; materials and natural resource handling equipment; construction and power transmission products; and government and municipal equipment. The flexibility to explore new markets is provided by a Special Products Group.

The impetus for the location decision at FMC comes from each of the many operating divisions and their higher level Groups in the course of the formal business planning cycle, which occurs every other year with a time horizon of 5 years. The business plan, which starts at the division level and works upward through Groups to the vice president for planning and the president, normally identifies potential capacity shortfalls and outlines a remedy. This remedy generally indicates the product to be manufactured in any new plant, the production technology to be used, the rough square footage required, the number of people involved, and a general location which is supported by some rationale. Informal communication normally precedes and accompanies the business plan so that upper management is not confronted with any surprises during its review.

Once the business plan is approved, it is the division's responsibility to develop the capital appropriation request and its supporting documents. Nevertheless, it is corporate policy that staff from the corporate level machinery manufacturing department direct all location searches and studies. Thus, once a new plant proposal is an approved part of the business plan, the machinery manufacturing staff, on seeing the approved plan, normally contacts the operating division about those plans. Machinery manufacturing presents the division with a "plant site specification survey" which queries the division about its projected requirements for the new plant: size, utilities needed, personnel, training, potential environmental problems, interplant communications needs, transportation/logistics aspects of supply and distribution, as well as how the division management is organizing itself to study and start-up the new plant and whether it has any suitable locations already in mind. Answering this survey not only serves as the basis for the initial search for sites but serves a role in readying the division itself for planning and implementing the start-up of the new plant. For many FMC divisions, the establishment of a new plant may occur only once in the corporate lifetime of its key management figures. Because of this, the staff from machinery manufacturing views its role as that of a "missionary" to the divisions so that they can "see the light", as it were, about all the needs of the new plant they are proposing.

The machinery manufacturing staff analyzes the implications of the survey responses for location, is the first to look at candidate sites, and begins the sorting process. Often the machinery manufacturing team invites some industrial relations staff people into this sorting process, and later into site visitations.

With the major culling of candidate towns accomplished, the operating division and its plant start-up team are invited back into the process to visit the towns that are still in contention and to evaluate them. While machinery manufacturing may have its own idea about which town to select, the division managers are usually permitted to make the choice among towns without any overt recommendation. When the division makes its selection, an option is taken on the preferred site.

The Staff-Led Study, as exemplified by General Foods and FMC, has six distinguishing characteristics all its own.

- The need for a new plant is initiated by the operating division, either through periodic business planning or through an ad hoc procedure.
- Once the proposal has received a go-ahead from senior management, corporate staff takes over the location study. Whereas the corporate staff may perform much of the study itself (typically the generation of potential sites and the initial site screenings) the operating divisions are permitted more influence in the decision than the veto authority characteristic of a Staff-Controlled Study.
- The division's influence most always includes final evaluation of a slate of sites and may include a delineation of potential areas at the start of the search.
- The corporate staff coordinates the study, largely determining its timetable and who should be contacted when.
- Often, more people become involved in this type of Staff-Led Study than in the Staff-Controlled Study.
- Corporate staff may contribute key segments of the capital appropriations request and its supporting documents.

We now pass into consideration of those joint division-corporate staff interactions where the operating division plays a stronger role in the study and choice of location.

The division-led study

UNION CARBIDE CORPORATION

Union Carbide Corporation is a large chemical company organized into several major Groups of divisions: chemicals and plastics; gases, carbons and metals; and batteries and consumer specialty products. Relative to many chemicals companies, Union Carbide is positioned "downstream" in the process, closer to the consumer than to many basic chemicals processes. The company makes and markets such well-known products as Eveready batteries, Prestone anti-freeze, Simonize car waxes, and Glad plastic bags.

Most of the company's location decisions are initiated by an annual long-range planning process, which employs a 5-year horizon. Some location decisions surface outside the planning process, notably those that involve R&D breakthroughs or acquisitions, but most are the result of a long series of discussions and debates on how to cope with capacity shortfalls. During the planning process, decisions are reached on whether or not to seek expansion at an existing site or at a new location, and, if the latter, what products and size should be assigned to it.

In these matters, the operating Groups (the several listed above) and the divisions which comprise them enjoy a great deal of autonomy. Once it is decided that a new plant is to be established, it is the division's responsibility to study the matter. Typically, a project manager is appointed within the division involved to carry on the thinking on plant location, as well as to supervise the development of the capital appropriations request. This manager chairs a committee drawn largely from the division itself, customarily including representation from division engineering, division production, division industrial relations, division transportation/logistics, and representation from the corporate real estate department. It is company policy to involve the real estate department on all major location decisions.

This committee functions first to develop guidelines to control the location search and under which the real estate representative can generate candidate sites. It is this individual's task to present a handful of sites for evaluation by the committee which meet the working guidelines that the committee has established. These promising sites are visited by various committee members—particularly engineering, production, and industrial relations—who then make a recommendation to the general manager of the division. If the general manager concurs, an option is taken on the land, and the capital appropriations request is developed and ushered through the approval process.

INTERNATIONAL BUSINESS MACHINES CORPORATION

The need for additional production space at IBM is expressed in the company's formal planning process, with its 5-year horizon. The company's various operating divisions are responsible for these plans, and the divisions, in consultation with senior management in the review of these plans, decide whether new facilities are warranted or whether on-site expansion will suffice. The plan can include a statement of division preference for location.

If a new plant is to be built, the division's responsibility turns to the study and decision on location once its plan is approved. The first step in the search process is to ascertain which sites are already available. IBM is among those companies which "land bank", that is, which build up an inventory of suitable locations in anticipation of need. A division seeking a new site thus has the opportunity of reviewing what IBM's real estate and construction division has already put "on the shelf."

If the division opts for a site already in the land bank, the decision can draw to a close rapidly. For such properties rezoning is completed, and construction can begin almost immediately. The division must still develop a capital appropriations request, of course, and shepherd it through the corporate management committee and the board of directors. These bodies have final say on the matter.

If the division decides against the suggested land bank properties, usually because of particular ideas about the location desired and the time to wait for it, the real estate and construction division, acting as a resource in concert with the operating division, begins to generate a list of sites that meet the operating division's requirements. Final decision is made by the corporate management committee.

The real estate and construction division may act on its own to recommend that a site to be placed in the land bank for possible future use. In the absence of a definite user for a site, the real estate and construction division relies on the advice, and ultimately, the consent of the corporate management committee. The real estate and construction division typically calls in corporate staff people from manufacturing and personnel on such a land bank issue, but it is the management committee which is apt to review the proposal several times before authorization to purchase is given. The corporate management committee takes the place of an operating division in those instances where a property is to be placed in the land bank for future use by any division.

These two examples—Union Carbide and IBM—and others suggest several features which distinguish the Division Led Study from others.

● The division is responsible for initiating the proposal for a new plant, for coordinating the study and evaluating potential locations, and for choosing (or acceding to) the preferred site. The capital appropriation request is strictly the work of the division.

• Typically, a team is assembled for the study, mostly drawn from the division itself. There is a strong precedent, or even a formal corporate mandate however, for someone on the corporate staff to get involved in the location study.

• The corporate staff is viewed, and frequently views themselves, as technocrats who provide information and only occasionally influence key aspects of the decision or the decision process. Most often, the corporate staff is used to generate lists of potential sites, or to counsel on environmental matters or some other field requiring special expertise.

The division controlled study

A Division Controlled Study is very much like the Division Only Study in that it is strictly the division's responsibility to initiate, study, decide, and champion the location of new capacity. Like the Division Only Study, the Division Controlled Study is likely to occur infrequently; to involve more informal communication, discussion, and approval than more staff-dominated organization schemes; to depend more on the performance record of the managers involved than does a more formal study; and to be merely one function of a division team which is charged with plant start-up in addition to location search and selection.

What sets a Division Controlled Study apart from a Division Only Study is the inclusion of some small, but important hurdles which the division must negotiate if it is to earn corporate approval for its choice. Some of these hurdles are discussed in the following two examples.

LEVI STRAUSS AND CO.

Levi Strauss is the nation's largest apparel company, known internationally for its blue jeans. The company is active in more than merely jeans manufacture, however. The company has six product divisions organized into two Groups: the Jeanswear Group (Jeanswear, Youthwear), and the Sportswear Group (Sportswear, Womenswear, Accessories, Activewear). In matters like capacity planning and plant location, each division is autonomous except that the need for space by one division typically triggers a company-wide check of available space in existing factories, space that may be leased from one division to another for as short a time as 20 weeks. Except for this cross-divisional hurdle, the operating divisions of Levi Strauss are essentially on their own for the location decision.

TRW, INC.

TRW is a highly diversified corporation with broad interests in car and truck components (steering gears, pumps, hydraulic motors, piston rings, and valves), electronics and space systems (capacitors, motors, communication equipment, point-of-sale terminals, space craft), and industrial and energy products (fasteners, tools, submersible pumps, airfoils for airplanes). The many divisions that comprise these three broad business segments exercise a great deal of autonomy over their operations, including location decisions. However, to assure some degree of uniformity throughout TRW's divisions in their handling of location decisions, there is a company manual which outlines some of the coordination required in the decision process. In addition, a director of facilities planning on the corporate manufacturing staff is responsible for overseeing all plans for new facility locations. Otherwise, the divisions act on their own in these matters and in planning and executing the start-up of a new plant.

Types of companies and the organizational forms for the location decision

What kinds of companies adopt which kinds of organizational form for their location decision? While my series of 60 Fortune 500 company interviews is not conclusive, there are some common threads among companies which are very suggestive and appear to be worth stating.

• As one might expect, the most capital-intensive industries are the most likely to adopt the Centralized, Large Group Study of location. This formal organizational form lends itself readily to comprehensive, expertise-laden location studies, and serves well these companies which cannot afford to make mistakes since so many dollars must be devoted to a new location.

• As a general rule, companies which tend toward staff domination of the location decision exhibit characteristics such as significant intra-company interdependence and coordination fostered say, by considerable vertical integration, and/or a concern for the efficient use of available space or land at existing company sites, often as a means to reduce overhead expenses, and/or a particular sensitivity to labor costs and unionization.

• To handle these needs, then, companies often develop corporate staff specialists to take such burdens off their operating managers who often do not have the time nor budget to generate the needed expertise and experience.

• More entrepreneurial companies often adopt the Centralized, Small Group Study which is less formal. These entrepreneurial companies include agribusiness cooperatives and companies still managed by a founder/builder or a closely-knit family.

• Division-Led domination of new site studies tends to occur in corporations such as consumer goods companies (except for some nationally distributed food processors and some apparel manufacturers for which intracompany coordination is essential) and conglomerates, which tend to have few cross-divisional interactions.

• A number of companies have adopted different organizational forms for different kinds of location decisions and thus have spread themselves over more than one category. Typically, large new plants or complexes are studied by staff-dominated teams while smaller, satellite facilities are left to the divisions more or less. Examples include vertically integrated companies whose "upstream" plants are large, state-of-the-art, capital-intensive operations but whose "downstream" plants are smaller, more conventional operations. Paper companies like Union Camp and Crown Zellerbach fit this description, with their paper mills demanding centralized study but many of their smaller, converting plants sited through division work and study.

● For many companies, the trend over time has been from division domination to staff domination of location decisions. This movement seems to reflect, in part, the increasing complexity of location decisions and the corporations' improved abilities to control a network of sometimes far-flung plants.

A spectrum of these organizational schemes is displayed in Chart 3-1. On this chart are listed many of the companies interviewed and my evaluation of the organizational forms for the location search which prevail at those companies. It should be stressed that Chart 3-1 should be viewed as a *spectrum* of location search forms rather than a listing of self-contained boxes or categories. There are shades of organizational difference which simply cannot be completely captured by rigid categorization. The categories described have been created largely for expository purposes and are not intended to be all-encompassing. Again, it should be observed that not all managers in these companies would agree with the categorization displayed; time naturally shifts companies along the spectrum. Thus Chart 3-1 should be viewed as suggestive rather than definitive.

Survey results: decision process character and timing

Various plant surveys provide additional data about the character of the location decisions mechanism among companies and the length of time each major segment of the location decision process takes. Table 3-1 reveals that in about three-fourths of the companies, the operating division first proposes a new plant and goes on to lead the site selection phase. A division/corporate staff team is formed in most circumstances, however, so the division does not usually register total control over the day-to-day workings of the decision process. Corporate staff input appears to be less pronounced in plant relocations, suggesting that a relocation decision is more an individual decision than is the more prevalent new plant opening. This finding is reinforced by the Fortune 500 figures on the average and median months of time required to debate the need for a new plant and to search for a suitable site. Median figures for the debate and search both indicate that most relocations are decided more quickly than plant openings, something one could expect if the division had more control of the decision process. The Cincinnati and New England survey results, encompassing more small companies, demonstrate even quicker decision-making than is true for the larger companies. This is also a consistent finding.

For larger companies, the site search typically takes half the time the decision on the need for the plant takes, with a total of a year and a half or more passing from the initial movement for a new plant until its location is approved. This estimate of time for these decisions holds true for most industry groups. The High Technology group, with its extraordinarily fast growth, cuts this average time down to 13 months however. No other group

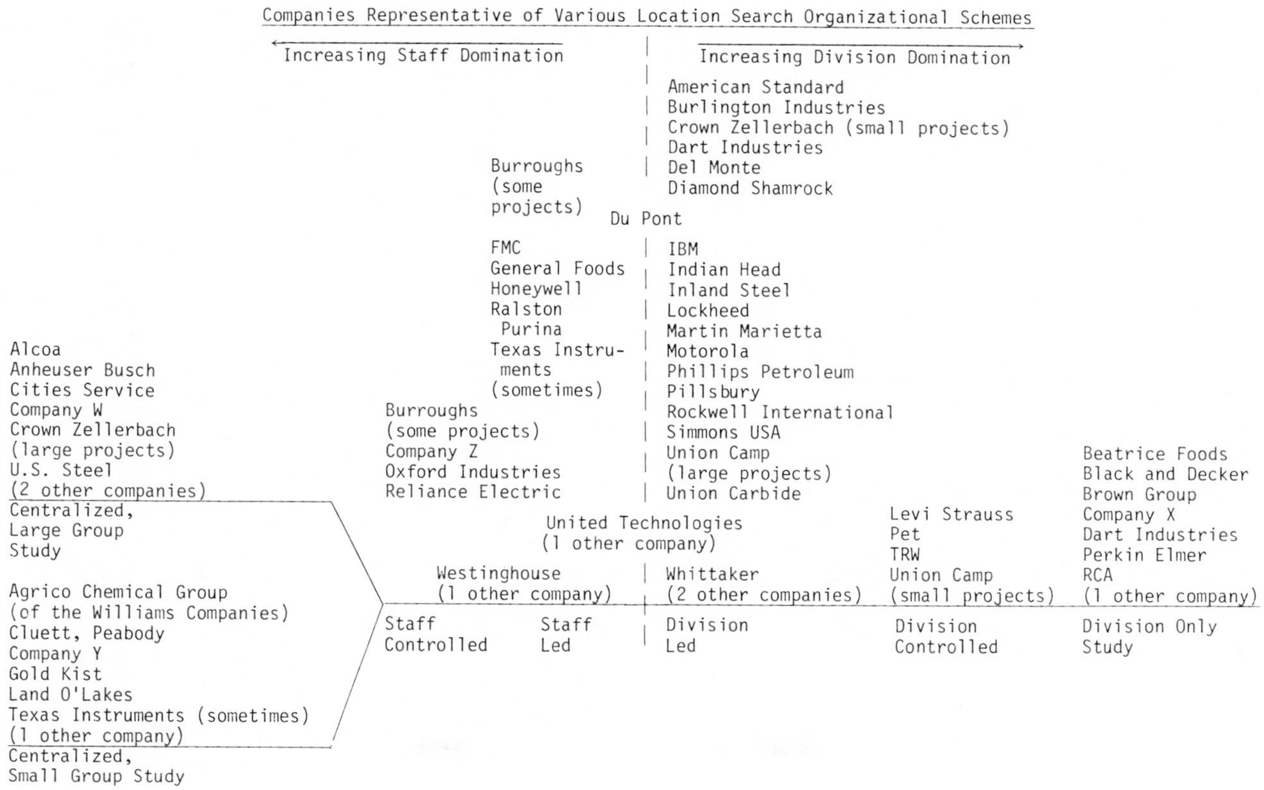

Companies Representative of Various Location Search Organizational Schemes

← Increasing Staff Domination   Increasing Division Domination →

Alcoa
Anheuser Busch
Cities Service
Company W
Crown Zellerbach
(large projects)
U.S. Steel
(2 other companies)

Centralized,
Large Group
Study

Agrico Chemical Group
(of the Williams Companies)
Cluett, Peabody
Company Y
Gold Kist
Land O'Lakes
Texas Instruments (sometimes)
(1 other company)

Centralized,
Small Group Study

Burroughs
(some projects)
Company Z
Oxford Industries
Reliance Electric

United Technologies
(1 other company)

Westinghouse
(1 other company)

Staff
Controlled

Staff
Led

FMC
General Foods
Honeywell
Ralston
Purina
Texas Instru-
ments
(sometimes)

Burroughs
(some
projects)   Du Pont

American Standard
Burlington Industries
Crown Zellerbach (small projects)
Dart Industries
Del Monte
Diamond Shamrock

IBM
Indian Head
Inland Steel
Lockheed
Martin Marietta
Motorola
Phillips Petroleum
Pillsbury
Rockwell International
Simmons USA
Union Camp
(large projects)
Union Carbide

Whittaker
(2 other companies)

Division
Led

Levi Strauss
Pet
TRW

Union Camp
(small projects)

Division
Controlled

Beatrice Foods
Black and Decker
Brown Group
Company X
Dart Industries
Perkin Elmer
RCA
(1 other company)

Division Only
Study

Chart 3-1. **Spectrum of organizational forms for location search which prevail at companies surveyed**

Table 3-1

The Character and Timing of the Location Decision Process: Survey Results

Panel A: Corporate Organization for the Decision

	Percentage for Each Item	
Item	Fortune 500 Plant Openings	Fortune 500 Relocations
Who first proposed a new plant?		
Division	73%	77%
Corporate Management	27%	23%
Was a team from both the division and corporate staff formed?		
Yes	61%	50%
Who led the site selection process?		
Division	72%	71%
Corporate Management	28%	29%

Panel B: Months Taken in Each Major Phase of the Decision Process

Item	Fortune 500 Plant Openings	Fortune 500 Relocations
How long was the need for a new plant debated before a decision was reached?		
Average (months)	13.4	14.2
Median (months)	12	10
How long did the search for a new site take?		
Average (months)	7.1	7.0
Median (months)	6	4

	Plant Openings		Relocations			
			Cincinnati		New England	
	Cincinnati	New England	< 40 Workers	≥ 40 Workers	< 100 Workers	≥ 100 Workers
Median number of months for decision on adding capacity	NA	5	NA	NA	6	6
Median number of months for site search	NA	5	6	10	3.5	7

comes close to that average, and the Agriculture and Forest-Tied industries may take well over two years to decide on the new plant and its location.

Survey results: new plant start-up

How content are companies about the start-up of new facilities? How much more costly than expected are they? How long does start-up take and what is the extent of any delay? How do companies view the effectiveness of the start-up and their new labor situation? The figures of Table 3-2 reflect the answers to these questions for new Fortune 500 plants.

As shown there, most companies match their actual start-up costs and speeds to their prior expectations quite satisfactorily. For new plant openings, start-up takes a little more than one year, on average. Relocations are typically quicker, primarily because relocations usually require moves of less than 20 miles. Cost overruns are inevitable, it seems, and Table 3-2 reveals that plant start-ups are not immune to them. These overruns are very modest for new plant openings, however, and only somewhat less so for relocations. Government regulations seem to cause a month or two average delay, although most plants, happily, remain unaffected.

In general, the speed and effectiveness of relocation plant start-ups seem to be more satisfactory than at new plants although markedly less

Table 3-2

The Costs, Speeds, and Success of New Fortune 500 Plant Start-Ups

Item	Plant Openings		Relocations	
	Average	Median	Average	Median
Costs				
Costs of construction/staffing (Percent of expected)	105.1	100	115.7	105.5
Labor costs (Percent of expected)	101.4	100	103.5	100
Speed				
Months from site selection to start-up	13.3	11	11.5	8
Speed of construction/ staffing-Months planned	12.0	12	8.1	6
-Months actual	13.6	12	9	6.5
Delays due to government regulation-Months planned	0.6	0	0.7	0
-Months actual	1.4	0	1.9	0

Success	Plant Openings		Relocations	
	Better than Expected	Worse than Expected	Better than Expected	Worse than Expected
Speed/effectiveness of start-up?	37%	32%	62%	24%
Labor productivity?	39%	14%	16%	22%
Absenteeism, turnover, attitudes?	45%	21%	19%	31%

satisfactory with regard to labor productivity, absenteeism, turnover, and attitudes.

Among industry groups, there is little pattern to be found in the responses. The speediest industries in start-up are in the High Technology and Labor Cost-Sensitive groups, and this latter group is most apt to rate its plant and labor start-up costs as higher than expected. (This may not be an unnatural response from an industry which is most eager to trim every cost it can and which may be more likely than other groups to hold unrealistic expectations about costs). Otherwise, there are no discernible trends.

Among regions, too, there are few significant trends. It is clear however, that speed and effectiveness of start-up are most likely to fall below expectations on the West Coast. There delays due to government regulations were most pronounced. Start-up costs are more likely to be greater than expected in New England, the East North Central region, and along the Pacific.

The On-Site Expansion—Plant Opening— Relocation Choice: Survey Results

Most companies, when confronted with the need to expand capacity, think first about expanding on-site, a very natural tendency, because on-site expansion is often low cost and not too disruptive of the existing management controls. However, as Chapter 1 argued in some detail, on-site expansion is fraught with diseconomies, especially if it has been repeated. New plant opening and relocation may offer various remedies to the diseconomies encountered with on-site expansion. As noted earlier, opening a new plant is to be preferred if the problems encountered involve product proliferation, workforce size, and meeting anticipated growth. Plant relocation is to be preferred if the problems involve the production process itself (layout, materials handling, production and inventory control, blocked adoption of new process technology) and lack of management depth.

This section investigates the strengths of these arguments for one form of new capacity or another and the characters of new plants, plant relocations, and on-site plant expansions.

Before examining the data that contrasts the characters of the plants variously expanding on-site, establishing new branches, or relocating, let us review how frequently each option is both thought about seriously and actually acted upon. As Chapter 1 suggested and as Chapter 4 documents, on-site expansion is more popular than either opening a new plant or relocating one. Of 9499 stay-put plants in the Fortune 500 plant census, 1704 (18%) of them were determined to have expanded on-site during the 1970s. This number compares to 1611 new plant openings and 450 relocations. The Cincinnati plant census results are even more indicative of the popularity of on-site expansion. Over the period 1971–1975, about 30% of the Cincinnati area's plants expanded on-site versus about 19% which were new plant openings and 11% which were relocations.

What fraction of the expansions on-site thought seriously of the alternatives of opening a new branch plant or relocating? What fraction of the new plants opened were only done so after careful consideration of on-site expansion or relocating? What of the relocations and their alternatives? In short, to what degree were on-site expansion, new plant opening, and relocation considered as substitutes for one another?

Table 3-3's results address these questions for Fortune 500 plants. It is fairly clear from these results that expansion on-site, new plant opening, and relocation are rather imperfect substitutes. Between 50% and 62% of the plants eventually acting one way or another did not think seriously about any alternative remedies. On-site expansions, at 62%, seem particularly unfettered by examining alternatives. Relocation, as we might expect, is the least considered alternative—a kind of last resort—but never-

Table 3-3

Capacity Alternatives Confronted by Expanding, Opening, and Relocating
Plants of the Fortune 500

Plants Actually Expanding On-Site	Number	Percent of Total	Average Employment
Thought seriously of plant opening and relocation	10	6%	631
Thought seriously of opening but not relocation	46	27%	1592
Thought seriously of relocation but not opening	9	5%	151
Did not consider alternatives seriously	105	62%	789
Plants Actually Opening			
Thought seriously of expansion and of relocation	25	17%	316
Thought seriously of expansion but not relocation	35	24%	346
Thought seriously of relocation but not expansion	11	8%	264
Did not consider alternatives seriously	72	50%	288
Plants Actually Relocating			
Thought seriously of expansion and of opening	4	12%	274
Thought seriously of expansion but not opening	5	15%	175
Thought seriously of opening but not expansion	6	18%	190
Did not consider alternatives seriously	18	55%	244

theless, 11% of even the actual on-site expansions considered relocation seriously. This group is dominated by smaller plants. Opening a new plant or expanding an existing one are pondered in about equal measure by the large companies represented in the sample. Not surprisingly, the plants actually expanding on-site are larger than the others. However, concern for large size does show up in the figures; the largest plants, while expanding on-site, at least look at spinning off a new plant.

The extent to which management contemplates one or the other option is reflected in as well Figure 3-2, which is a Venn diagram indicating the sets of responding stay-put plants in New England that (i) expanded on-site, (ii) thought seriously of relocating their plant, or (iii) thought seriously of or actually established a new branch plant. Accompanying the plant counts in the diagram are average employment levels for the plants in each subset.

The data reveal a good deal of overlap in considering capacity and location. Of those plants that either thought seriously of moving or branching or that actually expanded on-site, 45 percent considered more than one alternative, although only 5 percent thought or acted on all three. Yet, the fact remains that the management of a majority of plants seriously considered or acted on only a single choice, if they considered any choices at all. On-site expansion, branching, and plant relocation do appear to be allied but not perfectly substitutable means of augmenting capacity.

The confirmation of expectations is reinforced by the employment data in the diagram. Those managers contemplating more than one means

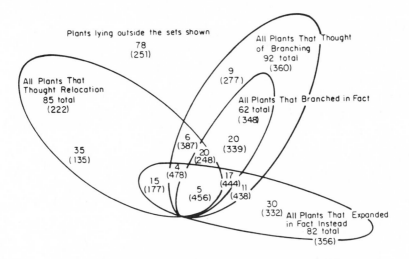

Figure 3-2.   **New England stay-put plants' capacity considerations. (Stay-put plants in diagram total 250. Num-
bers shown in parentheses are average employment figures.)**

of augmenting capacity have, on average, larger plants than the managers who consider only one or the other. Size definitely complicates the scope of the decision. Furthermore, as expected, those managers who contemplate a new branch have, on average, larger plants to man than those who contemplate relocation.

On-Site Expansion

The inherent advantages of on-site expansion are mirrored by Table 3-4's results which document the frequency various reasons for on-site expansion were cited by sampled plants that had actually done so. Four reasons for expansion are recognized by half or more of the responding Fortune 500 plants: keeping management together, realizing economies of scale, adding capacity quickly, and spreading overhead over more units of output. These concerns, plus the inconvenience of splitting product lines or processes, are confirmed in some other results (Panel B) from companies operating one or more plants in New England. Other reasons for on-site

Table 3-4

Reasons Given for Expanding On-Site Rather Than Opening a New Plant or Relocating

Panel A. Fortune 500 Plants

Reasons (Listed in descending order of frequency answered)	Number Citing Reason	Percent of Those Checking Off at Least One Reason
Keeps management together at a single location	103	61%
Economies of scale realized with on-site expansion	92	54%
Needed capacity quickly and quicker to expand on-site	87	51%
Spreads overhead costs over more units of output	85	50%
Cheaper construction costs, land available	66	39%
Difficult to separate out a product for manufacture elsewhere	49	29%
Difficult to separate out a portion of the production process	48	28%
Good existing workforce, technical support, wage rates	16	9%
Raw materials availability	3	2%
Others (modernization, warehousing, vertical integration, business climate, excess capacity, etc.)	8	5%

Note: Number of plants citing at least
      1 reason = 170

Table 3-4(b)

Reasons for Choosing On-Site Expansion

Panel B: New England Corporation Headquarters Survey Results

Reason	Percent Citing Reason
Low cost for expansion	68.5
Important to keep labor force intact	40.7
Product line and/or production process could not be divided conveniently	50.0
Economies of scale realized with expansion on-site	66.7
Change to aid proximity to markets either not needed or of low value	7.4
No transportation advantages to new site	3.7
Suppliers nearby anyway or proximity to suppliers of low value	1.9
Any labor cost improvements not particularly important to company	1.9
Improved energy availability elsewhere not strong enough a consideration	1.9
Other (includes raw material availability, high relocation costs, warehousing, expansion of existing markets, taxes, fuel)	11.1

NOTE: 54 companies responding

expansion are less frequently mentioned. These reasons reflect both the positive elements of on-site expansion (exploiting scale economies, adding capacity quickly and cheaply, spreading out overhead costs) and the negative elements of pursuing some alternative (diluting the management ranks, troublesome separation of product and/or process segments).

On-site expansion is frequently not without its own peculiar problems, especially if expansion has been repeated. Table 3-5 analyzes some of the typical problems cited by 57% of the Fortune 500 sample. Poor materials handling and factory layout head this list, followed by excessive job "bumping" among labor grades and assignments, excessive outside warehousing (a concomitant of factory layout problems), too complex a production control system (a concomitant of poor materials handling and of the other problems stated, such as too many products on the factory floor, too much work-in-process inventory, and too many workers to manage effectively).

Indeed, among plants that have repeatedly expanded on-site (i.e., those expanding during two or more years of the past decade), perceptions of poor materials handling and factory layout, job bumping, and too many workers in the factory are more acute than average. What keeps such plants expanding on-site appears to be their relatively more frequent assertions that it is the quickest way to add capacity and that they cannot easily separate out products or process segments for manufacture elsewhere.

Table 3-5

Problems Caused/Aggravated by Expansion On-Site
Fortune 500 Plants

Problem	Number Citing Problem	Percent of All Expansions	Percent of All Expansions Citing a Problem
Poor materials handling, layout	43	41%	72%
Job "bumping" around the factory	30	28%	50%
Excessive outside warehousing	28	26%	47%
Production control too complex	26	25%	43%
Too many products on the factory floor	23	22%	38%
Too much work-in-process inventory	20	19%	33%
Too many workers to manage effectively	18	17%	30%
Counter-productive work rules	11	10%	18%
Inability to adopt latest technology	6	6%	10%
Number of plants citing at least 1 problem	106	57%	

Opening a new plant

Establishing a new plant has been viewed as a remedy for many of the pitfalls of on-site expansion. Support for this point of view is found in Table 3-6 which documents the frequency of various reasons for opening a new Fortune 500 plant. Unlike in the similar table referring to on-site expansion, no one reason commands even 50% of the possible responses. Apparently, the reasons for a new plant opening are considerably more diverse in character than is true for expansions on-site. The most common reason for a new plant is simply that no space exists at the old plant for expansion. Following that rather straightforward explanation comes a handful of others which are more subtle. Of these, the most commonly cited relates to the vulnerability of a plant to labor strife or natural disaster (fire, flood, tornado, etc.). Many new plants (33% of the sample) have been

Table 3-6

Reasons Given for Opening a New Plant Rather Than Expanding On-Site or Relocating
Fortune 500 Plants

Reasons (Listed in descending order of frequency answered)	Number Citing Reason	Percent of Those Checking Off at Least One Reason
No space to expand at existing plant	74	47%
Desire not to have "all your eggs in one basket") hedge against labor strife or natural disaster	52	33%
Desire to escape an unproductive labor situation at an existing plant	41	26%
Too many workers at existing plant(s)	39	25%
Improved proximity to markets, lower transporation costs	36	23%
New production technology required a new facility	32	20%
Urgency of space need argued for buying an existing structure	20	13%
Improved proximity to supplies	8	5%
Better labor rates, availability	6	4%
Environmental considerations	3	2%
Escape high taxes, bad economic climate	2	1%
Other (building problems, general cost reductions, etc.)	9	6%
Note: Number of plants citing at least 1 reason =	158	

opened, at least in part, because a company did not want to risk having all its capacity in one place in case a strike or an Act of God should disrupt production for an extended period.

A new plant also permits a manufacturer to do some things it would not ordinarily be able to do. Four of these constitute the next most frequently mentioned reasons for opening a new plant: escaping an unproductive labor situation, avoiding a situation of too many workers at the existing facility, improving proximity to markets and transportation costs, and permitting the use of new production technology which could not be put in place at the existing plant. Other reasons for opening a new plant are less frequently cited.

These distinguishing characteristics mesh well with expectations about the new plant designed to remedy some deficiencies of on-site expansion. These findings, and understandings, are reinforced by the probit analyses reported in Tables 3-7 to 3-8.[1] These probit analyses are limited

[1]Probit analysis is much like regression analysis, although instead of fitting a straight line (or plane) to the observed data, a cumulative normal probability function is fit to the data. Probit analysis is the preferred technique when the dependent variable is restricted to

to plants which have stayed put, differentiating between those which "spun off" new branch plants over the past decade and those which did not.

Table 3-7's probit analysis addresses New England sample stay-put plants that actually opened new branch plants. Broadly interpreted, the results suggest that plants of multi-plant operations with rapid growth, lots of new product development, and a low labor skill, high capital investment process technology are more likely to open a new branch facility. Moreover, the base plant that establishes a new branch plant is not only growing, but is already big. Further, it is largely self-sufficient, and thereby an ideal base plant for spinning off branch or satellite plants producing more well-established products than can be supported from the base plant. Nevertheless, despite its size the base plant manufactures a relatively low number of products. This is an important consideration. Despite a strong tradition of new product development, the base plant spinning off a branch appears devoted to a narrow product line itself and a capital-intensive, low labor skill production process. One other variable is conspicuous by its absence: apparently the extent of room for expansion on-site has no bearing on a plant's branching. New branches are established even when sufficient space exists for on-site expansion. As we shall see, this is not the case for relocating plants.

An underlying theme supported by these results and corroborated by company interviews is the company's pursuit of a specific multiplant manufacturing strategy. The probit analysis suggest two distinct multi-plant strategies, one of placing different products in separate plants, and one of separating plants geographically into market areas. The former strategy is supported by evidence of new product development coupled with narrow product lines at the base plant. The latter is supported by the revealed unimportance of locating close to suppliers.

The success of the model in classifying plants can be gauged by how much better it does relative to the simple decision role of classifying every plant as one that followed the rule of the majority. In this case, 72% of the sample did not spin off a new branch plant, so under the simple decision rule, the 28% that did branch would have been misclassified. In contrast the model misclassifies only 17% of the plants, which is a definite improvement.

Table 3-8's results capture the character of Fortune 500 plants which have "spun off" such new branch operations. As the results suggest, the

either 0 or 1 for each observation. In these cases, the dependent variable is 1 if the plant has spun off a new branch plant and is 0 otherwise. The estimated coefficients reported are the so-called C-standardized coefficients that represent the rate of change of the probability, P, evaluated at $P = 0.5$, for a change of one standard deviation in the value of the independent variable in question when all other independent variables are held fixed. This coefficient, then, can be interpreted as the loss of explanatory power that would result if the particular variable in question were dropped from the model. Thus, the larger this C-standardized coefficient, the more important the variable is to our ability to differentiate between types of plants. Each table of results lists the variables in descending order of importance.

Table 3-7

Differentiating Plants That Have Opened Branch Plants From Other Plants That Have Remained at the Same Location

Summary of Probit Analysis for New England
(only significant coefficients retained)

Variables (in order of importance)	C-standardized Coefficient	Level of Significance
Multi-plant status (0 = single-plant company, 1 = multi-plant)	0.293	0.998
Capital-to-labor ratio	0.165	0.919
Change in sales (low value = steadily increasing sales)	-0.146	0.990
New product development (high value = all the time)	0.130	0.974
Employment	0.123	0.987
Number of products produced at plant	-0.121	0.964
Self-sufficiency (high value = more corporate functions performed at plant)	0.114	0.962
Value of proximity to suppliers (low value = proximity valued)	0.099	0.958
Kind of labor (low value = high skilled)	0.083	0.926

Goodness of fit: $R^2 = 0.339$ Number of observations = 115

Splitting at $P = 0.5$: Predicted

True	No Branching	Branched	Totals
No branching	78	5	83
Branched	15	17	32
Totals	93	22	115

Probability of error = 0.174

Peeling off the top: Predicted

True	No Branching	Branched	Totals
No branching	73	10	83
Branched	10	22	32
Totals	83	32	115

Probability of error = 0.174

Table 3-8

The Character of Plants Which Have "Spun Off" New Plant Openings:
Probit Analysis (only significant coefficients retained)

Variable (Listed in decreasing Level of importance)	C-Standardized Coefficient	Level of Significance
Rigidity of process flow (low value= less rigid, more flexible process over time)	-.228	.997
Shifts run	.174	.969
Marketing/Sales on site? (High value=Yes)	..170	.985
Union attitude (High values=militant, history of work stoppages)	.169	.984
Percent of supplies classed as really "raw" materials	-.125	.960
Company built plant? (High value=yes)	.114	.917

Number of observations: 74

Goodness of fit: $R^2 = .364$

Splitting at P=0.5

Predicted

True	No Spin Offs	Spun Off	Totals
No spin offs	54	3	57
Spun off	7	10	17
Totals	61	13	74

Probability of Error = .135
Sample fraction Spun Off = .230

Peeling Off the Top

Predicted

True	No Spin Off	Spun Off	Totals
No spin offs	50	7	57
Spun off	7	10	17
Totals	57	17	74

Probability of Error = .189
Sample fraction Spun Off = .230

Fortune 500 plants which have established branch operations, unlike their New England sample counterparts, are not any larger than others (the employment variable was not found to be significant). Rather, the most telling distinguishing characteristic is whether, over the past decade, the flow of the plant's production process was perceived to have become less rigid and more flexible. The need to become more flexible may be due, for example, to product proliferation or more customizing of what is produced. The result is a loss of focus on a particular manufacturing task. This loss may well explain why such a plant spins off a new branch plant, namely, to re-establish a more narrow purpose or focus to its operations. This finding is very much in concert with the perils of on-site expansion recounted above and with Table 3-7's results.

Another key influence in establishing a new branch plant is simply a lack of capacity. This is indicated by the importance of the "shifts run" variable; the greater the number of shifts run, the more likely a new branch was spun off. The results also indicate that plants which are home to a marketing and sales effort are more likely to spin off new branch plants, which is not surprising and again in concert with Table 3-7's findings. Also not surprising, given some of the decision rules cited above about unionism and capacity expansion, is the finding that the more militant, uncompromising, and prone to work stoppages is the union attitude at a plant, the greater the probability that the plant spun off a new branch operation over the course of the past decade.

The two other variables found to be important to this analysis also make a great deal of sense. First, the higher the percentage of supplies classed as really "raw" materials (an indication of how vertically integrated backward the facility is) the less likely is the spin-off of a new branch plant. Put another way, the less committed the plant to vertical integration, the more likely it will feel free enough to establish a separate operation somewhere else. And, the final significant variable relates to whether the company built the plant, the implication being that the more well-established company-built plants are likely to be the ones from which new branch operations are spun off.

The character of plants actually opened

The analysis of Table 3-9 differentiates actual Fortune 500 plant openings from the remainder of that sample, namely expanding or relocating plants. The most important differentiating variable of Table 3-9 exactly mirrors the chief reason found for opening a new plant; in almost half the cases, a new plant was opened for lack of space at an old one. As Table 3-9 indicates, new plant openings are apt to remedy that situation and have substantial room for expansion, even though such plants are more likely than others to be leased. That the company wants to diversify its capacity by establishing new plants is not readily apparent in the results, but it may be hinted at by the finding that the new plant is more likely to be a cost center than a profit center, more likely not to have industrial engineering at the plant, and more likely to draw its supplies from far away. A plant that management viewed as "auxiliary capacity" could be expected to demonstrate those traits.

It is much clearer from the results that the company is improving its labor situation and simplifying its operations by establishing a new plant. The new plant opening is apt to be non-union and to have lower worker turnover over time than other plants. And, despite a higher growth rate, the newly opened plant is likely to manufacture a narrower range of products and to be more stable in its mix of products. These results are reasonably clear indications of the restricted plant charters and the simplified, more clearly defined operations of the typical newly opened plant.

Table 3-9

The Character of Actual New Plant Openings:
Probit Analysis (only significant coefficients retained)

Variables (in order of importance)	C-Standardized Coefficient	Level of Significance
Room to expand? (Low value=substantial)	-.131	1.000
Unionized? (High value=no)	.120	1.000
Industrial engineering at site? (High value=yes)	-.094	.999
Changed product mix (High value=lots of change to product mix over time)	-.091	.998
Building leased? (High value=yes)	.077	.994
Profit or cost center? (High value=cost center, low value=profit center)	.069	.988
Miles from within which 1/2 of plant's supplies are shipped	.067	.986
Growth rate	.065	.982
Product lines manufactured	-.062	.962
Worker turnover (Higher value=lower over time)	.061	.972
Number of observations	316	
Goodness of fit: R^2	0.259	

Splitting at P=0.5				Peeling Off the Top			
	Predicted				Predicted		
True	Not Opened	Opened	Totals	True	Not Opened	Opened	Totals
Not opened	153	40	193	Not opened	149	44	193
Opened	49	74	123	Opened	44	79	123
Totals	202	114	316	Totals	193	123	316

Probability of Error = .282
Sample fraction Opened = .389

Probability of Error = .278
Sample fraction Opened = .389

It should be noted that the variables reported in Table 3-9 unquestionably improve our ability to discriminate between new plants and others. The probit analysis as reported misclassified plants with a probability of about 28%. This error rate however is a distinct improvement over the simple decision rule of classifying every plant as "not an opening". That decision rule would be in error about 39% of the time.

More reinforcing evidence still on the character of the newly opened plant is available from the Cincinnati and New England area surveys. From cross-tabulations too voluminous to print here, three major themes spring out as distinguishing these samples' newly opened plants from stay-put or relocating plants:

(1) The newly opened plant is smaller in size and simpler in organization.

Newly opened plants are only about 40% the size of established plants and are responsible for fewer product lines. They are more likely to lease their production space, less likely to be organized by a union, and less likely to run multiple production shifts. Warehousing is apt to be done on-site. Logistics are simpler, with tendencies to use truck transportation exclusively and to sell products directly to customers, rather than through wholesaler channels.

The Fortune 500 data corroborate these Cincinnati/New England findings about plant size. While Fortune 500 company plants tend to be larger than smaller company plants, their new plant openings are still only 38% the size of stay-put plants on average (244 workers versus 645). Plant closings, acquisitions, divestitures, and relocations are all just slightly smaller than openings, averaging 210, 225, 232 and 217 workers, respectively. Median plant sizes are even smaller, about ⅓ the average size for stay-puts and ½ the average size for all others. Even for the transportation equipment industry, with more than twice the average employment at stay-put plants (2654) as any other major industry, the average employment at plant openings is only 456. Only four other major industries—primary metals, textiles, machinery, and electrical machinery—have new plant employment averages exceeding 300.

(2) The newly opened plant is dependent on other company plants.

Relatively fewer of the major overhead functions (e.g., industrial engineering, marketing and sales) are based in the new plant, so that other plants or headquarters must cover these tasks for the newly opened plant.

(3) The newly opened plant makes use of modern facilities and technology.

As compared to other types of plants, the newly opened plant is more likely to occupy a single story structure on a previously vacant lot that offers substantial room for expansion. In addition, the newly opened plant exhibits a higher capital-to-labor ratio and a somewhat higher incidence of line flow process characteristics.

These results are very much in concert with the Fortune 500 plant data.

Relocating an existing plant

Like opening a new plant, relocating a plant was argued above to be a way of remedying some of the pitfalls of on-site expansion, particularly those dealing with deficiencies in the production process itself. Table 3-10 provides evidence that this is in fact the case in over half the relocations in the Fortune 500 sample. Fifty-eight percent of the relocations in that sample viewed moving as an "opportunity to redesign/modernize the production process, equipment, and materials flow". Even more important to

Table 3-10

Reasons Given for Relocating a Plant Rather Than Expanding On-Site
or Opening a New Plant

Reasons (Listed in descending order of frequency answered)	Number Citing Reason	Percent of Those Checking Off At Least One Reason
Cramped production space at former location	26	68%
Opportunity to redesign/modernize the production process, equipment, and materials flow	22	58%
Opportunity to consolidate corporate functions and activities at the same location	8	21%
Lease ended, plant burned down	5	13%
Opportunity to escape an unproductive labor situation	4	11%
Opportunity to escape high non-labor costs	4	11%
Forced by government action (highways, renewal)	2	5%
Change of location closer to market	2	5%
Crime/vandalism	1	3%
Environmental compliance	1	3%
Quality of life	1	3%
Better morale	1	3%
Too many products in the plant	1	3%
Opportunity to own rather than lease	1	3%

Note Number of plants citing at least
1 reason = 38

the relocating plant is extricating itself from cramped production space at its former location. Sixty-eight percent of the relocations cited this reason, a higher percentage, it should be noted, than was cited by newly opened plants. Smaller percentages cited apply to other reasons for relocating, although relocation as a means to consolidate corporate functions and activities is a significant reason for 21% of the sample. Moreover, 21 of 31 responding to the question indicated that two or more operations at former plant sites were consolidated into the new location's facility, an even more impressive indication of this particular argument for relocating. The Cincinnati and New England data support this observation since ¼ to ⅓ of the relocations in those areas consolidated two or more plants.

What characterizes the relocating plant? As Chapter 4's results make clear, there are really two different kinds of mover plant: the local mover plant (relocation of less than 20 miles) and the long distance mover plant (relocation of more than 20 miles). The local mover plant is by far the more prevalent. Judging from the New England and Fortune 500 data, local movers account for 80 to 90 percent of all relocations and 80 to 90 percent of all relocating employment. Let us consider their strikingly different characters in turn.

The character of the local mover plant

As revealed by simple cross-tabulations of the data, the local mover plant displays five major distinguishing characteristics:

(i) On average, local mover plants are small. For example, during the period 1971–1975 in Cincinnati, only 3.1 percent of the plants of over 100 employees relocated as opposed to 12.1 percent of all the plants under 100 employees.

(ii) Local mover plants are more independent and footloose than other plants. For every size class of plant, the mover evidences a greater degree of leasing, shared occupancy of a site, and unspecialized space needs than its stay-put counterpart. Mover plants are also more self-contained, performing more corporate functions such as industrial engineering, new product engineering, finance, and marketing themselves. The mover plant is more likely to be a job shop, and a non-union one at that, with a marked lack of dependence on nontruck transportation.

(iii) Prior to their moves, local mover plants suffered from cramped production space. Mover plants are more likely to claim that their former sites and plants had insufficient room for expansion. And, indeed, as a result of their moves, almost all mover plants are housed in larger quarters.

(iv) The supply and distribution systems of mover plants are simpler. This is a corollary to the independence and footlooseness of mover plants. The typical relocation, while selling output and buying inputs from a very broad geographic area, nevertheless is more likely to sell directly to customers and not through wholesalers. Almost no off-site warehousing is done.

(v) Local mover plants show definite signs of increasing growth and complexity. Relocating plants generally are growing at above average rates, are expanding their product offerings more than stay-put plants, and often have increasing, although still low, capital-to-labor ratios.

The evidence for these five broad statements about the character of local mover plants comes from cross-tabulations of survey data. These individual cross-tabulations, however, do not consider the strength of the associations among the variables when they are grouped together. To gauge the importance of some of the individual effects which differentiate mover plants from others, some probit analyses have been undertaken (Tables 3–11 through 3–13). These probit results confirm the cross-tabulations. Space considerations, small size, growth, footlooseness, and simplicity are all evident in the results. Consider the results in turn, beginning with the Cincinnati data.

As Table 3–11 indicates, the probability of being a mover plant in Cincinnati is enhanced the smaller the plant is. This is the single most important differentiating characteristic between mover and stay-put plants, a not-too-surprising result considering the statistics evident in Chapter 4. The other variables are listed in Table 3–11 in the order of their impor-

Table 3-11

Differentiating Mover from Stay-put Plants

Summary of Probit Analysis for Cincinnati
(only significant coefficients retained)

Variables (in order of importance)	C-Standardized Coefficient	Level of Significance
Employment	-0.517	.991
Room to expand, before move	-0.347	1.000
K/L ratio	-0.300	.992
Build-buy-lease (high value: lease)	0.167	.996
Sales in metropolitan area	-0.158	.998
Self-sufficiency in corporate functions	0.144	.992
Sq. ft. per worker	-0.141	.943
Sole occupant of site (1 = yes, 0 = no)	-0.126	.996
Type of space (high value: specialized space)	-0.119	.960
Type of process (high value: continuous flow process)	-0.113	.965
Value of proximity to suppliers	0.097	.953
Change in rate of profit	0.090	.934
Value of proximity to special business services	-0.079	.919
Change of suppliers (high value: lots of change)	-0.078	.900
Proportion retail or direct customer sales	0.076	.928

Goodness of fit: R^2 = 0.511   Number of observations = 255

Splitting at P = 0.5: Predicted

True	Stay-Put Plant	Mover Plant	Totals
Stay-Put Plant	194	13	207
Mover Plant	16	32	48
Totals	210	45	255

Probability of Error = .114

Peeling off the top: Predicted

True	Stay-Put Plant	Mover Plant	Totals
Stay-Put Plant	194	13	207
Mover Plant	13	35	48
Totals	207	48	255

Probability of Error = .102

tance, an order which is distinctly plausible. For example, the absence of room to expand greatly adds to a plant's probability of relocating. By the same token, if its capital-to-labor ratio is small, if it leases its production space, if it sells outside the Cincinnati metropolitan area, or if it performs a number of corporate functions, the plant is more likely to relocate. If the square feet of plant space per worker is low, if the space is less specialized, if the process is a job shop, if supplier proximity is valued, if profits have been growing, if proximity to special business services is not valued, if the supplier group is stable over time, and if direct customer sales are high, the greater is the probability of a relocation. These variables cut the error rate in classifying mover plants to 10 to 11 percent from the 19 percent error rate implied by simply classifying all plants as non-movers.

To interpret Table 3–11's results more liberally, a rough order of importance can be ascribed to the five broad statements made above. The prime differentiating characteristic is the mover plant's relatively small size. Next in importance is its perceived need to improve its crowded, cramped condition. Of third-level importance is the mover plant's relative independence, which permits it the luxury of relocating without much uncertainty. Of less importance are indications of increasing growth and complexity and the simplicity of the supply and distribution systems.

Turn now to Table 3–12 and the New England results. The New England mover plant also tends to be small, in need of increased production space, independent of other plants, growing, but tied to an unsophisticated logistics system. The fundamental impact of the need for additional space is demonstrated by the importance of the "room to expand" and "square feet of plant per worker" variable coefficients. That mover plants are generally smaller than others is signaled by the employment variable and its high rank in the variable list.

The independent nature of mover plants and thus their ability to be footloose in their locations is confirmed in several ways. For one, the more the plant engages in sales or purchases outside New England, the more likely it is to be a mover plant. Plants with lower labor costs as a percent of sales and plants that have experienced declines in materials costs as a percent of sales over the last ten years, both signs of independence, are more likely to relocate. Single-plant companies, typically more independent than branch plants, emerge, too, as more likely movers, as do plants that have not pursued radical changes in their product offerings.

The immaturity of the logistics systems for mover plants is evident by the result that the more complex and geographically dispersed the warehousing, the less likely the plant is to relocate. Finally, the positive and significant coefficient for the growth rate variable confirms that mover plants are those that are typically growing more rapidly than stay-put plants, in many instances, no doubt, forcing space problems on the firm.

This probit model halves the error rate implied by a simple look at the relative magnitudes of movers and stationary plants in the sample; from 38 percent, the error rate is reduced to between 19 percent and 20 percent.

What is striking about these results is that the typical mover plant is characterized so much by managerial considerations and not by more factor-related items such as rising labor costs or transportation costs. Moreover, that space problems and not product change loom so large for the mover plant is confirmation of some of the relative advantages of relocation versus new branch opening or on-site expansion.

Table 3–13 displays the results of probit analysis which differentiates the relocating Fortune 500 plant from other capacity changing plants in that sample, those expanding on-site and those newly opened. These results do not speak as much to the cramped-space/need-to-modernize na-

Table 3-12

Differentiating Mover from Stay-Put Plants

Summary of Probit Analysis for New England
(only significant coefficients retained)

Variables (in order of importance)	C-standardized Coefficient	Level of Significance
Room to expand, before move (high value = none)	0.216	1.000
Employment	-0.141	0.978
Percent of output sold nationally outside New England	0.111	0.997
Square feet of plant per worker, before move	-0.095	0.996
Multi-plant status (0 = single-plant company, 1 = multi-plant)	-0.095	0.993
10-year change in materials as percent of sales (high value = decreasing percent)	0.090	0.991
Labor as percent of sales	-0.084	0.984
Degree of product change (low value = no change)	-0.074	0.970
Percent of input value bought nationally outside New England	0.069	0.964
Growth rate of sales over last 5-10 years	0.055	0.926
Degree of warehousing off-site (low value = none off-site)	-0.068	0.956

Number of observations = 253

Goodness of fit: R^2 = 0.408
Splitting at P = 0.5: Predicted

True	Stay-Put Plant	Mover Plant	Totals
Stay-Put plant	135	21	156
Mover plant	27	70	97
Totals	162	91	253

Probability of error = 0.190

Peeling off the top: Predicted

True	Stay-Put Plant	Mover Plant	Totals
Stay-Put plant	131	25	156
Mover plant	25	72	97
Totals	156	97	253

Probability of error = 0.198

Table 3-13

The Character of the Plant That Actually Relocates
Probit Analysis (only significant coefficients retained)

Variables (in order of importance)	C-Standardized Coefficient	Level of Significance
More product? (High value=more products offered over time)	.182	.995
Plant independence (High value=more functions at plant)	.150	.997
Changed product responsibilities for plant (High value=product responsibilities changed)	.128	.999
Number of shifts run	-.121	.997
Profit or cost center? (High value= cost center, low value=profit center)	-.120	.986
Company built plant? (High value=yes)	-.102	.992
Railroad siding at site (High value=no)	.079	.954
Number of observations	354	
Goodness of fit: R^2	0.250	

Splitting at P=0.5				Peeling Off the Top			
	Predicted				Predicted		
True	Non-Mover	Mover	Totals	True	Non-Mover	Mover	Totals
Non-mover	318	3	321	Non-Mover	303	18	321
Mover	26	7	33	Mover	18	15	33
Totals	344	10	354	Totals	321	33	354

Probability of Error = .082   Probability of Error = .102
Sample fraction Movers = .093   Sample fraction Movers = .093

ture of the relocating plant as they do to its footlooseness. The results do single out relocating plants as having higher than average levels of product proliferation and changing product responsibilities, both of which suggest the need for more space. Significantly, too, in answer to a separate question asking mover plants to describe the condition of their former plant, 75% described their former plants as "cramped", as compared to 34% which rated those plants as still serviceable and 37% which termed the plants "worn out and in poor condition". Only 3% termed their former plants "in good condition with enough room for expansion, but obsolete".

The mobility of the relocating plant is highlighted by the following general characteristics which shine through the estimations of Table 3–13.

• The independence of the relocating plant as gauged by the number of functions (of the group: industrial engineering, new product engineering, mar-

keting and sales, purchasing of major raw materials, direct receipt of customer orders) which it performs for itself.
- The high probability that the plant operates only one shift a day.
- The plant's status as a profit center.
- Its occupancy of a building which it likely did not build itself.
- No dependence on railroad service.

Each of these characteristics aids a plant in being footloose.

How the local mover plant changes as a result of relocation

The results discussed in the previous section illustrate how mover plants differ from other kinds of plants and suggest what might foster relocation. These results do not address the issues of where managements decide to relocate their plants and how operations change as a consequence. These topics are addressed in this section by investigating "before and after" profiles of mover plants in Cincinnati and New England.

As one might expect, if certain "conditions" are important "triggers" for a relocation, the relocation itself should result in significantly improved "conditions." We have already broached our expectations that mover plants would enlarge their production space appreciably and would display some clear signs of increasing their size and complexity.

These expectations are in fact rewarded as Tables 3–14 and 3–15 attest. Over 80% of relocating plants in both Cincinnati and New England samples increase the square footage of their plant space. This increase in space goes hand-in-hand with results such as shown in Panel C of Table 3–15 for New England. Whereas 88.6% of the within-New England mover plants judged their space to be insufficient for on-site expansion prior to their relocation, only 20.5% judged their new space in the same way. For mover plants into New England the drop is even more dramatic, from 85.7% to a mere 7.1%. The results bear out as well that an increase in plant size often means that the average square footage for each worker increases.

For about two-thirds of the mover plants represented in both surveys, employment increased as well from the time immediately prior to their move until 1976. This finding not only underlines the space concerns of mover plants but emphasizes the growth aspects of most mover plants. Employment growth for mover plants averaged 39.5% in Cincinnati and 36.8% in New England for the relevant time spans in each area.

Not only does the survey sample's mover increase its space and employment but it displays some distinct signs of increased complexity. In contrasting their former sites with their present ones, a sizable fraction of the plants (Cincinnati: about two-fifths; New England: about one-half) acknowledge that they now produce a greater number of products; none

Table 3-14

Selected Comparison Iyems for Within Cincinnati Area Mover Plants
(Entries are Percentages, > = more than; < = less than)

	By Size Class		By Multiplant Status	
	< 40 Workers	40 Workers or more	Single Plant Companies	Plants of Multiplant Companies
Panel A. Size and Site Costs				
Employment Changes				
Present < Previous	8.9	0	7.8	0
Present About Same as Previous	24.4	29.4	19.6	54.5
Present > Previous	66.7	70.6	72.5	45.5
Change in Plant Square Feet				
Present < Previous	4.5	12.0	0	
Present About Same as Previous	5.3	9.1	2.0	30.0
Present > Previous	81.6	86.4	86.0	70.0
Average Plant Square Feet Per Worker				
Former Site	705	387	658	396
New Site	773	548	754	520
Change in Rent or Land Value Per Square Foot				
Present < Previous	44.4	33.3	41.9	50.0
Present About Same as Previous	7.4	0	3.2	50.0
Present > Previous	48.1	66.7	54.8	0
Change in Property Tax Rates				
Present < Previous	27.7	23.5	20.8	54.5
Present About Same as Previous	46.8	41.2	50.9	18.2
Present > Previous	25.5	35.3	28.3	27.3
Change in Local Income Tax Rates				
Present < Previous	37.1	42.9	28.9	72.7
Present About Same as Previous	51.4	50.0	63.2	9.1
Present > Previous	11.4	7.1	7.9	18.2
Panel B. Plant and Market Changes				
Combining Two or More Plants	20.9	40.0	25.0	30.0
Change in Production Process				
No Change	44.2	29.4	36.0	60.0
Slight Alteration	41.9	47.1	44.0	40.0
Fundamental Alteration	14.0	23.5	20.0	0

Table 3-14 (continued)

	By Size Class		By Multiplant Status	
	< 40 Workers	40 Workers or More	Single Plant Companies	Plants of Multiplant Companies
Locations in Industrial Parks				
No Park to No Park	68.2	43.8	66.0	40.0
No Park to Park	20.5	43.8	22.0	50.0
Park to Park	9.1	12.5	10.0	10.0
Park to No Park	2.3	0	2.0	0
Variety of Products Made				
Same as Before	58.1	58.8	54.0	80.0
More After Move	41.9	41.2	46.0	20.0
Corporate Functions Performed				
Same as Before	76.7	75.0	75.5	80.0
More After Move	23.3	25.0	24.5	20.0
Community Attitude Towards Business				
Same as Before	50.0	47.1	47.1	60.0
More Conducive to Industry	43.2	47.1	45.1	40.0
Supplier Retention				
All	40.9	17.6	33.3	40.0
Almost all	50.0	47.1	47.1	60.0
Customer Retention				
All	63.6	35.3	52.9	70.0
Almost All	31.8	52.9	39.2	30.0
Markets Reached				
Broader	34.1	41.2	41.2	10.0
Narrower	0	0	0	0
Transportation				
Better	29.5	11.8	29.4	0
Worse	6.8	0	3.9	10.0
Panel C. Labor and Energy				
Wage Levels				
Same	34.1	29.4	27.5	60.0
Higher	65.9	70.6	72.5	40.0
Labor Availability				
Same	65.9	64.7	66.7	60.0
Better	29.5	23.5	27.5	30.0
Worse	4.5	11.8	5.9	10.0

109

Table 3-14 (continued)

| | By Size Class | | By Multiplant Status | |
	< 40 Workers	40 Workers or More	Single Plant Companies	Plants of Multiplant Companies
Labor Skills				
Higher	22.7	17.6	23.5	10.0
Lower	4.5	5.9	5.9	0
Energy Availability and Rates				
Better	9.1	5.9	9.8	0
Worse	20.5	35.3	27.5	10.0
Unionization				
Union → Union	4.7	41.2	12.0	30.0
No Union → No Union	86.0	52.9	78.0	70.0
Union → No Union	4.7	5.9	6.0	0
No Union → Union	4.7	0	4.0	0
Panel D. Aspects of Former Plant and Location				
Condition of the Former Plant				
Cramped	80.9	76.5	77.4	90.9
Good Condition but Obsolete	6.4	11.8	9.4	0
Worn Out	12.8	23.5	15.1	18.2
Still Serviceable	14.9	11.8	13.2	18.2
Distance Now From Former Plant				
Median Distance				
Percent Moving More than 5 Miles	57.8	81.2	57.8	90.9
Percent Moving More than 10 Miles	31.1	50.0	30.0	63.6
Crime an Influence on Relocation	17.0	23.5	20.8	9.1
Relocation Forced by Public Action	8.5	23.5	11.3	18.2

state that they have reduced the breadth of their product lines. About a quarter state that their new locations encompass more corporate functions or divisions than before and none indicate that the new location is more specialized functionally than before. Apparently, mover plants, already more self-contained than stay-put plants, take the opportunity of the move to become even more self-contained. This result is buttressed by the fact that roughly a quarter of the responding plants, in moving, combined the operations of two or more old plants into the new plant. For multiplant company movers and for mover plants of greater than 100 employees identified in the New England sample, plant consolidation prevails in over a third of the mover plants.

One may wonder, however, if the consolidation found among mover plants is any more pronounced than consolidation among plants which have remained at the same location. For the Cincinnati sample, 25.8% of the mover plants combined the operations of two or more of their plants in making their move. At the same time, only 9.2% of the plants which

Table 3-15

Selected Comparison Items for New England Mover Plants
(Entries are Percentages; > = more than; < = less than; → = to)

| | By Size Class | | By Multiplant Status | |
| | | | Single Plant Companies | Plants of Multiplant Companies |
	< 100 Workers	100 Workers or More		
Panel A. Size and Site Costs				
Employment Changes				
Present < Previous	15.5	11.9	15.3	9.8
Present About Same as Previous	22.5	11.9	20.0	14.6
Present > Previous	62.0	76.2	64.7	75.6
Change in Plant Square Feet				
Present < Previous	11.9	21.4	13.9	17.5
Present About Same as Previous	0	2.4	1.3	0
Present > Previous	88.1	76.2	84.8	82.5
Plant Square Feet Per Worker				
Former Site	807	545	711	753
New Site	831	411	747	631
Change in Rent or Land Value Per Square Foot				
Present < Previous	24.7	38.1	18.6	44.4
Present About Same as Previous	23.5	16.7	24.3	15.6
Present > Previous	51.8	45.2	57.1	40.0
Change in Property Tax Rates				
Present < Previous	33.7	29.5	26.5	34.0
Present About Same as Previous	39.8	43.2	47.1	40.4
Present > Previous	26.5	27.3	26.5	25.5
Change in Income Tax Rates				
Present < Previous	12.9	23.8	10.0	28.5
Present About Same as Previous	80.0	66.7	82.9	60.0
Present > Previous	7.1	9.5	7.1	11.1
Panel B. Plant and Market Changes				
Combining of 2 or More Plants	22.8	38.5	24.2	34.9
Combining of 2 or More Warehouses	16.7	17.1	10.7	22.5

Table 3-15 (continued)

| | By Size Class | | By Multiplant Status | |
	< 100 Workers	100 Workers or More	Single Plant Companies	Plants of Multiplant Companies
Change in Production Process				
No Change	42.9	46.5	42.9	44.7
Slight Alteration	34.5	41.9	37.1	34.0
Fundamental Alteration	22.6	11.6	20.0	21.3
Locations in Industrial Parks				
No Park to No Park	43.0	57.1	43.7	53.3
No Park to Park	48.8	31.0	49.3	33.3
Park to Park	3.5	7.1	2.8	6.7
Park to No Park	4.7	4.8	4.2	6.7
Variety of Products Made				
Same as Before	56.5	56.8	57.7	63.0
More After Move	37.6	40.9	38.0	30.4
Corporate Functions Performed				
Same as Before	74.4	68.2	85.3	55.5
More After Move	20.7	31.8	13.2	42.2
Community Attitude Toward Business				
Same as Before	51.8	57.1	50.7	56.8
More Conducive to Industry	42.2	35.7	43.5	36.4
Customer Retention				
All	63.2	69.0	68.1	62.2
Almost All	27.6	16.7	22.2	26.7
Supplier Retention				
All	27.6	39.5	36.1	23.9
Almost All	42.5	34.9	38.9	41.3
Markets Reached				
Broader	12.9	6.8	12.9	9.7
Narrower	4.7	0	5.7	0
Expressway Access				
Better	51.2	51.2	46.5	56.5
Worse	5.8	4.7	4.2	6.5
Loading Dock Operations				
Easier, Less Costly	73.3	58.1	70.4	63.0
More Difficult and Costly	1.2	0	1.4	0

Table 3-15 (continued)

| | By Size Class | | By Multiplant Status | |
	< 100 Workers	100 Workers or more	Single Plant Companies	Plants of Multiplant Companies
Panel C. Labor and Energy				
Wage Levels				
Same	56.0	54.5	1.4	47.8
Higher	29.8	20.5	28.6	21.7
Lower	14.3	25.0	10.0	30.4
Labor Availability				
Same	51.2	55.8	54.9	52.2
Better	41.9	30.2	38.0	34.8
Worse	7.0	4.0	7.0	13.0
Labor Skills	69.8	79.1	73.2	71.7
Higher	18.6	11.6	18.3	13.0
Lower	11.6	9.3	8.5	15.2
Energy Availability and Rates				
Better	20.0	20.5	18.3	26.1
Worse	10.6	13.6	12.7	6.5
Unionization				
Union → Union	17.6	34.1	15.5	34.8
No Union → No Union	70.6	47.7	73.2	45.7
Union → No Union	5.9	11.4	4.2	10.9
No Union → Union	5.9	6.8	7.0	8.7
Panel D. Aspects of Former Plant and Location				
Condition of the Former Plant				
Cramped	63.2	75.6	66.7	58.3
Good Condition but Obsolete	19.5	8.9	15.3	16.7
Worn Out	29.9	13.3	33.3	14.6
Still Serviceable	18.4	26.7	16.7	33.3
Distance Now From Former Plant				
Median Distance	10.0	15.0	10.0	17.5
Percent Moving More Than 20 Miles	25.0	50.0	32.2	42.2
Percent Moving More Than 50 miles	6.9	37.5	14.9	26.7
Crime an Influence on Relocation	17.2	11.1	20.8	8.3
Relocation Forced by Public Action	18.4	6.7	19.4	6.3
Relocation Forced by Private Action (expired lease, landlord action, etc.)	22.4	11.9	18.6	21.7

113

stayed put absorbed the operations of plants which were then abandoned. The same finding holds, although less dramatically, for the New England sample. Of all responding mover plants, 28.0% combined operations from two or more plants in making their moves, while only 18.9% of all responding stay-put plants absorbed any operations from plants which subsequently closed.

To provide some further insights into this issue of plant consolidation, the New England survey sample data have been used to isolate the differences between mover and stay-put plants which have consolidated. Both groups of consolidating plants differ from their peers in noticeable ways. For example, compared to other mover plants settling in New England, the consolidating mover plant is more apt to:

- move farther
- consolidate warehousing activities as well
- sell more of its output to geographically dispersed markets
- be growing less rapidly
- have falling profits
- move to sites with lower prevailing wage levels and tax rates
- change its process technology fundamentally in making its move
- leave a plant which was less worn out and more serviceable

These differences are persuasive evidence that relocations which consolidate plants are more apt to be part of some business efforts to retrench. They appear less likely to be triggered by space shortages and more likely to be maneuvers to bolster profits.

Stay-put plants which have recently consolidated their operations, on the other hand, are not distinguished by the same characteristics. Rather, such stay-put plants are more likely to be the base plant of a multiplant operation whose function is, in large part, to breed new products which may then be spun off to new branch plants. More specifically, compared to other stay-put plants, those plants which have absorbed operations from other plants which subsequently closed are more likely to:

- be a base plant rather than a branch
- have experienced more expansion in the past and to have spun off more branch plants
- have built or bought
- have built on a previously vacant site
- be nonunion
- use lots of water
- value surrounding business services
- have exhibited more new product development
- have experienced more changes to the product mix
- have become more line-flow-like and to have lowered labor costs more over time.

Results from the previous sections suggest that the bulk of mover plants invested in new and more technologically advanced equipment over the decade 1966–1976. This technological advance is supported by the fact that about three-fifths of the responding plants in both Cincinnati and New England altered their production technologies as a result of their relocations, 15% to 20% of them fundamentally. It seems unmistakable to conclude that a relocation offers the firm a very convenient opportunity to improve the organization and process technology of its plant. Nevertheless, this significant opportunity appears to "tag along" with the decision to relocate and is not often itself the major reason for the relocation. If we can rely on the probit analyses, the cross-tabulation of the disappointments with the current site, and the interviews, space considerations appear to be a much more important influence in the decision to seek a relocation. Apparently, only after the need for additional space is recognized does the opportunity to alter production enter prominently into corporate thought.

These space and process changes occur amidst some impressive swings toward single-story production, space built expressly for the company (as opposed to leased space or existing space purchased by the company), and locations in industrial parks, as documented in the tables.

Other results of these before-and-after profiles document a number of other improvements to plant operations. Markets appear to have broadened modestly while at the same time retaining a substantial majority of former customers and the bulk of former suppliers as well. Transportation is certainly improved; both expressway access and loading dock operations show considerable improvement. Energy availability and/or rates also appear, on balance, to improve as a result of relocation, although, for most mover plants, energy factors remain the same. There is evidence as well that on balance labor availability and labor skills are generally enhanced at the new location, although for most mover plants, labor skills, wages and availability stay roughly the same as a consequence of the move. Unionization is another, related factor which, with only minor perturbations, remains the same. Significantly, too, the plant perceives that its relocation has placed it in a town whose attitude is more conducive to industry.

While plant operations, by many measures, are improved as a consequence of relocation, site-specific costs are not affected much. Rents or land values per square foot are higher in general at the new site and property taxes are almost as likely to be higher as lower. As for income taxes, most stay the same, although changes are more apt to lead to lower tax rates. It is really only for the branch plant mover that one can associate even a weak tendency to lower site-specific costs. Only the multiplant company is more apt to situate its relocating plant to a lower rent, lower tax site, and even here there are many cases where the reverse holds.

This characterization of the typical mover plant in both Cincinnati and New England is consistent with three major influences on the plant's decision to move—space needs, production technology advances, and consolidation. It is only for a fourth influence—escape—that the results for the typical mover fail to be supported. As we shall see, this failure results solely from the scarce numbers of longer distance industrial relocations.

Long- versus short-distance moves

The relatively broad geographic scope of the New England survey sample has permitted the comparison of plants which have moved longer distances, say 20 miles or more, with the more numerous set of short distance mover plants. The comparison is instructive for the long distance mover is revealed to be much more cost-conscious and even less tied to specific geographic, especially metropolitan, areas than the more prevalent shorter distance mover.

A number of cross-tabulations reveal that longer distance mover plants are much less likely to have leased space prior to their moves and more likely to have built their former factories. They were more likely to have been a sole occupant as well. The capital-labor ratios of longer distance movers are somewhat higher than those of short-distance movers and this appears to be the result of labor costs which are somewhat lower a percentage of total costs, on average, and materials costs which are somewhat higher a percent, on average. Longer distance mover plants, although most often performing a full range of corporate functions, are slightly less likely than shorter distance mover plants to perform functions such as personnel, order processing, purchasing, finance, and marketing themselves.

Longer distance movers are perceptively different in the nature of the labor they utilize. Plants employing high skilled labor are much less likely to move great distances, a thoroughly understandable result since such plants would resist losing such a precious resource. Long distance movers within New England are more likely to employ low-skilled labor, run more than one shift, and move to new locations where wage rates are lower than before. This finding is particularly true of mover plants into New England. Interestingly, with such a concentration on lower wages, and to a lesser extent with lower-skilled labor, long distance plants are more careful to locate in close proximity to their labor supply than are more local movers.

Predictably, long distance mover plants are less likely to value close proximity to customers and a greater fraction of them are content to locate more than two miles from an expressway interchange. More of them use rail transport as well. As anticipated, a smaller fraction of their products' sales are within New England, although the geographic pattern of their input purchases is the same as that for short distance movers.

Nearly one-third of all the movers of 20 miles or more seriously considered establishing a branch operation instead, more than twice the rate of shorter distance movers. For inter-regional mover plants, however, this desire for further decentralization of manufacturing is countered by an even stronger tendency for the new locations of such plants to represent corporate consolidations. Well over half of the surveyed moves into New England combined the operations from two or more plants and about 30% combined the operations from two or more warehouses. This function of the inter-regional move is supported by the fact that over 50% of such mover plants claim that the corporate functions they perform have increased as a result of the move. This figure is two to three times as high as that claimed by mover plants within New England.

Investigation of the many changes plants experience as a consequence of their relocation lends considerable support to the views that shorter distance mover plants are conscious of space and operations considerations almost exclusively while longer distance mover plants, especially interregional ones, are relatively more conscious of cost and consolidation factors. In general, longer distance movers are more likely to alter their production processes fundamentally; more likely to improve labor availability while at the same time reducing labor skills; more likely to lower wage rates, rents or land values, property tax rates, and income tax rates; and more likely to view its new location as in a community whose attitudes are more conducive to industry.

These results derive from simple cross-tabulations. The relative importance of certain characteristics of long vs. short distance mover plants is better gauged through the use of a multivariate technique such as probit analysis. Table 3–16 exhibits the results of a probit analysis of all New England mover plants, employing a dummy dependent variable which took the value 1 if the move was 20 miles or more (including inter-regional moves) and 0 if the move was under 20 miles.

Many of the cross-tabulation results are confirmed by this probit analysis. Again, the probit model succeeds in slicing in half the error rate implied by a simple categorization of the move as a short distance one (from 35% to 18% or 19%). The long distance mover is particularly footloose, selling little to its local area, willing to change its customers, and content to lease property, other things equal. The long distance mover is also more apt to be a part of a multiplant company.

Other coefficients attest to the cost consciousness of the longer distance mover. The longer distance mover plant is more likely to settle at a location whose income tax rates, rents or land values, and labor skills are all lower than its previous location. The attitude of the new town is thought to be more conducive to industry and the production process is more likely to be altered fundamentally as a result of the move, all other things equal.

Two coefficient signs are perplexing. While both the "change in wage rate" and "change in products made" variables are individually negatively correlated with the 0-1 dependent variable, although only mildly so, when

Table 3-16

Differentiating Long-Distance Moves (≥ 20 miles) from Short Distance Moves

Summary of Probit Analysis for New England
(only significant coefficients retained)

Variables (in order of importance)	C-Standardized Coefficient	Level of Significance
Percent of output sold within destination metropolitan area	-0.271	.956
Change in income tax rates (low value = lower rates)	-0.162	.998
Change in town's attitude (low value = more conducive to industry)	-0.154	.992
Change in customers (low value = all same as before)	0.141	.981
Build-buy-lease at new site (high value = lease)	0.125	.974
Multiplant status (0 = simple plant company, 1 = multiplant)	0.119	.972
Change in process (low value = no change, high value = fundamental change)	0.103	.951
Change in wage rate (low value = lower wages)	0.099	.921
Change in products made (low value = less variety)	0.093	.918
Change in rents or land values (low value = lower rents)	-0.086	.891
Change in labor skills (low value = lower skills)	-0.080	.890

Goodness of fit: R^2 = 0.435   Number of observations = 101

Splitting at P = 0.5: Predicted

True	Short Move	Long Move	Totals
Short Move	56	10	66
Long Move	9	26	35
Totals	65	36	101

Probability of Error = 0.188

Peeling off the top: Predicted

True	Short Move	Long Move	Totals
Short Move	57	9	66
Long Move	9	26	35
Totals	66	35	101

Probability of Error = 0.178

introduced into the estimation the correlation reverses itself; other things equal, long distance mover plants relocate to higher wages and more products. Covariances with other variables never exceed values of about 0.2 for the simple r. These unanticipated results remain unexplained and unsettling.

THE LONG DISTANCE FORTUNE 500 MOVER PLANT

The Fortune 500 company data provides another means to investigate the long distance mover plant. As the probit analysis reported in Table 3–17 indicates, three changes occurring as a result of the move are the most significant in differentiating between the long and the short distance Fortune 500 move:

- Breaking off old ties with suppliers
- Hiring lower cost labor
- Experiencing worse energy availability and rates

Table 3-17

The Character of the Long Distance Mover Plant: Probit Analysis
for Fortune 500 Data (only significant coefficients retained)

Variables (in order of importance)	C-Standardized Coefficient	Level of Significance
Some supplier at new plant versus old? (high value = change in suppliers)	0.332	.985
Wage rate at new plant versus old (high value = higher wages here)	-0.219	.985
Energy availability (rates at new plant versus old) (high value = better here)	-0.173	.949

Goodness of fit: R^2 = 0.588   Number of observatins = 32

Splitting at P = 0.5: Predicted				Peeling off the top: Predicted			
True	Short	Long	Totals	True	Short	Long	Totals
Short	18	2	20	Short	18	2	20
Long	3	5	12	Long	2	10	12
Totals	21	7	32	Totals	20	12	32

Probability of Error = 0.156   Probability of Error = 0.125

Sample fraction
    Long Distance Movers = 0.375

Sample fraction
    Long Distance Movers = 0.375

The willingness to change suppliers is quite understandable in a long move and probably offers little penalty. Paying lower wages is plausibly the most important single reason for a long distance move, although moving from cramped conditions and having the chance to redesign/modernize the production process still overshadow the wage issue in absolute terms as the reasons for moving in the first place. Six of the 14 long-distance moves surveyed were to lower wage rate areas versus none for the short distance moves. From other Fortune 500 data we know that the longer distance mover is more apt to want to relocate to lower non-labor costs (25% indicate that versus 0% for the short distance mover), to escape from an "unproductive labor situation" (18.8% vs. 5%), and to consolidate corporate functions and activities at the same location (31.3% vs. 15%). The long distance mover is growing more slowly than the short distance mover (and movers grow more slowly, on average, than expansions on-site and newly opened plants), and rates its relative profitability/effectiveness far worse. The definite theme of the long distance mover in the data is one of relocating to lower its costs, consolidate its operations, and return to greater profitability. It is somewhat strange then to see that long distance movers are more likely to experience worse energy availability and rates, but that may simply be the price of moving to lower wage rate areas or other desirable areas. This result seems to suggest that lowering energy costs themselves are of comparatively low concern to relocating plants.

Interplant relationships

Surfacing at various points in the discussion of the most appropriate form for new capacity has been the issue of how plants in a multiplant company interact with each other and how they compare against each other. Indeed, much of the analysis of the newly opened plant has focused on the reasons why it might be "spun off" from a base or "mother" plant. The Fortune 500 survey data permit us to examine the frequency with which plants have been spun off from one another and how such plants compare with the mother plant.

As we might expect, newly opened plants are far more likely to be spin-offs from some other plant. The following table compares the three classes of plant on this score:

Class of Plant	Percentage Viewing Themselves as Spin-Offs
On-site Expansion	22%
Newly Opened Plant	60%
Relocation	26%

And, among the newly opened plants those considered spin-offs are more apt to include above-average numbers of market area plants and process plants.

Contrasting the plant spin-offs against their mother plants yields some intriguing relationships. Compared to the spin-off, the following characteristics can generally be ascribed to the mother plant:

● Larger in size—For on-site expansions, the mother plant is half again larger; for newly opened and relocating plants, the mother plant is two and a half times larger.

● Manufactures a broader product line composed generally of more mature products.

● The production process is more capital-intensive (although it is less so for the Heavy Metals, Heavy Chemicals/Oil/Glass, and Agriculture-Tied industry groups) and operates longer production runs.

● Uses more skilled labor but is perceived to have lower labor productivity than the spin-off plant.

● Its workforce is more likely to be unionized (especially in the heavy industrial plants and in the Industrial Machinery/Transportation Equipment groups). Union militancy is apt to show up more in the Labor-Cost Sensitive, Heavy Metals, and Industrial Machinery/Transportation Equipment groups.

These findings are much in line with expectations and with other results. It is not difficult to believe that mother plants with these general characteristics would want to spin-off new plants that have smaller, non-union, more productive workforces concentrating on fewer, and newer, products.

Influences on the Location Search Itself:
Company Examples

The location decision is a non-standard, complex, and trying one for many managers largely because the factors that affect it can be quite numerous, and not easily quantified. For these reasons, checklists are often devised. Often these lists are valued more for their use in reminding managers of something that might be overlooked, rather than for their influence in structuring the search process. Checklists, especially in the initial stages of a location search, must be simplified if they are to provide much assistance.

To appreciate how a number of companies have tried to simplify and control the search for a new site, this section presents some company examples and survey results.

Simplifying the decision: primary concerns for particular factors

LABOR COSTS   The apparel and shoe industries are classic examples of industries which must seek low labor cost locations in order to remain competitive. Production of these consumer items is still more labor-intensive and less skill demanding than other industries. Despite continued advances in mechanization, reducing costs by locating in lower wage areas remains a critical factor in location decisions made by these U.S. manufacturers. Consumer resistance to high prices, plus substantial domestic and foreign competition puts severe pressure on these industries to keep costs low. Imports, particularly apparel from the Far East and shoes from Europe, have taken larger and larger percentages of the U.S. markets. In 1979, imported shoes captured 54% of U.S. sales, and apparel imports constituted about 22% versus 6% in 1967.

Given these realities, American-based companies have countered in several ways. Some have joined the movement overseas by establishing factories in lower wage countries. Some have pushed technological advance in equipment and techniques. Some have pushed brand name marketing and other selling innovations to ward off the effect of other companies' lower prices. Almost all, however, have located their U.S. production in low-wage areas with a ready supply of female labor—isolated rural areas, many in mountain regions like the Appalachians and Ozarks; Mexican border communities; and large cities with substantial poor and/or immigrant populations.

This predominant concern for labor costs, by both union and non-union companies, greatly simplifies the location searches of apparel and shoe companies. For the most part, this has meant a search through isolated rural areas not previously industrialized or industrialized by firms that employ overwhelmingly more men than women. Concern for any other influence on location is forced into the background.

While labor cost is the driving concern in their location searches, for many such companies the proximity to another company plant, warehouse, or distribution center, may also be important. Most of these companies operate clusters of plants which perform similar but not identical tasks. In the shoe industry these clusters typically revolve around the mixing warehouses which fill orders from retailers. Each plant is scheduled by headquarters and materials are controlled centrally. And, most plants are dedicated to a particular type of shoe, requiring specialized equipment, materials, and techniques (e.g., crepe-soled men's shoes vs. wood wedge women's shoes vs. mocassin-type footwear). The charter for each plant is subject to change over time, as fashion and sales dictate, but companies generally like to load their plants with as much of the same kind of product (or, equivalently, process characteristic, like fabric type) as possible. This helps worker productivity at the plant and aids production control and scheduling, which is usually done centrally.

In the apparel industry, the clusters may also feed separate warehouses or distribution centers, but need not. Most often the clusters are identified with particular classes of apparel (e.g., men's sport shirts, men's dress shirts, women's sports wear) which can be expected to follow the same fashion and sales trends. Clustering in this manner has permitted the centralization of engineering, and of fabric cutting within the cluster. Centralizing engineering saves overhead and centralizing fabric cutting saves raw materials inventory and enables the firm to run efficiently the latest automatic machinery in designing and sizing patterns and in cutting fabric. Cluett, Peabody and Co., the makers of Arrow shirts, can foresee a time when the plants within any cluster may be even more specialized by segment of the manufacturing process, incorporating, for example, a cutting facility, a parts facility (e.g., collars, cuffs), and a number of assembly plants within the same cluster. This kind of process segment specialization within clusters can be seen in the Brown Shoe Company, as well, which has a number of "component plants" that feed the assembly plants within a given cluster.

The typical apparel/shoe company search for a new plant location begins with the determination of which cluster the new plant should be a part of, a decision which is often dictated by product line growth (e.g., need sports shirt capacity) or by available central warehouse space. Given the cluster choice, the location search then fans out from the cluster's center. The search is governed almost exclusively by concern for low labor costs. The communities seriously considered are thus apt to be small, remote, and sparsely industrialized. No large employer, especially one paying high wages and/or organized by a national union, is likely to be within 30 or 40 miles.

Candidate communities are identified by a variety of means. A common technique is to contact state economic development agencies and to ask them for a list of communities which satisfy the basic criteria, namely access to the cluster's warehouse/distribution center and low labor costs. Often, however, because of past searches or general familiarity with a cluster's geographic area, the company can develop a list of candidate communities on its own. Frequently census data on population, employment, and other demographic items are joined with the state- or company-generated data to identify those communities which merit second looks. Sometimes local development commissions are contacted directly, foregoing the state development agency, and sometimes subcontracting agents or sewing machine company representatives with knowledge of "where the needles are" are used to uncover sites.

Those communities whose workforce characteristics (e.g., availability indicated by population, population growth, unemployment, isolation from high-paying alternatives, low level of union activity) appear most promising are visited. Sometimes the initial visit is made by the plant manager closest to the community in question, but most often it is the corporate manufacturing manager responsible for the operation who makes the initial site visit. During this visit, population and other statistics are checked; other manufacturers in the area are visited and polled about labor availability at various skill levels, absenteeism, turnover, workforce attitudes, unionism, and wage rates (sometimes this polling of other area manufacturers is done by phone prior to any visit to the town); the quality of life in the town is assessed in rough terms through travel around the community and talks with various representatives (local government, realtors, bankers, school officials, clergy, average citizens); and available buildings, sites, and utilities are scouted.

As a result of this first site visit, if the community still looks promising, a detailed examination of the labor force is accomplished by the corporate personnel staff. Ads are taken out in community newspapers and/or radio, announcing that a manufacturer in the apparel/shoe industry will be holding employment interviews for a period of several days or a week (and, invariably over at least one Saturday). Prospective employees are then questioned about acceptable wage rates, availability, skill levels, worker attitudes, experience. The overall response to the interview announcement as well as the individual responses of the prospective employees interviewed are evaluated, and the handful of communities so examined are then ranked by the personnel staff.

For many companies within the apparel and shoe industries the assessment of the community's labor force does not end here. Based largely on the interviewing but also on other factors mentioned below, a community is chosen for the new manufacturing plant, but usually only on a provisional basis. Manufacturing space in town is typically leased for a number of months and hiring and training commenced in that leased space. If the response continues satisfactorily, a new, permanent facility is either constructed or purchased and renovated, and the pilot plant's operations are transferred to the new building.

LABOR UNIONIZATION   There is scarcely a manufacturer in any industry which would not choose to remain non-union. For the most part, this preference is not predicated on the avoidance of higher wages, since the price a firm may have to pay to remain non-union is a wage plus benefit schedule comparable to those of union companies. Rather, it springs from the inflexibility which union-negotiated work rules, such as manning requirements, job classifications, advancement procedures, and task definitions bring to the manufacturing operation. The inability of the managers to pursue technological advance or enhanced productivity because of a contract clause acceded to years prior but whose importance was not recognized until a change in techniques is entertained frustrates the managers' effective control of the operation. In the end, it means higher total costs than are implied by the wages themselves.

Some industries and companies are more sensitive to labor unionization than others. The capital-intensive industries such as petroleum refining, chemicals, food processing, basic metals, and paper-making are less concerned about the unionization of their employees. The labor-intensive industries—furniture, apparel, and shoes—are most likely to locate in the smallest most rural towns where wages rates and, incidentally, unionization are lowest. Other labor-intensive industries, such as printing and rubber manufacturing require proximity to larger, metropolitan areas because of market and logistics considerations. Effectively barred from using location choice to avoid or impede unionization, many companies in these industries have had to confront their unions with the urgent need to accept and adopt new technology. Some of these confrontations, particularly in newspaper printing, have been difficult, even ugly, but in the main successful at revising past union labor restrictions and enabling production technology to advance.

As the survey shows, the industries falling between the extremes of capital-intensity and labor-intensity are those most apt to evidence their primary concern for labor unionization, as opposed to costs, when making new facility decisions. The fabricated metal and the equipment manufacturers are those which my research has indicated are most likely to seek non-union locations specifically for their new capacity. In these industries the labor content of the products is high enough to trigger concern and, where technological advances, both to the products and to the process, are frequent enough to cause management concern about the impact of union work rules. In these industries, too, the workforce tends to be low or semi-skilled, and thus more likely to be unionized. Many of the high technology companies, while falling into the classification of equipment manufacturers, employ skilled workers whose predisposition to unionization is lower to begin with. In broad strokes, then, it is those lower technology companies in the metal fabrication and equipment industries, where no other single factor like transportation expense is especially important, for which non-union locations are most prized.

Often, of course, a company's past history with its unions and/or with union certification elections colors its attitudes, no matter what its industry. There are numerous companies for which a work stoppage or a successful organization attempt fingers that plant for no additional expansion on-site. It is this type of company which is also likely to make union avoidance a primary concern of its location decision-making.

How does a corporation screen locations which are least likely to present labor unionization problems? For most corporations, the initial screening tool is whether or not the state has a so-called right-to-work law, where the union shop is outlawed.[2] There are currently 20 right-to-work states, concentrated primarily in the Southeast and in the Plains States.[3] Some of the corporations interviewed look first to one of the 20 right-to-work states. Only if a division makes a particular, and strong, request to be somewhere else, or if some other special factor (such as a natural resource constraint) intercedes, does the location search team consent to look in other than a right-to-work state.

At the same time, many of these same companies recognize the difference between *average* unionization in a state or area and *incremental* unionization there. Thus, there are locations within right-to-work states where unionism and/or union organization activity is low. Sophisticated corporations try to identify these differences by three major means: (1) use of National Labor Relations Board data on certification and decertification elections and their outcomes by area (say, a county); (2) use of labor survey data supplied by some state industrial development agencies indicating union or non-union status among major employers within an area and the history of work stoppages there, as well as certification elections held and their outcomes; and (3) telephone polls of selected manufacturers already in the area about their views on the local labor force—its attitude toward unionization, its productivity, its absenteeism, turnover, and skill levels. With this data, the likelihood of plant unionization can be gauged fairly well. More precise indications of union sentiment are usually gleaned only from site visits.

Most capital-intensive industries are relatively unconcerned by the unionization of their own employees. However, many of them become very concerned about the unionization of the construction crews which erect their new plants. With so much money tied up in plant and equipment, it is understandable that some companies in these capital-intensive corporations resolutely avoid locating in areas in which the plant construction labor is unionized because the chance of work stoppages or exceptionally high construction costs are greater there. Construction labor unionization

[2]In a union shop, new employees are required, by management consent with the union, to join the union after a short probationary period of usually 30–90 days.

[3]The 20 "right-to-work" states are Alabama, Arizona, Arkansas, Florida, Georgia, Iowa, Kansas, Louisiana, Mississippi, Nebraska, Nevada, North Carolina, North Dakota, South Carolina, South Dakota, Tennessee, Texas, Utah, Virginia and Wyoming.

tends to be even more spotty and localized than industrial labor unionization, and thus requires the location team to secure detailed information about the geographic pattern of unionism in the construction trades.

Non-union status is valued so much by many companies that unionized companies in many industries are reluctant to enter non-union communities, especially in the South, for fear of antagonizing these communities or other manufacturers in the area. They want to avoid importing labor organization attempts and thus they are generally careful to declare their union status early so that town-company compatibility can be established.

TRANSPORTATION COSTS FROM PLANT TO MARKET   Industries that serve broad geographic markets with commodity or near-commodity products for which the transportation costs are significant, find that these expenses can be reduced with careful choice of location. Many companies in food processing, lumber or paper converting; and common chemicals, plastics, glass, metals, and metal fabricating are constrained by transportation costs from competing successfully in distant markets. These are the companies whose divisions are most likely to adopt a market area multiplant manufacturing strategy and thus are most apt to place their next increments to capacity so as to reduce their total transportation bill.

Anheuser-Busch Inc.

Anheuser-Busch Inc., the St. Louis-based brewer, is an excellent example of a company where concern for transportation costs shapes the location decision process and simplifies it. Beer is subject to considerable freight costs. In fact, finished goods freight expenses are by far the largest location-influenced cost incurred by brewers. The costs of materials and their transportation to the brewery are likewise of only small concern; water is nearly ubiquitous and of low cost, and freight expenses on the malts, hops, and rice for the beer are relatively insignificant. The significant expense is transporting the beer itself to market.

The problem Anheuser-Busch faces is intriguing. Population migration patterns, differences in regional market penetration, and changes in tastes, and thus the mix of products to be brewed, can have profound effects on the geographic pattern of demand over time. Such a growing, but geographically changing, demand requires a carefully planned program of capacity addition if Anheuser-Busch is to keep its freight costs low. The challenge of this problem has spurred Anheuser-Busch to adopt a very sophisticated analysis of its brewery locations and of the transportation network implied by them.

The location decision process begins with the corporation's 5-year planning exercise. As with most other companies, the marketing forecast drives the plan and it is here that potential geographic and product mix shifts in demand are identified. The expected level and pattern of demand

is then overlaid against the existing geographic pattern of supply. Anheuser-Busch services about 1000 wholesale distributors scattered across the country in distinct geographic areas. At any time, each area's demand is filled by only one brewery. Given marketing's forecast of sales by area, the expected demand on any existing brewery can be computed. If a brewery's existing capacity falls short of meeting this expected demand, a number of changes can be instituted: (1) adding equipment and/or labor to break an existing bottleneck, (2) rearranging the market areas served by the brewery so that some other brewery with surplus capacity picks up the slack, (3) building an expansion onto the existing brewery, or (4) building a new brewery elsewhere.

If the management committee decides that the capacity shortfall can be effectively countered only by new construction, either on-site or at a new location, then the corporate planning department is called in to analyze the problem and to suggest the metropolitan area in the country in which the additional capacity would be best placed. The first stage of this analysis is an examination of the freight cost implications for the company nationwide which stem from the alternative site selections for the new capacity.

A linear programming model, similar to the classic transportation problem example found in the literature, is the means by which company freight costs are examined. The linear programming model is a sophisticated mathematical technique which minimizes the freight costs incurred in shipping beer from the set of geographically dispersed breweries (including the introduction of the new capacity) to a set of market areas. The company presently operates 10 breweries in St. Louis, Newark (NJ), Los Angeles, Tampa, Houston, Columbus (OH), Jacksonville, Merrimack (NH), Williamsburg (VA), and Fairfield (CA). Together these breweries serve about 1000 distributors which, for the purpose of the linear programming model, are aggregated into 200 geographic centers. The model requires information on the estimated demand, by product, for each of the 200 areas; the freight costs between area and breweries; shipping weights for particular product mixes (cans versus bottles); and the current production capacity of each brewery. The resulting linear program, when run on a computer, calculates the best match of demand areas to breweries so as to minimize the company's total cost of transporting beer, given the existing constraints on brewery capacities.

A linear programming model of this type is a powerful tool for analyzing the desirability of particular, suggested brewery locations. A potential new brewery location can be specified, a linear program incorporating it run on the computer, and the company's lowest possible transportation cost calculated. This cost can then be compared against those calculated for other potential brewery locations and the results ranked. The linear programming model will compute the total company transportation expense for any number and geographic spread of breweries. By this means, a transportation-effective network of breweries can be developed. Moreover, the linear programming model permits considerable sensitivity analysis—showing, for example, how different levels and patterns of demand affect the relative rankings of potential locations.

To make such a model truly useful, Anheuser-Busch must suggest a series of potentially attractive brewery locations as input for the linear program. Three major sources of potentially attractive locations are suggested for the analysis: (1) expansions at existing breweries; (2) sites that ranked high in the last analysis; and (3) locations near the intersection of freight advantage lines.

This last source deserves more explanation. Around each brewery, Anheuser-Busch draws iso-cost freight lines. These lines are roughly the shape of concentric circles centered on each existing brewery. Through logic and experience, the company has determined that good potential locations are often found along or in the neighborhood of the intersections of two or more sets of such iso-cost freight lines.

While concern for keeping transportation expenses as low as possible guides the selection of candidate sites and their ranking, more than transportation expense is examined by the Anheuser-Busch planning department in recommending a location for additional brewing capacity. The annual freight cost disadvantages of the prospective locations relative to the lowest cost location investigated by the linear programming model are calculated and considered. To these disadvantage figures are added other annual and one-time costs, as input to a net present value analysis of each location. Thus, freight costs direct the initial screening of potential locations, but serve only as one input to overall evaluation of those locations. The list of other costs considered include energy; raw materials freight (malt, barley, rice, etc.); any cost difference likely to be incurred (or saved) by building at a new location versus expanding at an existing brewery, including construction costs, spreading of overhead, plant start-up expenses, and the like; taxes; and any other expenses that are thought to vary by location. It is usually assumed that cans and bottles would be readily available nearby. Since breweries are now being built with capacities on the order of 5-6 million barrels of beer a year, if neither a can plant nor a bottle plant is located nearby, it is likely that one can be justified merely to supply the brewery.

The end result of the consideration of these costs is a net present value analysis of every cost that can be assigned straightforwardly to each potential location. To these after-tax present value calculations of total costs some qualitative assessments are added as well, before a final site decision is reached. Among the more subjective considerations are the quantity and quality of the water supply and any potential environmental regulations which could influence the decision.

The corporate planning department's recommendation of a metropolitan area for a new brewery or an expansion must be approved by the company's management committee. Other corporate staff groups are involved as well. Engineering is charged with championing the capital appropriations request and for gathering much of the data for it (although corporate planning performs the financial calculations for it). Other staff members become involved in selecting the particular site for the brewery within the approved metropolitan area.

General Foods Corporation

Some, although by no means all, of the product divisions of the General Foods Corporation—marketers of Maxwell House coffee, Post cereals, Birdseye frozen foods, Kool-Aid, Jell-O, Gaines pet foods, and a wide assortment of other staples of the American household—are affected by transportation expenses, plant to distribution center, in much the same way that Anheuser-Busch is. For these divisions, the first task in the location search is to see how transportation costs vary with different choices of location. A computer model is used to calculate a weighted sum of the transportation costs from selected new plant locations to the 20 distribution centers operated by General Foods. If a considerable mix of products is involved, a linear programming model is invoked to minimize transportation expenses.

This concern for transportation is enhanced by the use of railroads as the principal source for identifying potential sites. General Foods is a large rail user, and most of the company's plants have been sited along rail lines on property owned by the railroads. The initial site visits typically involve a senior staff consultant in industrial engineering (central engineering is the lead staff group in the study of alternative locations at General Foods) and a representative from the traffic department.

Whereas transportation factors guide the initial site identification and screening process, other location-related influences serve in the evaluation of sites that have not been screened out. These influences include labor rates, environmental factors, freight costs of raw material, supplies, economies of scale, and taxes, among others.

PROXIMITY TO RAW MATERIALS SOURCES   For several types of companies, a new location is geographically constrained by the need to be close to raw materials. This is particularly true for plants which process agricultural, mining, or forest products, or which depend on bulk shipments from outside the country. In these instances, the spoilage inherent in long-range transportation, and the freight costs, especially if the product is lighter in weight or less bulky than the raw materials, preclude locating the processing plants far away from the raw materials. Locations outside those of the resource areas are typically dismissed out of hand by the managers involved in such a location search.

Examples abound:

Del Monte's newest green bean packing plant is sited in Wisconsin, amidst sizable green bean growing acreage, in a northern state which does not suffer weather too hot for the long green bean growing season. There are other green bean growing areas in the nation, of course, but Del Monte did not have a green bean packing plant in the center of the country and wanted to complement its East and West Coast facilities.

For similar reasons, General Foods' Birdseye division located its new frozen vegetable packaging plants in the heart of the growing region of the vegetable being packaged.

Both tuna packing and foreign-grown sugar processing are effectively constrained to large port facilities. For example, Ralston Purina's Chicken of the Sea brand tuna fish is packed in San Diego, the chief port of the American tuna fishing fleet. And, what processing of imported sugar General Foods does can best be accomplished at large ports specializing in that trade, such as Baltimore or ports along the Gulf Coast or the West Coast.

Most of the nation's agricultural cooperatives, owned as they are by their farmer suppliers, are concentrated in particular regions of the country. Even within regions there are crop specializations implied in part by soil conditions, climate, and terrain, and in part by traditional patterns of farming.

What complicates this materials availability constraint on location is that, over time, the siting of a processing plant can stimulate agricultural production in an area. With some products there is an interdependency between plant location and crop selection that must be considered by the cooperative. For example, Gold Kist's choice of southern Georgia and northern Alabama for soybean processing plants had to be predicated on the suitability of that soil and location for soybean growing, since soybean production in the Southeast prior to Gold Kist's entry into the business was relatively minor.

For the forest products companies such as Union Camp and Crown Zellerbach, the region choice for a new, primary manufacturing facility (a pulp, paper, or saw mill in contrast to a converting facility like a corrugated box plant) is dictated by the availability of trees. Often the choice is further constrained to areas where the company itself owns a sizable fraction of the trees. In the case of a pulp and/or paper mill, the required raw materials include water as well as wood and this need, in turn, limits the possible location of a new mill to the banks of rivers or large lakes.

PROXIMITY TO EXISTING COMPANY FACILITIES   A sizable number of facilities in a broad spectrum of industries must be located within a given radius of one or more other company facilities. For these plants, the size of the radius of constraint may differ widely—within a hour's drive, within a day's truck drive, within two hours by company jet—but the existence of very real geographic bounds on the location search is most important.

Three major classes of location decision share this concern for proximity to existing company facilities.

The first class springs from the cluster concept as exemplified by the shoe and apparel industries. There the cluster revolves around the mixing warehouse (or, in a technical industry, the research and development center) and the plants within the cluster specialize in certain finished products which are shipped to the warehouse (or, alternatively, which emanate from the research and development center).

The second class springs from a process plant multiplant manufacturing strategy. A number of companies, especially those producing complex or high technology products, have found it effective to split their manufacturing operations into distinct segments, each assigned to a particular plant or set of plants. This assignment may involve one or more assembly plants and a set of feeder plants, or perhaps, a series of plants which feed one another with work-in-progress. Many computer and electronics firms, machine tool manufacturers, and auto companies organize their manufacturing operations this way.

Because of the frequent shipment of work-in-process among plants; the considerable managerial and engineering troubleshooting needed to coordinate complex product manufacturing; and the sustained attention across plants which managers and engineers must give to new product introduction or product modification under such a multiplant strategy, it is frequently the case that such plants are located in close proximity to one another. The location of a new plant conforming to this multiplant strategy is thus constrained to a given radius from the cluster's other plants.

The third class sharing a concern for intracompany proximity is more ad hoc in character. Sometimes a plant cannot expand on-site because of space limitations but the capacity that must overflow to a new location is so closely allied to the plant's existing capacity that the management cannot bear to see the new capacity venture too far away. In a very real sense, the new capacity is a satellite plant, which by design, must revolve around the base or mother plant out of which it sprang. The satellite plant thus depends on the mother plant for a good many overhead functions such as purchasing, engineering, and production scheduling while it fulfills its limited mission of manufacturing.

Examples of these three classes of location decision vary markedly.

Clusters of Plants Producing Different Products Revolving Around a Warehouse/Distribution Center, R&D Center, or Something Similar

Already discussed are the Brown Shoe Company's policy of placing plants within either of its two clusters, one centered on St. Louis and the other on western Tennessee. The center of these clusters are mixing warehouses which fill retailer orders. The shoe assembly plants are located within a day or night's truck drive from the warehouse and concentrate on specific product types requiring similar production technology.

The same sort of cluster around a distribution center is characteristic of the Women's Wear Division of Levi Strauss. Most of the division's plants are in Texas, many in South Texas within easy driving distance of the distribution center in Amarillo. Similar clustering is common to Oxford Industries whose plants are all in the Southeast.

Cluett, Peabody offers a variation on the cluster concept. Its four clusters in New York State, Pennsylvania, North Carolina, and Georgia-Alabama manufacture different shirt styles (e.g., sports shirts in Pennsylvania, dress shirts in Georgia-Alabama) but they tend not to revolve around distribution centers (the company now has only two). Rather, the clusters revolve around cutting plants which parcel out materials to the assembly plants within the cluster, themselves differentiated largely by fabric type.

The successful defense contractors are exceedingly flexible. The high technology and grand scale of the products, as well as the well-established fickleness of the U.S. Department of Defense, argues for a manufacturing organization that can adapt quickly to changes in the engineering or the number of products demanded. Often, a company's ability to offer existing space and people enough to perform a given contract is a prerequisite for being granted that contract. It is understandable then why most defense contractors operate manufacturing plants of huge size, among the very largest plants in the country. These large facilities enable management to shift people and equipment among contracts of varying sizes and durations with a comparatively low amount of disruption and overhead expense incurred.

These requirements for flexibility in product design and production volumes have also influenced the location of smaller manufacturing facilities for these defense contractors. These smaller facilities tend to concentrate on very specialized, although related, functions to those performed in the huge manufacturing complexes of each company: (for example, electronics components, test sites, product options assembly). In order to monitor and control these operations effectively such facilities are often located close to the larger complex so that managers and engineers have ready access to them.

Not all of the small defense plants can be regarded in these terms, of course, but it is worth noting that there is some clustering of plants in companies like:

- Martin Marietta Aerospace—a cluster in Florida, and another in the Mountain states
  - Lockheed—a cluster in California
  - United Technologies (Pratt and Whitney Aircraft Group)—a cluster in New England.

Clusters of Plants, Each Concentrating on a Segment of the Process

This clustering of process plants is used by companies as diverse as Digital Equipment Corporation, Black and Decker, and Alcoa. For example, the computers manufactured by DEC are complex products. Digital Equipment's plants serve largely as feeders to one another and to final assembly and test facilities. This transfer of work-in-process encourages clustering, and, so Digital's facilities are concentrated in eastern New England and in the Southwest. Clustering not only reduces the cost and complexity of work-in-process shipment but facilitates the troubleshooting that managers and engineers in high technology industries are compelled to do all the time.

Black and Decker's plants also engage in a non-trivial amount of cross-shipment. For example, within Black and Decker's Consumer Products Division, the plants at Fayetteville and Tarboro, North Carolina ship 15-20% of their output (largely motors at Fayetteville, and cordless chargers and cord sets at Tarboro) to other Black and Decker plants, some outside the division. It is not surprising then to find that the Consumer Product division's plants are either in North Carolina or Maryland.

A similar story can be told of some major fabricating plants of Alcoa, which are located conveniently near other Alcoa plants which feed them with raw materials.

Clusters of Plants, The Satellite Relationship

A number of companies, particularly those like Burroughs, Honeywell, and Polaroid, operate clusters of facilities which resemble the relationship of a sun to its satellites. The sun plant tends to be the largest in the cluster and the one which the major overhead functions call home. The bulk of new product engineering, engineering and management troubleshooting, production and inventory control, scheduling, and kindred functions are based at the main plant. The satellites are strictly manufacturing facilities, often of the highest volume items produced. Typically the satellite plants are designed and staffed to perform a limited number of tasks, with the sun plant handling the low volume, highly engineered products or components.

The satellite plant is often a creation of the sun plant itself. The following scenario is common: Sales are growing rapidly and the sun plant keeps introducing new products which are well received. The sun plant has already undergone expansion on-site, but further on-site expansion appears less desirable. The sun plant's management wants to establish a new plant but does not want to lose too much control over the new plant's operation. Sometimes a mature product or component can be split off from the sun plant's portfolio of responsibilities and transferred to a new satellite plant; other times the satellite is assigned a new product or component. The satellite's product line and management, however, remain linked to the sun plant.

Perhaps the clearest example of this multiplant strategy is Texas Instruments, Incorporated. This major producer of semiconductors, consumer electronics, minicomputers, and peripherals, with plants located mainly in Texas, has adopted an explicit pattern of technology centers and satellites. Product development is housed at the technology centers, at least one of which exists for each major business unit of the corporation. Allied to each technology center is at least one satellite which is charged with manufacturing, often of only a single product line. The technology centers are large operations, employing up to 8,000 to 10,000 people, while the satellite plants are smaller, although still large in comparison with many other companies' plants.

Motorola, Inc. operates a similar dichotomy of plants. The largest facilities—100 acres of campus and 2,000–3,000 people per plant—are reserved for integrated operations including engineering and administration. In contrast to the campuses are the feeder factories—20 acres, 800 people, and 200,000 square feet under roof—which are sited within a truck-day of the integrated facilities and concentrate on low cost manufacturing, rather than engineering.

QUALITY OF LIFE IN AN AREA   Several industries, notably those in high technology areas, have no particular location-sensitive costs such as transportation or labor which constrain their location decisions in important ways. Companies such as Motorola, IBM, Burroughs, Perkin-Elmer, and Honeywell are remarkably free to locate their production capacity almost anywhere in the United States.

In the absence of some primary concerns that affect location, such firms usually consider certain subjective aspects when generating and evaluating potential sites. In assessing the competitive demands placed upon their manufacturing operations, many high technology companies have concluded that the best locations for their plants are those most likely to be attractive environments for their engineers and managers. After all, broad-ranging and rapid new product development, effective engineering, and timely delivery are the salient competitive weapons in these companies; and these weapons are fashioned by a talented, dedicated, and happy corps of engineers and managers. Their plant location decision is one of analyzing where the most attractive places to live in the United States are located.

Being a highly subjective exercise, there are no universal screening mechanisms that apply. The most common screening mechanism is to consider only metropolitan areas, and frequently, only the larger metropolitan areas. Two concerns argue for such a screening mechanism: (1) the breadth of educational, cultural, and recreational amenities prized by many engineers, managers, and their families is usually found only in metropolitan areas of a certain minimum size, and (2) such corporations often erect large plants designed to employ thousands of people yet do not usually wish to be the dominant employer in a community, which implies that large metropolitan areas must be sought. Many such companies adopt rules of thumb for screening metropolitan area size. Typical rules of thumb are that the company should not employ more than 2–4% of the population

(or, sometimes, the employable population) in the metropolitan area (or, sometimes, within the commuting radius around a proposed site, ordinarily 15–25 miles).

Beyond this screening by size, quantitative measures of an area's attractiveness are neither universally sought nor applied in significant and consistent ways. Depending on the company and the situation, some of the following criteria may be considered in the initial location screening process:

- Cost of living data, including housing availability and cost
- Right-to-work state data and/or NLRB certification election data
- Area work stoppages
- School system data (dropout rates, percent going on to college, national test scores)
- Numbers and sizes of colleges and universities in the area
- Cultural measures: Art museum? Symphony? Theatre?
- Sports teams?
- Transportation system: Service quality and frequency of airlines and railroads, area highway network
- Mean January temperature

Even here the evaluation of some of these topics is left for the site visit.

The screening process inevitably turns to subjective evaluations as well. Presented with a choice, many high technology companies would like to locate their operations in those regions and metropolitan areas which are perceived as exciting and congenial places to live. With this in mind, some companies look to various polls which have rated area attractiveness or to polls they conduct themselves among their white-collar workforce, young engineers, or among engineering/management candidates who are still in school.

SCREENING LOCATIONS WHEN THERE ARE NO PRIMARY CONCERNS

Most of the corporate managers I have talked with can casually tick off the one or two key concerns that control the initial screening of new locations. These primary concerns are usually those dictated by the economics of the products produced and by the industry of which they are a part. However, for some companies (between ¼ and ⅓ of those interviewed), representing a variety of industries, there are no easily established primary concerns which control the location screening process. In such instances, the initial screening of potential locations, becomes a more arbitrary exercise.

Most of these companies cope with the ambiguity by adopting a set *initial screening procedure*, as opposed to the application of a *controlling consideration*, such as labor costs or proximity to other company plants. Such an initial screening procedure need not be elaborate, but it does serve to simplify the list of possible locations to evaluate.

Three major initial screening procedures were unearthed in the interviews:

Initial Transportation Analysis Followed By Sensitivity Analysis

This rather inelegant label is used to identify a procedure which first calculates the geographic centers of the source of supply and of the market. These geographic centers are usually weighted by the dollar amounts associated with each geographic subdivision used in the calculation. Often they are also calculated to reflect likely or planned shifts in the geography of both demand and supply. The geographic center of the market is of interest since it is likely to be close to the spot where the freight costs incurred in serving the market are lowest. Similarly, the geographic center of supply is likely to be near the lowest cost spot for assembling a plant's supplies. Furthermore, the line between these two geographic centers is likely to pass near where the plant's total costs of transportation, in and out, are lowest. Wander too far away from these two geographic centers and from the line connecting them, and the company can expect to pay a transportation penalty for locating there. Sometimes the penalties rise sharply as one proceeds away from the geographic centers; other times the penalties rise only modestly. This initial calculation is similar to what some companies which are sensitive to transportation costs do to simplify their own location screening.

After this transport cost analysis, this particular screening procedure uses other criteria, such as labor availability or costs, energy availability, or taxes. Typically, sample locations are selected at varying distances from the two geographic centers calculated and data are assembled about them. The extent of the transportation penalties suggests how far location decision-makers can wander from the lowest freight cost locations in search of sites with markedly better labor availability, labor costs, environmental properties, quality of life amenities, or whatever.

Essentially, this is a two-part comparative procedure which first identifies a focal group of locations on the basis of freight costs and then examines neighboring locations systematically in ever-widening rings (ellipses) to test the attractiveness of those locations along various quantitative and qualitative dimensions apart from transportation costs. The companies that use this method are seeking locations whose attractions more than overcome any freight cost penalties the company would incur by locating a new plant there. Representative companies that use this general approach to the initial site screening include Westinghouse Electric, FMC, and Company Z.

MULTIDIVISION SHARING OF A PRODUCTION COMPLEX

Some corporations attempt to deal with the ambiguity associated with the absence of clearly established controlling considerations by concentrating the activity of different divisions on the same site. In most large corporations the autonomy granted the various operating divisions is such that a division may refuse to share a production complex with another division, although persuasion and pressure from corporate level managers can be brought to bear. Thus, in some companies the initial phases of a division's search for additional capacity includes a critical look at space for expansion on sites already occupied by plants of other company divisions.

This policy prevails only in capital-intensive operations which are less susceptible to the particular diseconomies of scale that argue strongly against on-site expansion. In these diversified complexes, increased size and production volumes may, in fact, lead to some economies, particularly plant power, maintenance, and pollution control, which often have high capital expense and declining marginal unit costs. Chemical companies like DuPont have, and are, encouraging multidivision sharing, as is General Foods in many of its divisions. At one company interviewed, the manufacturing managers are free to poll the other division managers about producing given products with any spare capacity the latter may have.

It should be recognized that one of the difficulties to overcome in such a situation is the aversion of some division managers to enter into a tenant-landlord relationship. In many of these situations, one division bears the responsibility for the site and overhead functions, and the other division is charged for their use. Depending upon the arrangement and how the division's performance is evaluated, some division managers resist accepting tenant status since they may feel less in control of their destiny there or evaluated less satisfactorily. Some companies overcome such resistance by having the corporation assume the capital and overhead costs common to the divisions on-site so that all are, in a sense, tenants of the complex.

REGIONAL LIMITS

Still a third way to deal with the ambiguity of location screening is to limit the search to a particular set of states. While this may sound like an unnecessarily arbitrary policy it need not be. For example, one company limits its initial location screening to a corridor of Plains states stretching down from the Dakotas, Minnesota, and Wisconsin, to Texas and Louisiana. Historically, many of the company's plants have been located in this corridor, and its boundaries make sense for future plants as well. After an analysis of the key factors, company managers have concluded that this corridor of states best fits the company's present and future distribution needs, as well as company attitudes concerning population/industrial density, growth rate of industrialization (not too high in the Plains states), labor availability and quality, technical training, labor costs, and other factors.

Furthermore, this limited designation of the Plains states' corridor has permitted the company to compile a library of sites with good potential. This library helps to speed the site selection process and new plant start-up, which is very desirable for this innovative corporation.

Emotion and personal preference

For many of the corporate staff professionals interviewed, the scourges of the location decision process are emotion and personal preference. Much of the role these staff people see themselves performing is squeezing these out of a location decision. This is all the harder to accomplish when there are no controlling considerations to the initial screening of potential locations.

It is interesting to note that most of the companies/divisions interviewed which did not have any controlling considerations in location screening have adopted decision teams that are dominated more by division managers than by corporate staff people. Put in other terms, staff-dominated location decisions tend to have more clear-cut criteria than division dominated processes. Furthermore, many of the companies/divisions which locate sites without a controlling concern but with a set initial screening procedure, and which have also adopted a strong corporate staff-dominated organization, have done so comparatively recently. Perhaps these companies, more than others, have recognized the vulnerability of past location decisions to the personal preference of individuals. At present, their more staff-dominated teams and set screening procedures help keep emotion out of the decision process.

Pursuing the specific location

To this point, the discussion has focused on how companies simplify the checklist length of factors that influence location and how some controlling considerations can effectively screen potential regions and locations within regions. To round out the description of the location choice process at major corporations, three topics merit further discussion: (1) how sites are generated initially, (2) what the routine of the site visit includes, and (3) how a site selection is consummated. These topics are addressed in turn.

GENERATING POTENTIAL SITES

Most companies rely on organizations outside their own to uncover communities which might host their operations. Popular sources of available site information include:

- state government industrial development agencies
- railroad company departments of real estate
- power company departments of industrial development

Less popular sources of manufacturing sites include:

- location consulting firms, such as Fantus, and A.T. Kearney
- community-based industrial development commissions
- chambers of commerce

- industrial realtors or developers
- specific industry-affiliated consultants or middlemen

In recent years, state industrial development agencies have become increasingly popular as site sources. This is due in part to the resources and professionalism which some states have tried to bring to these agencies and in part to the decreased rail transportation needs of most manufacturers today. Power companies, the traditional exponents of industrial development, remain active but have had some of their roles usurped by the rising state agencies. There are a variety of frequently alleged reasons why the less popular site sources are avoided: location consultants are expensive, community-based commissions and Chambers of Commerce cannot keep a secret, realtors and developers are too intent on selling their own properties, and industry-affiliated consultants with expertise often are not available. Still, these less popular site sources are used in many instances and can be expected to play continuing roles in location searches.

Some companies uncover new plant locations through their own research. For the most part this is done either by companies with many plants in a given region and thus great familiarity with towns there, or by companies which are attracted only to large, visible metropolitan areas.

A source like a state industrial development agency is apt to be telephoned by a member of the company team working on location, often a staff executive in real estate, manufacturing, or industrial engineering. Sometimes the approach is made anonymously; almost always, absolute confidence is requested. The site source is given some criteria for guiding its review of communities within its jurisdiction. The criteria may be broad or exceedingly detailed, depending on the company, the location study team working on the project, the team's progress on the project, and whether an existing building is requested. Typical examples of a guiding criteria for towns/sites follow.

- Towns between 25,000 and 100,000 population served by at least two railroads, one north-south and the other east-west. Site must be at least 100 acres.
- Towns within 200 miles of city X and within 20 miles of a commercial airport, situated on an interstate highway, and within 10 miles of a truck terminal which can serve the entire country.
- Rural towns of less than 10,000 population, with higher than average unemployment, no history of labor organization, a structure of at least 15,000 sq. ft. available for lease immediately, industrial revenue bonding opportunities, and a vocational/technical school within 20 miles.

Within several weeks the agency is usually requested to provide information on, say, 5 to 20 towns (or sites) which fit, or come close to fitting, the criteria established. The more complete the information on each community or site the better. A good town profile includes:

population and recent trends in population
area employment, and area unemployment rates

highway access
truck, rail, and airline service
schools and training programs in the area
wage information and extent of unionization
existing manufacturers
area industrial parks
available utilities and public service, and
tax rates

Good site information includes:

l ocation (map included)
acreage
land contour description
highway and rail access
available public services, with spare capacities of utilities indicated (a measure
of how much more development can be coped with readily), and asking price
of site.

A good building description would include all of this information plus all
of the structural data concerning the building itself.

THE SITE VISIT

After the towns/sites that have been screened, those that remain attractive are generally visited by one or two members of the location study
team. The first visit is usually a whirlwind affair, often with only one or
two days spent in any one town. Different companies naturally employ
different techniques in touring and evaluating communities. Permit me to
offer a kind of composite characterization of the site visit.

The company executives travel without disclosing the identity of their
company, carrying no business cards or anything that could be traced back
to the company, often going by an alias as well. The executives may travel
with state development officials or other local representatives to aid in
introductions, but they often travel alone, as well.

The purpose of the site visit tries to resolve questions left unanswered
by the initial screening process. The visit is in part designed to confirm
data and impressions and in part designed to catch the flavor and texture
of a community. A portion of the visit is thus spent touring the town—
looking at available industrial sites, confirming the presence and size of
the industry already located there, seeing what the existing housing stock
is like, and noting such relevant aspects of the town's physical infrastructure
as the quality of the roads, water and sewage systems, schools and town
shops and buildings.

Another portion of the visit is alloted to talking with townspeople:

Representatives from the community's own economic development body, such
as a local development authority or Chamber of Commerce—This is the

opportunity for the community to "sell itself" to the company representatives.

Other industrial employers, which have already been telephoned—Here data gathered about the workforce (rates of turnover, absenteeism, time it takes to fill vacant positions at different job skill levels, prevailing wage rates, perceived skills, attitudes about craftsmanship, attitudes toward unionization, prevalence and quality of area training programs, perimeter of commuting draw to the town), and about local and government attitudes and assistance to business.

Local government officials—How eager are the local elected officials for new business investment? How willing are they to make public investments that would benefit an in-coming manufacturer—roads, water mains, sewerage, waste treatment facilities, expansion, training programs? How willing are they to help with re-zoning, environmental permits, industrial revenue bond financing? What are the tax rates and assessment practices? Any tax concessions offered?

Town fathers—Some manufacturers are less interested in the elected town officials, who come and go, as they are in the town's Establishment, the movers and shakers who frequently stand behind the elected officials and who may largely determine their fate. These manufacturers want to ascertain the views of those town fathers toward new business investment, whether they would push for some of the public investments that a new manufacturing plant might acquire. The view here is that the town fathers will determine how progressive the town is.

Local transportation and utilities officials—Local railroad, trucking, and airline officials are questioned about service, schedules, and rates. Questions are posed as well about power, natural gas, and water availability rates.

Realtors—What does the housing market look like? How expensive is it? Are there class divisions within the town? What are the schools and hospitals like? How transient is the town? Where do people work?

School officials—How are the school offerings and facilities, class sizes, dropout rates, test scores, percent college-bound?

Bankers, Clergy—What are their impressions of this town versus others in which they have served? Problems in town? Does the town take pride in itself? Are the people active and willing to see progress, or do most people want to keep the town like it always was? What cultural, recreational, and community events are promoted?

Man on the Street (cab drivers, barbers, etc.) What is the average person's opinion of the town, its potential, and the role industry can play?

In an effort to gather accurate information from all these sources, some manufacturers I have talked with have their own techniques which they employ during a site visit. When visiting an area manufacturer to test labor availability, for example, a team of two may split up, one to talk with the manufacturer's personnel manager and the other to talk with the shop foremen and workers. Notes would then be compared on items like the length of time it took to fill the last vacancy in a certain job class.

For those companies seeking low labor costs, statistics and the opinions of existing manufacturers are not enough usually to convince management that enough quality labor at the right wage can be hired. To get a better understanding of the local labor market, the company generally takes out an ad in the local media which announces that job interviews are to be held for an unnamed company in such-and-such an industry. Then, for several days or a week, always including Saturday, company personnel people interview prospective employees, gauging the wage rate that would attract them from existing jobs, their experience and skill levels, their attitudes toward industry and unionization, and the number of employees that could be drawn from the area. This labor survey is an important test of a town but, even if the town is selected for the plant, some companies may first place a pilot facility in operation in rented space as a further test of the labor market, before scheduling the building of a new plant.

After the initial visits to the towns/sites which had looked most promising, another ranking is done, using the facts and impressions discovered or confirmed. It is at this point in the decision process that the location study team charged with developing the recommendation typically wants to limit the choices to six or fewer towns/sites and often just to two or three. Additional site visits are made, the original visitors usually return with others from the management team who are apt to have specialties— engineering, industrial relations/personnel, environmental affairs, logistics, among others. Questions that were not asked and people who were not seen are now asked and visited. This second round of visits usually takes longer than the initial round. The focus of the search becomes more critical and more detailed. The tone of the search shifts from a desire to discover all that is attractive about a town/site to a desire to uncover any "snakes lying under the rocks". The management team wants to avoid expensive surprises.

As a result of this second round of visits and concomitant development of a capital budget analysis of the various sites, the location study team deliberates and tries to reach a concensus on the ranking of at least the best site and, more often, on the best two or three sites. With the location study team for the decision all agreed (or reconciled to the selection), the division general manager and often the president and/or chief executive officer are brought more formally into the site selection process. For the most part, this means escorting this top rank of company management to the two or three best sites. These senior managers ordinarily must champion the capital appropriations request for the new plant through the board of directors, so they usually want some first hand knowledge of the proposed site before they can feel comfortable enough to approve the recommendation.

After the senior managers of a company have given their approval to a team's site recommendation, an option is almost always taken on the land. The optioning of a site permits the company to bring surveyors, geologists, and engineers onto a site to conduct specific tests of it and any structures on it. The option thus provides some insurance that the architectural/engineering designs contemplated can be successfully implemented without incurring any unanticipated expenses. In most cases, the price of the option can be applied to the sales price when the option is exercised.

The option is usually taken by a local attorney who is retained for just this purpose. Most large corporations are very reluctant to reveal their identities before a firm commitment on price has been legally contracted. It is only after the option has been negotiated that the corporation will identify itself, and sometimes it will not do so until it is actually constructing the plant. The secrecy also helps mitigate the disappointment towns might feel if they knew they had been passed over by a large, well-known company. In a similar vein, secrecy permits the corporation to assess the town in more leisurely fashion and dispassionately, without any of the extra "show" that might be put on it if the corporation's identity were known.

Most corporations will option only the first choice of the location team and the division manager, but some companies, looking to avoid wasted time if the first choice has to be discarded for one reason or another, will option 2 or more sites at the same time. Heavy industrial companies are more likely to option multiple sites.

Influences on Location Choice: Survey Evidence

It should be plain by now that a definitive assessment of the impact of any one factor on industry location is an extraordinarily difficult methodological task. As the foregoing pages have tried to make clear, manufacturers of different types see themselves constrained in different ways and thus limited in the geographical sweeps they can engage in when searching for new plant locations. Items like labor costs and transportation expenses to markets undoubtedly are more important for some industries—and for selected companies within these industries—than they are for others. Thus, speculating on what, say, a 10% labor rate shift would do to the industrial fortunes of an area depends not only on (1) with which other areas the area in question is being compared to, and (2) the strength of the changes induced by such a shift, other thing equal, but also on (3) the particular blend of industries and companies which could possibly be affected.

It seems a hopeless task to sort out all these effects in any thoroughly satisfactory way. Researchers have been obliged to selectively investigate

(1) geographical variations in industrial "densities" or (2) particular plant/company/industry location decisions. The research reported here has focused on what inferences can be drawn about the importance of particular factors, measured as straightforwardly and as objectively as possible, from actual, specific location decisions. This study's particular methodology includes (1) comparisons of plants in different places to see what differentiates facilities in one place from those in another, and (2) structured interrogations of location decision-makers themselves about the factors that influenced location choices and how important they were. Neither method is completely satisfactory, but together they offer the best means currently available of assessing the strengths of particular influences on the changing pattern of industry location.

The remainder of this chapter explores the importance of particular influences on decisions to locate in one place rather than another. The first of these explorations involves a comparison of Sunbelt and Frostbelt plants.

The regional characters of plants

Despite the increasing heterogeneity of industry within any region of the U.S., a certain degree of industrial specialization still persists in most regions. This industry specialization is bound to affect the general characters of the plants in a region. Nevertheless, I think it is useful to try to abstract from industry-specific features to consider the particular characteristics of a plant which may be different across regions. In particular, is a Sunbelt plant—especially a *new* Sunbelt plant—different in purpose and character from a Frostbelt plant? Do manufacturers envision different roles and operational choices for Sunbelt plants?

THE SUNBELT-FROSTBELT HYPOTHESIS

Several forces may act to differentiate the Sunbelt from the Frostbelt plant:

The Sunbelt has not had a long history of industrialization, therefore manufacturing skills must be learned by nearly all workers. While many manufacturers are no doubt pleased by the work ethic found in many parts of the Sunbelt (and the non-unionism and even anti-unionism of some sections), they cannot establish high labor skill operations there without expending considerable resources in training.

Because the Sunbelt has been poorer than the Frostbelt, labor rates have been lower and can be expected to remain low until the region is sufficiently developed. This argues for the assignment of specific manufacturing tasks to Sunbelt plants that can best exploit the labor cost differences between regions.

Because manufacturing has heretofore been concentrated in the Frostbelt, nearly all support operations for manufacturing have developed there as well. For most large Frostbelt companies, research and development activities, new products and processes, and similar innovations can be expected to remain at their traditional centers in the north. The implication is that Sunbelt plants are not well suited for developing new products or processes.

Although the manufacturer's Frostbelt facilities are likely to spawn the latest products and technologies, these plants are commonly restricted from using the latest manufacturing techniques and the best equipment simply because they are older and may employ equipment that the company finds easier to leave in place than to move. A Sunbelt plant can thus be expected to be more modern in facility design, and to incorporate the latest equipment and production techniques.

These forces might be expected to define a typical Sunbelt plant with the following general characteristics:

- Definite, fairly narrow production responsibilities with little or no product or process innovation.

- Strong ties to other company plants, mainly in the Frostbelt, especially for support functions like industrial engineering, major purchasing, order handling and scheduling, marketing and sales, in addition to new product engineering.

- A higher than average reliance on other company plants for specialized materials/components that might not be available locally in the Sunbelt.

- A high volume operation that can take advantage of the lower wages and any other lower costs which prevail, perhaps, in the Sunbelt. Such an operation may also offer considerable vertical integration.

- A thoroughly modern plant in design and equipment, often exhibiting a higher capital-labor ratio, because of more—and more sophisticated—equipment and lower labor expenses.

- A definite tendency to less unionization than in the Frostbelt.

TESTING THE CHARACTER OF THE SUNBELT PLANT

The sample of completed plant surveys, drawn as they are from Frostbelt and Sunbelt and encompassing both new and existing plants, has permitted an examination of the character of the Sunbelt plant. Probit analysis has been used to isolate those characteristics which differentiate and explain the variances between Sunbelt and Frostbelt plants. The surveys were sorted into two groups (Sunbelt and Frostbelt), with the Sunbelt identified as the following census regions: South Atlantic, East South Central, West South Central, and Mountain. The dependent variable is thus a 0-1 dummy variable that takes the value 1 when the survey is from the Sunbelt.

The results of the analysis of all existing Sunbelt versus Frostbelt plants in the survey are reported in Table 3-18. Only significant variable coefficients are included. Two separate analyses are provided, Form 1 includes the capital-labor ratio; Form 2 excludes it. Because potentially sensitive information is needed to construct the capital-labor ratio, key information for that analysis was frequently excluded from the surveys returned. Excluding the capital-labor ratio increased the number of observations available for the probit analysis from 197 to 324.

Table 3-18

The Character of the Sunbelt Plant: Probit Analysis
(Only significant coefficients retained)

Variables (in rough priority)	Form 1		Form 2	
	C-standardized Coefficient	Level of Significance	C-standardized Coefficient	Level of Significance
Unionized? (High value = no)	0.133	1.000	0.114	1.000
Plant independence (High value = more independent)	-0.106	0.997	-0.121	1.000
Percent of plant's supplies purchased from other company plants	0.080	0.983	0.071	0.993
Degree of product innovation (High value = lots)	-0.054	0.923	-0.068	0.991
Percent of supplies classed as really "raw" materials	0.050	0.900	0.051	0.955
Capital-labor ratio	0.047	0.877		
Number of observations	(197)		(324)	
Goodness of fit: R^2	0.182		0.158	

Splitting at $P = 0.5$

Predicted

True	Frostbelt	Sunbelt	Totals
Frostbelt	98	22	120
Sunbelt	38	39	77
Totals	136	61	197

Probability of Error = 0.305
Sample fraction Sunbelt = 0.391

Splitting at $P = 0.5$

Predicted

True	Frostbelt	Sunbelt	Totals
Frostbelt	154	37	191
Sunbelt	63	70	133
Totals	217	107	324

Probability of error = 0.309
Sample fraction Sunbelt = 0.410

Peeling off the Top

Predicted

True	Frostbelt	Sunbelt	Totals
Frostbelt	88	32	120
Sunbelt	32	45	77
Totals	120	77	197

Probability of Error = 0.325
Sample fraction Sunbelt = 0.391

Peeling off the Top

Predicted

True	Frostbelt	Sunbelt	Totals
Frostbelt	141	50	191
Sunbelt	50	83	133
Totals	191	133	324

Probability of error = 0.309
Sample fraction Sunbelt = 0.410

The variables in Table 3-18 are listed in declining priority as determined by the C-standardized coefficient, which expresses the rate of change of the probability of occurrence, P, evaluated at P = 0.5, per a one standard deviation change in the explanatory variable when all other explanatory variables are held fixed. The results largely confirm the hypothesis stated above. The typical Sunbelt plant has a character which is distinctly different from the Frostbelt plant, one that can be captured by survey responses. Foremost, the Sunbelt plant is differentiated by being non-union and by not having the independence more characteristic of the Frostbelt plant. (The plant independence variable was constructed as the sum of responses to the question of "which of the following functions are performed at this plant": industrial engineering, new product engineering, marketing and sales, purchasing of major raw materials, and direct receipt of customer orders. The more of these five functions performed at the plant, the greater the plant's independence is said to be.) In this sense, not only does the typical Sunbelt plant lack the functional independence of other plants, but a greater fraction of its supplies are purchased from other company plants. It appears to be dependent on other company facilities for manufacturing support services and for materials as well. A larger fraction of the Sunbelt plant's supplies are also termed "really 'raw' materials," which suggests that the Sunbelt plant may be vertically integrated backward more than the Frostbelt plant. This conclusion is not contradicted by evidence that the Sunbelt plant has a higher capital-labor ratio, which also supports the view that the Sunbelt plant houses a good deal of newer, more sophisticated equipment. The higher capital-labor ratio may indicate the industry mix in the Sunbelt also, since 57% of the chemical and petroleum plants surveyed were from Sunbelt states as opposed to about 40% of all plants surveyed. When the chemical and petroleum plants of the sample were excluded from the probit analysis, the significance of the capital-labor ratio falls substantially. Other results are not affected, however. Lastly, the probit analysis results point to an absence of innovation in the products manufactured by Sunbelt plants, suggesting that the products assigned to them are more stable, high volume ones.

In sum, results shown in Table 3-18 support the contention that Sunbelt plants are in general distinguished from Frostbelt plants by being more narrowly focused, more dependent on other company plants and functions, more non-union, and more a low-technology, high volume operation. The variables included in the results do a fair job of improving our ability to differentiate Sunbelt from Frostbelt plants. With the probit analysis, errors in differentiating are made about 30% of the time. This improves the 40% error rate implicit in the simple decision rule of classifying every plant as a Frostbelt one.

How is a *new* Sunbelt plant different from a new plant elsewhere? Table 3-19 shows the results of another probit analysis which was restricted to new plants (plant openings and relocations). The variables that could

Table 3-19

The Character of the Newly Sited Sunbelt Plant: Probit Analysis
(only significant coefficients retained)

Variable (in priority order)	C-standardized Coefficient	Level of Significance
Want low taxes? (High value = desired)	0.149	1.000
Plant independence (High value = more independent)	-0.126	.998
Warehousing (High value = more complex warehousing and distribution system)	0.119	.997
Percent of plant's supplies purchased from other company plants	0.098	.984
Must be near other company/division facilities? (High value = yes)	-0.096	.982
Want to be near college? (High value = desired)	0.088	.973
Transportation important to plant operations? (High value = less important)	-0.087	.975
Rigidity of process (High value = process has become less rigid over time)	-0.086	.972
Unionized? (High value = no)	0.082	.973
Miles from within which 3/4 of plant's supplies are shipped	-0.075	.953
Want cheap land? (High value = desired)	0.050	.875
Number of observations	(181)	
Goodness of fit: R^2	0.375	

Splitting at $P = 0.5$

Peeling off the Top

Predicted

True	Frostbelt	Sunbelt	Totals
Frostbelt	70	19	89
Sunbelt	19	73	92
Totals	89	92	181

Probability of error = 0.210
Sample fraction Sunbelt = 0.508

Predicted

True	Frostbelt	Sunbelt	Totals
Frostbelt	70	19	89
Sunbelt	19	93	92
Totals	89	112	181

Probability of error = 0.210
Sample fraction Sunbelt = 0.508

be included in this probit were more numerous than in the preceeding ones, because the search requirements for the new sites could be included.

As might be expected, some of the same character of the existing Sunbelt plant shows through in that of the newly sited Sunbelt plant. The new Sunbelt plant is likely to be less unionized, less functionally independent, and tied more to other company plants for its supplies than its Frostbelt counterpart, just like the sample of all plants, reported above. Other variables show up as important in Table 3-19 and many refine the story told by Table 3-18's results. While a new Sunbelt plant performs fewer specialized functions than a new Frostbelt plant, it can operate at quite some distance from other company facilities, as indicated by the hesitancy to claim that it must be located near other company/division facilities and by the likelihood that it is tied into a more elaborate, multifacility warehousing system. A new Sunbelt plant also shows definite signs of being a high volume operation producing products from readily available materials and with sales more apt to be subject to price competition. These interpretations are indicated by responses which show (1) that the new Sunbelt plant's operations have become "more rigid, more single purpose" over time than the new Frostbelt plant's, and that (2) its supplies are shipped from more local sources, and yet (3) it is more likely to consider itself "seriously impeded from competing in some geographical markets solely because of transport costs". Reflected through these results, the image of the new Sunbelt facility is of a plant whose charter is to produce a non-specialty product which can be consumed nearly everywhere but is subject to price pressures. The plant simply manufactures the product; it is not a development and innovation center for the company. The vulnerability to price pressure is underscored by the location search criteria for low taxes and cheap land to further reduce costs. The survey results indicate that college towns in the Sunbelt have a special allure as well.

The variables incorporated into Table 3-19's results do well in differentiating new Sunbelt plants from new Frostbelt ones. The error rate is 21%, substantially below the 49% error rate implicit with the simple decision rule of classifying every new plant as a Sunbelt one.

Constraints On and Desires For the Location Decision: What Manufacturers Say About Particular Plant Location Choices

Managers of all new plants surveyed, both newly added and relocating plants, were asked about particular influences on their choices of location. The questions posed stratified their decisions into region/state choice and particular site selection. Managers were asked to identify those factors, if any, which constrained them in their region/state choice, that is, which "were perceived as 'musts' ". They were similarly asked about "musts" in the final site selection. Subsequently they were asked "what factors were perceived as 'desirable, if available' and helped to tip the scales in favor of this site?" This stratification was developed to structure responses from plant managers in much the same way that the executives I interviewed discussed the steps taken in their site search processes.

The results of this series of survey questions, reported for all industries, are found in Tables 3-20 through 3-22. These findings are, in general, consistent with the others reported so far. Compiled, but not shown here, are results for broadly defined industry groups (see Chapter 4 for details of their definition). These industry group results highlight diversities across industries in the influences which guide the location choice.

For the most fundamental phase of the location search, that of selecting the region/state, two constraints ("musts") loom as particularly important: a favorable labor climate and being near the market for the prod-

Table 3-20

Constraints on the Region/State Choice: Factors Viewed as "Musts"—All Industries

Factor	Percent of Plant Openings Citing at Least 1 Factor	Percent of Movers Citing at Least 1 Factor
Favorable labor climate	76%	39%
Near market	55%	0%
Attractive place for engineers/ managers to live	35%	19%
Near supplies, resources (includes energy)	31%	28%
Low labor rates	30%	19%
Near existing facilities of division/ company	25%	17%
Environmental permits	17%	8%
Facility/land already available	3%	6%
Better transportation	2%	0%
Taxes, financing	1%	0%
Retaining current labor force	0%	56%
Community attitude	0%	3%
Number of plants citing at least one factor	159	36

Table 3-21

Constraints on Final Site Selection: Factors Viewed as "Musts"--All Industries

Factor	Percent of Plant Openings Citing at Least 1 Factor	Percent of Movers Citing at Least 1 Factor
Rail service	47%	25%
On expressway	42%	31%
Special provision of utilities (gas, sewerage, water)	34%	22%
Rural area	27%	19%
Environmental permits	23%	3%
Within metropolitan area	21%	39%
On water	16%	11%
Available land/building	8%	11%
Transportation (airport, truck service)	3%	3%
Community financing, support	1%	0%
Proximity to other division plant	1%	3%
Minimum acreage	1%	0%
Non-union site	1%	0%
Number of plants citing at least one factor	159	36

Table 3-22

Influences on Site Selection: Factors Viewed as "Desirable, if Available"
--All Industries

Factor	Percent of Plant Openings Citing at Least 1 Factor	Percent of Movers Citing at Least 1 Factor
Favorable labor climate	74%	44%
Low land costs	60%	50%
Near markets	42%	22%
Low taxes	35%	19%
On Expressway	35%	28%
Rail service	30%	22%
Low construction costs	29%	33%
Low wage rates	28%	25%
College nearby	26%	14%
Low energy costs	25%	14%
Government help with roads, sewerage, water, labor training	25%	3%
Near suppliers	23%	25%
Government financing	13%	6%
Available land/buildings	3%	11%
Near other division facilities	3%	3%
Air transportation	1%	0%
Quality of life	1%	0%
Retain labor force	0%	3%
Number of plants citing at least one factor	159	36

uct(s) manufactured. Other factors were cited much less frequently. These findings were supported as well by surveys of company headquarters that oversee operations in Cincinnati and New England. These latter surveys identified "proximity to markets" as the "single most important" factor affecting the region and metropolitan/rural area choice. The only other consideration that approached the importance of market proximity was the concern for labor wage rates (in the metropolitan versus rural area choice). All other considerations were dwarfed by these two.

Even though "favorable labor climate" was indicated by three-fourths of the sample's plants, however, there were marked variations in the frequency of response by industry group. Those industries labelled "Labor Cost Sensitive" (textiles, apparel, furniture, leather, and consumer electronics) placed the labor climate high on their lists of location "musts" (73%). But labor climate was cited by a even greater fraction of plants in the Specialty Chemicals/Metals group, in the Heavy Metals group (a slim sample of only 4), and in the large Industrial Machinery and Transportation Equipment group. Labor climate was relatively less important to Agriculture and Forest-tied plants and to those in the Heavy Chemicals/ Oil/Rubber/Glass group. These industries are all capital-intensive and thus less influenced by the labor climate.

Proximity to the market, is also the most frequently cited "must" for that group of industries labelled "Market Sensitive" (much of food processing, paper converting, printing, asphalt making, plastics fabrication, can making, and miscellaneous manufacturing). Proximity to the market is also valued by three other industries that deal largely in low value to weight of commodity or near-commodity products, namely the Heavy Metals, Forest-Tied, and Heavy Chemicals/Oil/Rubber/Glass. This is thoroughly consistent with expectations and the other findings. Market proximity is valued not at all by High Technology plants, and only moderately so by the Industrial Machinery/Transportation Equipment, the Specialty Chemicals/Metals, and Labor Cost Sensitive groups, all of which deal with more specialized items with broad geographic distribution.

Turning again to Table 3-20, three factors rate frequencies of about a third: the quality of life in an area, proximity to supplies and resources, and low labor rates. These influences, too, register pronounced differences across industry groups. The quality of life in an area receives a low level of response from nearly all the industry groups. However, quality of life rates nearly as high as "favorable labor climate", for the High Technology group, being cited by 5 of every 8 plants in the group. This agrees with the interview evidence introduced earlier. Quality of life also ranks rather high with the Industrial Machinery/Transportation Equipment group, perhaps the other group of the nine that is most dependent on engineering talent.

Proximity to supplies and resources receives a comparatively low level of response from most industries, however, the three groups most likely to value these proximities are those one might expect: Heavy Chemicals/Oil/Rubber/Glass, Forest-Tied, and Agriculture-Tied. Each of these industries are integrated backward into raw materials which are bulky and rather costly to ship great distances. Again, the specialty products groups place the lowest values on transportation-related concerns.

To some readers, the low labor rates' fifth ranking in Table 3-20's results may be surprising , but their relative ranking among industries makes eminent sense. As anticipated, low labor rates are valued most by the so-called "Labor Cost Sensitive" industry group and least by capital-intensive industry groups (Heavy Metals, Heavy Chemicals/Oil/Rubber/ Glass, Agriculture-Tied, and Forest-Tied). The more footloose industry groups (High Technology, Industrial Machinery/Transportation Equipment, and Specialty Chemicals/Metals) are those which, after the Labor Cost Sensitive group, attach the most influence to low labor rates, a finding that is not surprising.

The other two "musts" mentioned with some regularity are proximity to other division/company facilities and the securing of environmental permits. Cross-industry variations for these two factors meet one's expectations as well. The close plant-to-plant couplings of the High Technology and Heavy Chemicals/Oil/Rubber/Glass are reflected in the results, as well as the environmental needs of the chemicals industry and the water-using agriculture and forest-tied industries.

In sum, for newly opened plants, the wide diversity of location needs shows through in the frequencies by which various industry groups label certain factors as "musts" for the selection of regions and states. And the relative importance of certain factors in each industry make sense and help confirm the interview findings introduced previously.

Table 3-21 deals with "musts" for the site itself. Again, results for the nine broad industry groups have been compiled but are not shown. The responses of the plants surveyed underscore the many differences which exist across industries in search of new plant locations. For example, the results document the critical ties that certain industry groups (Heavy Metals, Forest and Agriculture-Tied) have to rail service. Less critical, but still significant, are the ties other industries have to water supplies (Heavy Chemicals/Oil/Rubber/Glass), expressways (Labor Cost Sensitive, Market Sensitive), and utilities (metals and chemicals).

Table 3-22 addresses those factors perceived as "desirable, if available" which "helped to tip the scales in favor of this site". This is where we glimpse the economic "margins" of a location decision, where at least some other factors have been held equal. Again, the cross-industry group results are especially revealing.

Favorable labor climate and low land cost considerations are the most frequently mentioned influences for all industries combined; indeed, a favorable labor climate is sought by a greater fraction of plants than any other influence in every industry group except Forest-Tied and Industrial Machinery/Transportation Equipment. Companies plainly want to locate in areas with recognized good work ethics and/or little unionism.

Low land costs are particularly important to the Labor Cost Sensitive, Heavy Metals, Industrial Machinery/Transportation Equipment, and Agriculture-Tied industry groups. Indeed low costs in general—low land costs, low construction costs, low wage rates, and low taxes—seem to be consistent desires for plants in the Labor Cost Sensitive group. Perhaps this category ought to be renamed simply as the Cost Sensitive industry group.

The relative frequencies by which other location influences were indicated by the various industries coincides for the most part with expectations. Proximity to markets is valued most by the Market Sensitive and the commodity goods manufacturers (Heavy Chemicals/Oil/Rubber/Glass, Forest and Agriculture-Tied groups). Proximity to supplies is valued most by the Forest-Tied and Heavy Chemicals/Oil/Rubber/Glass groups. Rail service is most popular with the Heavy Metals and Forest-Tied groups. Expressway access is most prized by the Market Sensitive Heavy Metals, and Specialty Chemicals/Metals groups. The Heavy Metals and Specialty Chemicals/Metals groups also value low energy costs most. Understandably, having a college nearby is prized most by the High Technology group.

Table 3-22 also offers some insight into the influence of public sector actions on industry location. Government financing does not seem to play an important role in "tipping the scales" toward particular sites in any industry. Government help with physical improvements like roads, sewerage, and water systems varies considerably by industry, and does seem to be more important for the Market Sensitive and Industrial Machinery/ Transportation Equipment groups. That such physical improvements are not more popular with the capital-intensive industries is surprising, although it may be that such industries are accustomed to providing all these kinds of physical necessities for themselves. More frequently mentioned than these government policies are low taxes, particularly for the Specialty Chemicals/Metals and the Labor Cost Sensitive industry groups. There is a tendency for low taxes to be valued more highly by the more footloose industries (High Technology, Industrial Machinery/Transportation Equipment, Specialty Chemicals/Metals, Labor Cost Sensitive, and Market Sensitive) than by others whose sites are constrained more by rail service, water use, and/or resource availability.

The influence of other factors on location choice

Labor climate and proximity to markets were uncovered as the two most important "musts" in the choice of region and state for newly locating plants. Other aspects of the survey permit the further investigation of these influences.

As the interviews revealed, the unionization or potential unionization of new facilities is an abiding consideration for a considerable number of companies. On average, industry in this country is about half union and half non-union.[4] In our sample 52% of the plants which had stayed put over the 1970s, involving 52% of their employment, were unionized.

This is dramatically not the case for new plants. Almost 80% of all new plant openings, involving three-fourths of all new plant employment, are non-union. This 80% figure holds for new plants in all regions except for the East North Central. Table 3-23 documents the unionism of plants by region of the country.

In every region, the unionism of plant openings is markedly below that of stay-put plants. Moreover, except for the East North Central region, the odds of opening a plant that will be non-union, at least for its early career, remain very good. Naturally, there is some erosion of non-union status over time, as labor organization attempts are given more time to succeed. In this sample, 85% of the new plants occupied since 1975 were non-union as opposed to 75% of the new plants occupied between 1970 and 1975. One might also expect organized labor to single out larger new plants for organization efforts; this is suggested in the data where 26% of

---

[4]See Richard B. Freeman and James L. Medoff, "New Estimate of Private Sector Unionism in the United States." *Industrial and Labor Relations*, vol. 32 no. 2 (January 1979), pp. 143–174.

Table 3-23

Unionism of Manufacturing Plants by Region and by Class

	New England	Mid-Atlantic	South Atlantic	East North Central	East South Central	West North Central	West South Central	Mountain	Pacific	Nationally
Stay-Put Plants Expanding On-Site										
Percent union	50%	47%	39%	71%	50%	50%	39%	33%	57%	52%
Number of plants in region	20	19	23	41	10	18	26	3	23	186
New Plant Openings										
Percent union	22%	29%	22%	60%	18%	7%	4%	0%	22%	21%
Number of plants in region	9	14	36	15	22	14	23	5	23	163
Plant Relocations										
Percent union	17%	33%	0%	75%	33%	100%	0%	100%	29%	38%
Number of plants in region	6	3	5	8	3	2	2	1	7	37

the 1970–1974 new plant employment was unionized but only 13% of the
new plant employment since 1975.

In business location decisions a good deal of attention is devoted to
the 20 right-to-work states. How do they do relative to others? Thirty-four
percent of the stay-put plants surveyed are located in right-to-work states;
44% of these are union, which compares with 57% union for non-right-to-
work states. As for new plants sited in the 1970s, again there is a distinct
difference between right-to-work and non-right-to-work states, although
not one of startling dimensions. In right-to-work states, only 14% of the
plant openings of the last decade were union as opposed to 29% in non-
right-to-work states. Apparently, locating in a right-to-work state does help
a plant stay non-union, but it is clear that plants can remain non-union
almost anywhere in the country.

There is no question, however, that the right-to-work states are booming: one half of all the new plants were sited in them as opposed to only
34% of the stay-put plants. Of the 76% of plant openings where non-

Table 3-24

Market and Supply Areas by Industry Group
and by Region

Averages for All Survey Responses

Industry Group	Miles Within Which 1/2 of Market Lies	Miles Within Which 3/4 of Market Lies	Miles Within Which 1/2 of Supplies Lie	Miles Within Which 3/4 of Supplies Lie
Agriculture-Tied	599	1018	415	596
Market-Sensitive	501	747	625	956
Forest-Tied	438	656	438	703
Labor-Rate Sensitive	724	1230	763	1138
Heavy Chemicals/ Oil/Rubber/Glass	687	1232	534	966
Specialty Chemi- cals/Metals	671	1238	435	834
Heavy Metals	743	978	550	1097
Industrial Machinery/ Transportation Equipment	851	1520	520	998
High Technology	1587	2954	800	1434
Region				
New England	1254	2074	589	1214
Mid-Atlantic	754	1430	452	970
South Atlantic	916	1360	659	1052
East North Central	539	1174	320	659
East South Central	510	822	540	726
West North Central	671	1000	477	995
West South Central	832	1505	515	966
Mountain	640	931	950	1266
Pacific	1120	2032	1066	1587

unionism was a "must" factor in location, 58% were sited in right-to-work states. The data suggest that the edge for non-unionism in right-to-work states has triggered a more-than-proportional degree of plant openings there. The data also suggest that companies are well aware of the advantages of right-to-work states; 88% of the managers of new plants so sited indicate that remaining non-union is a "must" for them. Of the 40 new plants where a "desire to escape an unproductive labor situation at an existing plant" argued for establishing a new plant in the first place, 27 (68%) opened in right-to-work states.

Because of geography and the mix of industries over the country, plants in different regions of the U.S. value proximity to markets or supplies differently. Table 3-24 presents data on the average number of miles within which selected industry groups' markets and supplies lie. These results indicate that supplies are collected from a closer range than prevails for product marketing. The influence of freight costs is thus more acute for shipping output to market than in gathering supplies.

The industries most sensitive to market proximity come as no surprise—Forest-Tied industries (lumber and paper) and Market-Sensitive industries (some food, paper converting, printing, asphalt, cans, miscellaneous manufacturing). They lie closest to their markets. These two groups are also the most apt to have answered that the "plant is seriously impeded from competing in some geographic markets solely because of transport costs". In fact, 47% of the Forest-Tied plants responded that way and 40% of the Market-Sensitive plants. In contrast, only 3% of the High Technology plants were "seriously impeded" by transport costs and only 9% of the Industrial Machinery/Transportation equipment plants.

Naturally, the region of the country has a bearing on the market and supply areas of plants. The central states enjoy some obvious geographic access. More plants that are most affected by transport costs tend to be found in the center of the U.S. than on its coasts. While 57% of the New England plants and 45% of the Pacific coast plants show that transport costs are "only slightly important", that statistic for plants in the East South Central region drops to 29%.

No matter what the industry or region, those plants for which freight costs are a primary concern have smaller market areas than others. The following small table documents just how constrained market areas are for some plants.

Importance of Transport Costs to Plant	Miles Within Which ½ of Market Lies	Miles Within Which ¾ of Market Lies
Serious impediment	447	814
Modest impediment	634	1132
Only slightly important	1198	1992

The influence of profit on location search

That plant location is even a topic of management concern stems largely from the belief that some locations afford more profitability than others and are therefore worth seeking out. Where have major manufacturers sought better, more profitable plant sites? Have those sites proven more profitable? The first portion of this section investigates the states and regions that came close to being chosen for new plants as well as those which actually won out. From there the study of a plant's profitability and effectiveness is taken up, with the purpose of uncovering whether some locations, such as Sunbelt ones, are inherently more profitable.

In the survey, manufacturers who were opening new plants were asked to list all of the states they were seriously considering for their new locations. This enabled us to identify which states are perused relatively more often than others, and how successful they are in landing new plants. Table 3-25 summarizes this information. For this sample of 161 responding plants, the most popular states for location searches are, in order, North Carolina, Texas, California, South Carolina, and Tennessee. Not an unanticipated collection.

For the most part, the regions most thoroughly searched, outside the own region, are the immediately adjacent ones. Of the 21 states searched by the 9 new plants locating in New England, for example, those most searched outside of New England were in the Mid-Atlantic states. The Mid-Atlantic plants, in turn, looked elsewhere most frequently to the South Atlantic and to New England. Regions like the West South Central and the East South Central have wide appeal, having been considered seriously by plants which decided to locate as far away as both coasts.

Profitability/effectiveness and location

With all the interest in and development of the Sunbelt states, are the facilities there, all things considered, really more profitable than plants elsewhere? The survey data permit at least one test of this. One question in the surveys asked respondents to rate their plant's "profitability/efficiency" relative to other plants in this division. Permitted responses were "top ⅓", "middle ⅓", and "bottom ⅓". Using this response with other descriptive information about the plant and its operations, we can test whether Sunbelt plants are more profitable.

Table 3-26 reports a probit analysis which differentiates between the Fortune 500 plants responding "top ⅓" to the profitability question and all other plants (nearly 60% rated their plants in the top third). Table 3-26's results are as interesting for the variable coefficients not found statistically significant as for those found to be. The size of the operation enters via significant variables specifying the number of product lines manufactured and the acreage on-site. Neither square footage nor employment

Table 3-25

Location Searches by State: Survey Evidence from New Plants

States and Regions	Times Sought	Actual Locations
New England		
Connecticut	6	3
Maine	1	1
Massachusetts	7	3
Rhode Island	1	0
Vermont	3	1
New Hampshire	1	1
Region Totals	19	9
Middle Atlantic		
New Jersey	9	4
New York	11	4
Pennsylvania	14	6
Region Totals	34	14
South Atlantic		
Delaware	0	0
District of Columbia	0	0
Florida	7	4
Georgia	16	7
Maryland	9	1
North Carolina	27	14
South Carolina	21	4
Virginia	12	6
West Virginia	3	0
Region Totals	95	36
East North Central		
Illinois	9	4
Indiana	12	2
Michigan	6	2
Ohio	9	4
Wisconsin	3	3
Region Totals	39	15
East South Central		
Alabama	16	3
Kentucky	11	5
Mississippi	16	9
Tennessee	17	5
Region Totals	60	22

Table 3-25 (cont'd.)

Location Searches by State: Survey Evidence from New Plants

States and Regions	Times Sought	Actual Locations
West North Central		
Iowa	8	4
Kansas	2	0
Minnesota	3	2
Missouri	10	5
Nebraska	4	1
North Dakota	3	1
South Dakota	3	1
Region Totals	33	14
West South Central		
Arkansas	14	4
Louisiana	6	0
Oklahoma	11	4
Texas	26	15
Region Totals	57	23
Mountain		
Arizona	12	2
Colorado	4	0
Idaho	3	2
Montana	1	1
Nevada	2	0
New Mexico	2	0
Utah	1	0
Wyoming	2	0
Region Totals	27	5
Pacific		
Alaska	0	0
California	22	16
Hawaii	0	0
Oregon	9	4
Washington	6	3
Region Totals	37	23
National Totals	401	161

Table 3-26

The Character of Plants With High Profitability/Effectiveness Ratings:
Probit Analysis (only significant coefficients retained)

Variable (in order of importance)	C-Standardized coefficient	Level of Significance
Product lines	.136	.968
Acres on site	.122	.943
More capital relative to labor over time? (High value=yes)	.091	.991
Company built plant? (High value=yes)	.089	.990
Miles within which three-fourths of the plant's output is shipped	.087	.980
Capital-labor ratio	-.075	.953

Number of observations = 184

Goodness of fit: R^2 = .137

Splitting at P=0.5

Predicted

True	Low Profit	High Profit	Totals
Low profit	40	37	77
High profit	24	83	107
Totals	64	120	184

Probability of Error = .332
Sample fraction High Profit = .582

Peeling Off the Top

Predicted

True	Low Profit	High Profit	Totals
Low profit	46	31	77
High profit	31	76	107
Totals	77	107	184

Probability of Error = .337
Sample fraction High Profit = .582

were significant, which suggests that those variables should be interpreted carefully. Size, per se, is probably not a factor, however the better performing plants are those which (1) are "home" to many different products, each of which may be quite specialized and thus high margin, and (2) are land-extensive, established enough so that they have their own "campuses" around them.

Other variables which show significant coefficients are more readily interpreted. The substitution of capital for labor over time is a standard argument for increased productivity. Company-built plants, where all the design innovations possible are coupled with the obvious profit stability such an option implies, are expected to outperform other plants easily. Plants with large market areas, are also expected to outperform other plants. And, finally lower capital-labor ratios may indicate non-commodity businesses where profitability has always been on the high side.

With some reflection, then, the variables which enter into Table 3-26's results are plausible. Importantly, however, other variables which could have entered prominently into the analysis do not. For example, location in the Sunbelt, the spur for this analysis, is not significant. This is not really surprising since it confirms what many think, that companies can be profitable in many locations throughout this country. It supports the view that the bulk of company plants have sorted themselves out among locations, as they should, to earn acceptable levels of profit. Also absent from the analysis is any indication of vertical integration or particular process characteristics. In reflection, this also seems proper; relative profitability in many industries may not lie with broad vertical integration or with production processes which fit into specific categories.

The influence of location to shorten the executive's commute

That manufacturing plants are located sometimes to satisfy the commuting needs of a company executive has long provided some amusing anecdotes. To my knowledge, no one has tested this hypothesis. All the surveys sent to plants of all types in Cincinnati and New England contained a question which read: It is often said that plants are located so that their chief officer(s) can enjoy a shorter commute. How true is (or was) that statement for this plant? Three responses were possible: very true, somewhat true, and not at all true.

The results show that 40% to 50% of all plant locations that responded to this question were influenced by the commute of the plant's chief officer(s). Moreover, a greater percentage of new plant and within Cincinnati area movers were influenced by such commuting considerations than were stationary plants or within New England area movers. About 10%–20% of those responding admitted that it was "very true" that their new location was determined at least in part by the executive's commute.

The importance of the commute does not cut evenly across all types of plants, however; the larger the plant the less likely that the executive's commute was a determining influence in its location. This result reinforces the notion that larger plants generally require more specialized space and must scout further distances to locate suitable space. Similarly, the plant locations of multiplant companies are less influenced by the executive's commute than those of single-plant companies. Overall, only 26.7% of the branch or subsidiary plants responding from Cincinnati and 34.7% from New England indicated that the executive's commute exerted an influence in the plant's location. The statistics for single-plant companies in these two areas are 57.3% and 48.4%, respectively.

The influence of executive commuting on plant location does not appear to be correlated with suburban locations as data from Cincinnati attest. In fact, the influence is better supported by plants located within the Cincinnati city limits or on the Kentucky side of the river. On the other hand, the commute influence does appear to be greater for companies whose founder came from Cincinnati.

That executive commuting appears to be as widespread as it is testifies to the flexibility of many plants in adapting to available sites and space. There appear to be few, if any, "optimal" sites for many plants. With several sites of high equivalent rank involved in a choice, it is not surprising that personal considerations are brought into the decision. That personal convenience does not outweigh the needs of the company is supported by the data. Since large facilities and branch plants—those requiring more space—are not governed by personal inclinations, it is difficult to believe that for smaller and/or single-plant companies executive convenience would dominate truly important business considerations.

4

What's Hot, What's Not: the changing geographic pattern of manufacturing in the United States

What happened over the course of the 1970s to the pattern of industrial location? How did major U.S. manufacturers shift their capacity and employment geographically? Which sections of the country were affected most? How did cities, suburbs, and rural areas fare? Which industries altered the pattern of their locations most? The answers to these and other questions are the province of this chapter, which uses the plant census data described in the Introduction, as well as selected information from the Census of Manufactures.

Census of Manufactures Data, 1977 and 1967

The broadest-based data which track manufacturing plants and employment are those provided by the Census of Manufactures. While allegedly offering full coverage of all the nation's manufacturing establishments, the Census reports only highly aggregated plant and employment data by region, state, and selected metropolitan areas and by 2-, 3-, and 4-digit Standard Industrial Classification codes. These data are useful in documenting major trends, but are of limited value in explaining their nature. Still, the Census data offer us a reasonable beginning for assessing what's hot and what's not.

Region and state comparisons

Table 4-1 displays state and regional data for the years 1967 and 1977. While total manufacturing employment grew by 1.4% during those

Table 4-1

EMPLOYMENT CHANGES FOR EACH STATE

Census of Manufactures Data

STATE BY REGION	Earlier Year Employment 1967	Later Year Employment 1977	Percent Change 1967-1977
New England			
Connecticut	477,700	412,100	-13.7
Maine	110,800	102,800	-7.2
Massachusetts	713,600	613,400	-14.0
New Hampshire	94,900	95,300	0.4
Rhode Island	122,300	125,000	2.2
Vermont	42,500	41,500	-2.4
TOTALS	1,561,800	1,390,100	-11.0
Middle Atlantic			
New Jersey	861,300	778,300	-9.6
New York	1,929,200	1,509,900	-21.7
Pennsylvania	1,549,500	1,329,200	-14.2
TOTALS	4,360,000	3,617,400	-17.0
East North Central			
Illinois	1,397,300	1,286,200	-8.0
Indiana	710,200	705,900	-0.6
Michigan	1,134,100	1,115,900	-1.6
Ohio	1,397,000	1,331,200	-4.7
Wisconsin	512,200	535,000	4.5
TOTALS	5,150,800	4,974,200	-3.4
West North Central			
Iowa	210,100	240,300	14.4
Kansas	143,800	168,100	16.9
Minnesota	299,800	331,700	10.6
Missouri	452,200	433,300	-4.2
Nebraska	77,000	87,700	13.9
North Dakota	7,500	13,800	84.0
South Dakota	15,500	22,500	45.2
TOTALS	1,205,900	1,297,400	7.6
South Atlantic			
Delaware	70,700	66,500	-5.9
District of Columbia	23,100	18,600	-19.5
Florida	285,100	358,000	25.6
Georgia	423,100	484,700	14.6
Maryland	287,600	243,200	-15.4
North Carolina	643,800	765,300	18.9
South Carolina	304,300	374,200	23.0
Virginia	339,800	395,200	16.3
West Virginia	124,000	117,000	-5.6
TOTALS	2,501,500	2,822,700	12.8

Table 4-1 (continued)

STATE BY REGION	Earlier Year Employment 1967	Later Year Employment 1977	Percent Change 1967-1977
East South Central			
Alabama	288,800	341,000	18.1
Kentucky	224,600	277,500	23.6
Mississippi	160,400	219,400	36.8
Tennessee	418,000	489,800	17.2
TOTALS	1,091,800	1,327,700	21.6
West South Central			
Arkansas	143,600	197,100	37.3
Louisiana	164,500	194,800	18.4
Oklahoma	117,700	164,400	39.7
Texas	657,500	886,400	34.8
TOTALS	1,083,300	1,442,700	33.2
Mountain			
Arizona	76,800	110,900	44.4
Colorado	104,000	152,500	46.6
Idaho	37,100	51,600	39.1
Montana	20,400	23,500	15.2
Nevada	7,000	15,000	114.3
New Mexico	16,900	29,000	71.6
Utah	47,000	70,200	49.4
Wyoming	5,900	8,500	44.1
TOTALS	315,100	461,200	46.4
Pacific			
Alaska	7,600	11,400	50.0
California	1,583,500	1,751,500	10.6
Hawaii	25,400	25,000	-1.6
Oregon	164,100	202,400	23.3
Washington	270,700	265,000	-2.1
TOTALS	2,050,300	2,255,300	10.0
ALL STATES TOTAL	19,323,200	19,588,700	1.4

ten years, the traditional manufacturing states of New England, the Mid-Atlantic, and the East North Central regions suffered absolute, as well as relative, declines in manufacturing employment. In sharp contrast is the substantial growth of the Mountain and West South Central regions. In general, the data make clear that the Sunbelt states do much better relatively than do the Frostbelt states. Nevertheless, there are pockets of absolute growth within the traditional manufacturing regions—Rhode Island, New Hampshire, Wisconsin, for example. But, it is clear that Texas, Florida, the Carolinas, the Deep South, Oklahoma, Arkansas, the Rocky Mountain states, and Oregon have been gaining manufacturing employment in a big way.

Region and industry cross tabulations

Table 4-2 explores the census data further by breaking down regional employment by major industries (2-digit SICs). Both Panels A and B point up the industries which each region depends on the most. A comparison of 1977 to 1967 data reveals that regions in 1977 were less dependent on their key industries than they were in 1967. In most regions, the loss of employment in key industries was accompanied by substantial relative gains of employment in previously under-represented industries. For example, there was a loss of employment in food processing in the western states (West North Central, West South Central, Mountain, and Pacific regions) and a concomitant increase in the importance of a host of other industries. The key industries of particular regions—fabricated metals in the Mid-Atlantic, textiles in the South Atlantic, apparel in the East South Central, transportation equipment in the West North Central and Pacific, and lumber in the Pacific—are not as important now, in a relative sense, as they were 10 years ago.

One can expect some industries and regions to vary from this trend, of course. Apparel became more important relatively to the Mid-Atlantic region and lumber to the mountain states. Furthermore, machinery (which includes office equipment and computers) became more important to the nation as a whole, increasing from a 9.7% share of total national manufacturing employment in 1967 to an 11.3% share in 1977. Particularly striking is the growth of machinery employment in the West South Central and Mountain regions.

These counter trends notwithstanding, on balance the shifts from 1967 to 1977 reflect a broadening of the industrial make-up of most regions in the country and a diminishing of the critical importance of certain industries in specific regions.

Table 4-3 examines the data in a different way—instead of showing the share of a region's manufacturing employment accounted for by each industry (columns summing to 100%), Table 4-3 shows the share of an industry's manufacturing employment accounted for by each region (rows summing to 100%). Table 4-3 demonstrates the West's greater relative importance to food processing, for example, as well as New England's relative importance in leather goods, instruments, paper, and in miscellaneous manufacturing such as jewelry, toys and sporting goods.

A comparison of Panel A (1977) with Panel B (1967) shows that, in most cases, the importance of one region to an industry has declined relatively over time. These comparisons must be tempered by the observation that the overall importance of New England, the Mid-Atlantic, and the East North Central regions to the rest of the country had diminished during those 10 years, decreasing from 57.4% of total manufacturing employment to 50.1%. Accompanying this general trend is the declining im-

Table 4-2

Percentage Distribution of Employment by Major Industry, For Each Region

Panel A. 1977 Census of Manufactures Data

Major Industry	New England	Middle Atlantic	South Atlantic	East North Central	East South Central	West North Central	West South Central	Mountain	Pacific	Nation
Food Processing	4.2	6.4	8.1	6.7	7.7	15.0	10.9	13.6	10.7	8.2
Tobacco	-	0.1	1.6		1.0				-	0.3
Textiles	4.9	3.4	20.3	0.4	6.5	0.4	1.1	0.3	0.9	4.7
Apparel	4.9	12.3	10.7	1.9	14.6	4.0	8.1	4.4	5.3	7.2
Lumber	2.2	1.2	4.4	1.8	5.5	2.9	5.1	10.1	9.1	3.7
Furniture	1.4	1.6	4.9	2.0	3.9	1.6	2.3	1.3	2.7	2.5
Paper	5.0	3.5	3.8	3.2	3.5	2.9	3.4	1.4	3.0	3.4
Printing	5.9	8.1	4.6	5.3	3.8	8.1	5.2	7.7	5.5	5.9
Chemicals	2.5	5.8	6.5	3.6	6.8	3.7	7.7	2.5	2.9	4.8
Petroleum	0.2	0.6	0.2	0.5	0.3	0.7	3.9	1.0	1.0	0.8
Rubber/Plastics	4.8	3.3	3.1	5.0	4.0	3.9	3.4	3.1	3.2	3.9
Leather Goods	4.3	1.7	0.8	0.6	1.9	2.0	1.1	1.2	0.6	1.3
Stone/Clay/Glass	2.0	3.5	3.5	3.3	3.1	3.6	4.1	5.0	3.0	3.1
Primary Metals	3.5	7.7	3.3	9.6	5.9	3.6	4.2	6.9	3.4	6.0
Fabricated Metals	9.3	7.4	4.4	12.1	6.9	8.6	9.1	8.2	7.4	8.5
Machinery	12.8	9.8	5.2	15.9	7.2	16.8	11.9	10.1	9.3	11.3
Electrical & Electronic Machinery	8.9	10.0	6.7	9.8	7.6	8.8	8.1	9.9	11.0	9.1
Transportation Equipment	8.5	5.0	5.3	14.4	6.8	10.8	7.3	6.3	15.0	9.5
Instruments	6.4	5.0	1.3	2.0	0.9	2.4	1.6	5.9	4.2	3.0
Misc. Manufacturing	5.9	3.6	1.3	1.8	1.7	2.0	1.4	2.7	2.2	2.4
Total Employment	1,318,200	3,317,100	2,710,900	4,651,100	1,299,600	1,206,500	1,377,300	442,600	2,171,100	18,494,400

Note: Total employment as allocated to individual industries is less than that allocated to states because of disclosure problems and other omissions in the industry-specific data. Total employment is less than that reported in Table 4-1 because administrative workers are excluded from these data.

Table 4-2(b)

Percentage Distribution of Employment by Major Industry, For Each Region
Panel B. 1967 Census of Manufactures Data

Major Industry	New England	Middle Atlantic	South Atlantic	East North Central	East South Central	West North Central	West South Central	Mountain	Pacific	Nation
Food Processing	4.7	6.5	9.0	6.8	8.6	16.8	13.3	17.2	11.1	8.5
Tobacco	0.0	0.2	1.9	0.0	1.1	0.0	-	-	-	0.4
Textiles	5.9	3.4	22.0	0.5	7.7	0.4	1.1	0.4	0.9	4.8
Apparel	5.1	12.3	10.1	1.9	15.5	4.4	7.3	3.1	3.8	7.0
Lumber	2.2	1.9	5.2	1.8	6.0	3.2	6.5	10.3	10.9	4.0
Furniture	1.4	1.6	4.4	1.9	4.0	1.2	2.4	1.1	2.0	2.2
Paper	4.6	3.1	3.7	3.1	3.4	3.1	3.5	1.3	3.0	3.3
Printing	4.9	6.8	4.0	5.0	3.4	7.2	4.8	7.1	4.9	5.3
Chemicals	2.1	4.8	6.4	3.4	7.5	3.8	6.7	3.0	2.5	4.4
Petroleum	0.1	0.5	0.2	0.6	0.3	0.6	4.6	1.5	0.9	0.7
Rubber/Plastics	5.2	4.6	2.8	4.5	3.1	3.1	2.7	2.4	3.2	3.9
Leather Goods	6.2	2.0	0.9	0.9	2.2	2.9	1.3	0.8	0.7	1.8
Stone/Clay/Glass	2.3	3.1	3.6	3.4	3.1	3.1	4.1	4.4	2.6	3.2
Primary Metals	4.2	7.9	3.4	10.1	6.9	3.1	4.5	8.2	3.8	6.6
Fabricated Metals	9.4	11.0	4.3	12.3	6.3	10.3	9.6	6.2	8.0	9.5
Machinery	11.4	8.2	3.6	15.2	5.0	12.7	7.4	9.9	6.9	9.7
Electrical and Electronic Machinery	12.1	8.6	6.3	10.6	7.7	8.4	8.2	10.0	10.7	9.3
Transportation Equipment	8.1	3.8	6.1	14.3	5.8	11.7	9.5	7.9	19.1	9.8
Instruments	5.4	6.4	1.1	2.0	0.8	2.0	1.4	3.5	3.5	3.2
Miscellaneous Manufacturing	4.6	3.3	1.1	1.7	1.6	1.9	1.2	1.6	1.7	2.2
Total Employment	1,561,800	4,360,000	2,501,500	5,150,800	1,091,800	1,205,900	1,083,300	315,100	2,050,300	19,320,500

Table 4-3

Percentage Distribution of Employment by Region, for Each Major Industry

Panel A. 1977 Census of Manufactures Data

Major Industry	New England	Middle Atlantic	South Atlantic	East North Central	East South Central	West North Central	West South Central	Mountain	Pacific	Total Employment
Food Processing	3.6	13.9	14.4	20.6	6.5	11.9	9.9	4.0	15.3	1,520,500
Tobacco	0.3	5.9	70.7	1.6	21.5	-	-	-	-	61,500
Textiles	7.4	12.9	63.0	2.2	9.6	-	1.8	0.2	2.3	875,800
Apparel	4.8	30.5	21.7	6.7	14.2	0.6	8.3	1.5	8.6	1,334,500
Lumber	4.2	5.9	17.2	12.3	10.3	3.7	10.2	6.4	28.4	692,500
Furniture	3.9	11.6	28.5	20.3	10.8	5.1	6.9	1.3	12.6	464,200
Paper	10.4	18.3	16.3	23.7	7.3	4.1	7.3	1.0	10.2	629,700
Printing	7.1	24.6	11.5	22.6	4.5	5.5	6.6	3.1	11.0	1,091,300
Chemicals	3.7	21.7	20.1	19.0	10.1	5.0	12.0	1.3	7.1	879,500
Petroleum	1.6	13.7	4.2	17.2	3.0	5.4	36.4	3.1	15.4	146,500
Rubber/Plastics	8.7	15.4	11.7	32.3	7.2	6.6	6.6	1.9	9.7	723,100
Leather Goods	23.5	22.8	8.5	11.5	10.3	10.1	6.1	2.1	5.1	243,600
Stone/Clay/Glass	4.6	20.5	16.4	27.1	6.9	7.7	10.0	3.9	3.0	572,100
Primary Metals	4.1	23.0	8.1	39.9	6.9	3.5	5.2	2.7	6.6	1,114,400
Fabricated Metals	7.9	15.7	7.6	35.8	5.8	6.7	8.0	2.3	10.2	1,565,100
Machinery	8.1	15.7	6.8	35.4	4.5	9.7	7.9	2.2	9.7	2,083,700
Electrical & Electronic Machinery	7.0	19.6	10.7	27.1	5.9	6.3	6.6	2.6	14.2	1,686,000
Transportation Equipment	6.3	9.4	8.2	37.9	5.0	7.4	5.7	1.6	18.5	1,762,600
Instruments	15.0	29.9	6.4	16.3	2.1	5.2	3.9	4.7	16.4	559,700
Misc. Manufacturing	17.6	27.0	7.8	19.0	5.1	5.4	4.4	2.7	10.9	440,300
All Industries	7.1	17.9	14.7	25.1	7.0	6.5	7.4	2.4	11.7	18,494,400

Note: Total employment as allocated to individual industries is less than that allocated to states because of disclosure problems and other omissions in the industry-specific data. Total employment for each industry excludes administrative workers.

Table 4-3 (cont'd.)

Percentage Distribution of Employment by Region, for Each Major Industry
Panel B. 1967 Census of Manufactures

Major Industry	New England	Middle Atlantic	South Atlantic	East North Central	East South Central	West North Central	West South Central	Mountain	Pacific	Total Employment
Food Processing	4.4	17.1	13.6	21.2	5.7	12.3	8.7	3.3	13.8	1,649,200
Tobacco	0.4	13.9	66.2	2.9	16.2	0.5	-	-	1.9	73,600
Textiles	9.8	15.9	58.8	2.7	8.9	0.5	1.3	0.1	1.9	936,400
Apparel	5.8	39.6	18.6	7.4	12.5	3.9	5.8	0.7	5.7	1,357,300
Lumber	4.5	10.9	16.8	12.2	8.5	4.9	9.1	4.2	29.0	773,900
Furniture	5.0	16.5	26.0	22.5	10.2	3.4	6.1	0.8	9.4	425,400
Paper	11.3	21.2	14.4	25.3	5.9	5.9	5.9	0.6	9.5	638,800
Printing	7.5	28.8	9.6	25.1	3.6	8.4	5.1	2.2	9.8	1,032,500
Chemicals	4.0	24.9	19.1	21.0	9.8	5.5	8.6	1.1	6.0	840,900
Petroleum	1.3	15.3	3.7	20.2	2.5	5.4	35.3	3.4	13.0	141,600
Rubber/Plastics	10.7	26.4	9.2	30.9	4.5	5.0	3.9	1.0	8.6	756,200
Leather Goods	28.2	25.9	6.4	13.0	7.0	10.3	4.1	0.7	4.3	343,400
Stone/Clay/Glass	5.1	21.9	14.5	28.2	5.5	6.0	7.1	2.3	8.7	616,500
Primary Metals	5.1	26.9	6.7	40.6	5.9	2.9	3.8	2.0	6.2	1,279,300
Fabricated Metals	7.9	26.0	5.8	34.4	3.7	6.7	5.6	1.1	8.9	1,844,600
Machinery	9.5	19.2	4.8	41.9	2.9	8.2	4.3	1.7	7.5	1,871,500
Electrical and Electronic Machinery	10.6	20.8	8.8	30.5	4.7	5.6	5.0	1.7	12.2	1,795,200
Transporation Equipment	6.7	8.6	8.0	38.6	3.4	7.4	5.4	1.3	20.6	1,901,300
Instruments	13.6	44.7	4.3	16.2	1.4	3.9	2.4	1.8	11.6	619,700
Miscellaneous Manufacturing	16.8	33.5	6.7	20.9	4.2	5.5	3.0	1.2	8.2	423,500
All Industries	8.1	22.6	12.9	26.7	5.7	6.2	5.6	1.6	10.6	19,320,500

portance of leather goods, paper, and textiles in New England; apparel, printing, rubber/plastics, fabricated metals, instruments, and miscellaneous manufacturing in the Mid-Atlantic; and furniture, machinery, and electrical machinery in the East North Central to mention a few.

Despite overall growth in regions outside the Northeast, even some of the relative importance of specific non-Northeastern regions to given industries has been attenuated. For example, while the Western states (West North Central, West South Central, Mountain, and Pacific regions) gained 4.0 percentage points (17%) in total manufacturing employment in 1967–1977, the food processing industry there gained only 3.0 percentage points (8%); despite enjoying a high and growing absolute share of the food processing industry. This relative decline is simply an indication that other manufacturing employment grew more rapidly than food processing. A similar story can be told of textiles in the South Atlantic. While the absolute importance of the region to the textile industry increased to 63.0%, its relative importance declined over the 10-year span of 1967–1977; the region's share of national manufacturing employment grew 14% while its share of the textile industry grew only 7%. Even in the growing, non-Northeastern regions of the U.S. some absolute declines in the importance of selected regions occurred for specific industries, such as lumber and transportation equipment in the Pacific.

While most regions and industries observe the general trend, there are exceptions. New England, East North Central, and the Pacific became relatively more important to the instruments industry, the East South Central became more important to the leather goods industry, the South Atlantic became more important to the electrical and electronic machinery industry, and the East North Central became more important to the rubber/plastics industry, to mention several. In general, however, industrial activity seems to be spreading out, thus evening out regions' relative shares of most industries.

From this broad overview of regions and industries, let us turn to the more detailed results possible from the plant census conducted of 410 of the nation's largest manufacturers.

Plant Census Data for 410 Major Manufacturers, Early 1970s and Late 1970s

Before presenting some results, it is worthwhile putting the independently developed "plant census" data into perspective. The data file contains 17,759 entries which represent all of the identified manufacturing sites operated by 410 major U.S. manufacturers at any time during the 1970s. Each entry lists company name, division/subsidiary name (if applicable), address, employment early in the 1970s, employment late in the 1970s, the two most important standard industrial classification (SIC) codes that describe what is manufactured (to 3 digits), any former addresses (if the plant had relocated or had absorbed operations from elsewhere), and two codes that categorize the plant and its growth or contraction during the 1970s. These codes merit some elaboration.

PLANT STATUS CATEGORIES:

Stay-Put Plant—A plant that has been established since about 1970 or before which has remained at the same site during the time period examined. This plant may have absorbed the operations of another plant or may have spun off operations to another, possibly new, plant.

Plant Opening—A new plant for the company that has been built, purchased, or leased since about 1970, which has usually hired new personnel and has purchased new equipment.

Acquisition—An on-going business's facility which has merged with or has been purchased by the corporation since about 1970 and has been operated usually within a separate division or subsidiary.

Divestiture—The sale of a plant of an existing business of the corporation to another company since about 1970. This plant can be expected to continue operations much as before, but under new management.

Plant Closing—The shut-down of a facility of the corporation since about 1970. The building may have been sold subsequently to another company, but the former operation is *not* continued.

Mover—A plant that has been closed since about 1970, which has been followed by the near-simultaneous opening of a new plant to perform essentially the same tasks, and has often employed some of the same people and equipment.

Opened/Closed—A plant that has been opened or acquired during the 1970s followed by the closing or divestiture of that plant, also within the decade.

Closed/Opened—A plant that has been closed (usually as the result of the 1974–5 recession), followed by its re-opening sometime later in the decade.

GROWTH/CONTRACTION INDICATION:

Expansion On-Site—An expansion of "bricks and mortar" at the plant site since about 1970. This expansion may have included a major increase in employment as well.

Contraction On-Site—A situation where some space at the plant site is no longer used for manufacturing, or has been sold, leased, or torn down. This contraction may have included a major decline in employment as well.

It is this information which has been assembled for 410 of the largest corporations in the United States. In the early 1970s for these major manufacturers, there were 31.2 domestic plants per company employing an average of 497.1 workers in each plant. In the late 1970s, there were 36.4 domestic plants per company, each employing an average of 492.6 workers. Thus, the number of plants per company went up substantially during the decade and average plant employment declined slightly. The late 1970s employment associated with these companies totalled 7,354,040, or 37% of the manufacturing employment accounted for by the 1977 Census of Manufactures. This is a measure of how important the companies in this plant census are to the country's economy. The extent of this private census coverage, and the quite reasonable congruence of this private plant census's data with the geographic and industrial breakdowns of the Census of Manufactures, lends credence to the results which follow, many of which go beyond the capabilities of the Census of Manufactures data.

Compensating Capacity Changes: An Aside

It is sometimes suggested that the foregoing categorization of plants into "components of change" (e.g. openings, closings, relocations, stay-puts) ignores a more subtle form of change, namely one where the corporation reduces employment at a site but does not close the operation there, and expands or opens a new plant elsewhere. In a sense, the corporation contracts operations at one location but compensates for it elsewhere. How prevalent is this practice?

To answer this question, the plant census data base was sorted by company and then by industry (3-digit SIC code) within each company. All instances of a drop in employment at one site accompanied by an increase, on-site expansion, or new plant in the same 3-digit SIC code industry (where the increase in employment elsewhere was 50% or greater of the employment decline) were tallied. Some industries have been excluded from consideration because their markets are so local that expansions and contractions could only be expected to be deliberately compensating occasionally: for example, bakeries, dairies, can making plants, paper converting plants, glass bottle plants, and commercial printers. The resulting list of instances where the contractions and expansions appear to be co-ordinated or compensating may overstate the number of times such a co-ordination of capacity changes actually occurs, but it provides some estimate at least. The results given by region of plant contraction are shown in Table 4-4.

The instances of compensating capacity changes are about one-third as numerous as plant closings but seven times as prevalent as inter-regional relocations, arguably the closest substitutes for these practices. Nevertheless, compensating capacity change is a fairly rare event, and with good reason. The instances where a corporation can even entertain this idea are limited, since many plants within company divisions are so specialized that their operations cannot be traded easily. Ordinarily, even if a trade of

Table 4-4

Compensating Contraction and Expansion

Region of Contraction	Number of Compensating Contractions and Expansions	Number of Relocations Out of the Region	As a Percent of Plant Closings	As a Percent of Stay-Put Plants
New England	32	3	36.8	5.5
Mid-Atlantic	61	17	34.1	4.5
South Atlantic	46	1	35.7	3.0
East North Central	111	23	44.6	5.0
East South Central	23	1	39.0	3.3
West North Central	18	1	25.7	2.4
West South Central	21	1	28.8	2.4
Mountain	11	0	47.8	3.6
Pacific	27	4	17.8	2.3
Nationally	350	51	34.3	3.7

responsibilities were possible, the corporation would have to be dissatisfied with performance at the base plant to think of changing capacity in compensating fashion. Because dissatisfaction of sufficient magnitude is probably found most readily around older and more unionized plants, the slightly higher incidence of compensating capacity changes in the traditional Northeast manufacturing belt is understandable.

Regional and state comparisons

For the large, multiplant corporations studied, the decade of the 1970s was one of impressive growth. The number of their domestic manufacturing plants increased by 16.8% to almost 15,000 and their employment increased 15.8% to more than 7,350,000. Yet, as Table 4-5 displays, this growth was not evenly spread among the regions of the country. The traditional industrial regions—New England, Mid-Atlantic, East North Central—grew at less than the national average, while the rest of the coun-

Table 4-5

Regional Growth in Manufacturing Plants and Employment for Large, Multiplant Companies

Region	Plants			Employment		
	Early 1970s	Late 1970s	Recent Growth	Early 1970s	Late 1970s	Recent Growth
New England	820	891	8.7%	427,344	490,956	14.9%
Mid-Atlantic	1,872	1,984	6.0%	1,109,352	1,123,041	1.2%
South Atlantic	2,019	2,384	18.1%	859,201	1,015,619	18.2%
East North Central	2,956	3,335	12.8%	2,016,396	2,165,076	7.4%
East South Central	908	1,200	32.2%	381,209	501,270	31.5%
West North Central	984	1,190	20.9%	417,743	523,300	25.3%
West South Central	1,148	1,513	31.8%	381,827	554,090	45.1%
Mountain	402	534	32.8%	136,112	201,235	47.8%
Pacific	1,669	1,899	13.8%	623,000	779,453	25.1%
Nation	12,778	14,930	16.8%	6,352,184	7,354,040	15.8%

try, and particularly the West South Central and Mountain regions, grew at a rate in excess of the national average.

The composition of this change is documented in Tables 4-6 and 4-7, which offer some intriguing insights. Acquisitions are the most important source of company employment gains, being responsible for twice the employment of plant openings and nearly two and a half times the employment growth found at stay-put plants. Acquisitions are spread fairly evenly across the country, although they are responsible for relatively more employment growth in the Mountain states and relatively less in the Mid-Atlantic and East North Central states. If it were not for acquisitions, major company manufacturing in the Mid-Atlantic region would, in fact, show no growth at all, since employment at stay-put plants actually dropped during the decade and employment at plant closings overshadowed that at plant openings.

Table 4-7 offers insight as well into the character of the significant gains made by the Sunbelt states during the past decade. Nationally, 60% of the gains in manufacturing employment are accounted for by on-site expansions net of contractions. Thirty-six percent of the employment gains were due to new plant employment exceeding that of plant closings. Growth in relocating plant employment accounts for the remainder. In the Sunbelt states on-site expansions net of contractions accounted for more than 45% of employment growth, with new plants net of closings accounting for 53%. The Sunbelt is thus characterized more by substantial numbers of new plants than by on-site expansion, which occurs more frequently in the Frostbelt.

The Mid-Atlantic region is clearly the worst off in the country. The two other traditionally industrial regions—New England and the East North Central states (the eastern Midwest)—managed to grow at modest rates in several ways. Employment at stay-put plants in those regions increased, and new plant openings' employment compensated for losses due to plant closings. Acquisitions far outdistanced divestitures there, as they did in all regions of the United States. Of the three traditionally industrial regions, New England is clearly the best off, showing total employment growth just shy of the national average. The East North Central region just managed to keep growing.

Employment growth for the South and West exceeds the national average, but the composition of this growth is not uniform. For example, the West South Central and Mountain states are gaining dramatically in every way—substantial expansion of existing plants, vast differentials between openings and closings and between acquisitions and divestitures. Not quite as dramatic but still most impressive is the diversified growth of the East South Central and West North Central regions. Both regions are doing very well along each component of change.

Table 4-6

The Composition of Location Change Over the 1970s, by Region (Plant Counts)
Changes of Various Types as a Percent of the Number of Stay-Put Plants

Region	Number of Stay-Put Plants	Plant Openings	Plant Closings	Acquisitions	Divestitures	Relocations	Open/Close
New England	577	13.3	15.1	35.0	12.7	6.1	8.3
Mid Atlantic	1343	10.2	13.3	34.1	14.7	3.4	8.0
South Atlantic	1539	20.2	8.4	29.5	11.0	5.0	6.8
East North Central	2231	11.3	11.2	34.5	10.7	3.7	6.9
East South Central	698	28.5	8.5	39.8	10.3	3.4	7.9
West North Central	754	16.6	9.3	36.2	9.7	4.9	6.6
West South Central	893	29.3	8.2	34.8	9.1	5.3	6.0
Mountain	307	27.0	7.5	40.4	12.1	6.2	5.2
Pacific	1157	14.3	13.1	42.3	14.2	7.2	9.8
Nation	9499	17.0	10.7	35.4	11.6	4.7	7.4

Table 4-7

The Composition of Location Change Over the 1970s by Region (Employment Counts)

Region	Employment At Stay-Put Plants Early 1970's	Employment Changes of Various Types as a Percent of Early 1970's Employment at Stay-Put Plants						
		Stay-Puts	Openings	Closings	Acquisitions	Divestitures	Relocations	Opens/Closes
New England	380,754	6.5	5.6	4.3	14.5	5.2	2.3	1.0
Mid Atlantic	1,012,484	-2.3	2.5	4.5	9.7	3.4	1.0	1.2
South Atlantic	782,087	4.3	11.2	3.2	12.2	4.8	2.1	1.6
East North Central	1,862,762	1.5	3.2	3.1	10.5	3.6	1.0	1.0
East South Central	384,177	10.8	14.3	2.8	17.7	3.9	1.0	2.6
West North Central	389,498	11.6	6.5	2.4	13.7	2.1	2.5	1.3
West South Central	356,154	17.0	18.3	2.0	18.4	3.4	1.9	1.8
Mountain	128,178	15.4	15.0	1.2	24.6	4.3	1.9	0.6
Pacific	553,061	14.3	6.1	5.7	16.9	4.0	3.6	1.9
Nation	5,813,155	5.3	6.7	3.5	12.9	3.8	1.7	1.4

In contrast, for the South Atlantic states, the employment growth rate at stay-put plants was less than the national average. The differential between acquisitions and divestitures was slightly less than the national figures, but the differential between plant openings and closings was much greater than average. Employment growth in the Pacific region is the mirror image of the South Atlantic; there both the growth of stay-put plants (generally the aerospace industry) and the differential between acquisitions and divestitures are much higher than the national average, but new employment from plant openings barely outweighs that lost to plant closings.

Table 4-8 details this same information for individual states, grouped into regions. Note that several states (Connecticut, Hawaii, Montana, New Jersey, and Pennsylvania) actually lost major company employment over the 1970s. In most of those states declines in stay-put plant employment were coupled with more employment being lost to plant closings than were gained by plant openings. Employment declines occurred as well at stay-put plants in Georgia, Maryland, Nevada, Virginia, and West Virginia. Plant closings overshadowed openings in even more states: Alaska, California, Connecticut, Hawaii, Illinois, Massachusetts, Michigan, New Jersey, New York, Pennsylvania, Vermont, West Virginia, and the District of Columbia. Acquisitions dominated divestitures everywhere. The growth in some of the other states during the past decade has been spectacular. Particularly noteworthy are Alabama, Arizona, Arkansas, Colorado, Florida, Idaho, Iowa, Kansas, Maine, Mississippi, New Hampshire, New Mexico, North Dakota, Oklahoma, Oregon, Rhode Island, South Dakota, Texas, Utah, and Wyoming—all twenty of which had 40% or more employment growth by the major companies tracked in this study. Observe that not all of these high-growth states are in the Sunbelt.

Table 4-7 also documents how small an influence relocation is, accounting for only about a quarter of the employment increase of newly opened plants. What is more, the vast majority of plant relocations are short-distance, as Tables 4-9 and 4-10 demonstrate. Only 11.5% of 445 traceable relocations of the major companies studied, involving only 10.7% of their total employment, crossed census region boundaries. And, only 13.7% of these relocations, involving just 14.4% of their total employment, crossed state boundaries. The interstate, inter-regional relocation is a rare event and accounts for a very small percentage of the growth in any area. Even in so popular a region as the South Atlantic, net in-migration of relocating firms accounted for only 3.8% of net new employment (that is, expansions at stay-put plants, openings less closings, relocations from out of region, but not acquisitions or in-region moves) there. This percentage is even smaller for other regions.

Table 4-8

Incidence of Plant Employment Changes by State
(Changes based on earlier year employment)

State by Region	Earlier Year Employment	Later Year Employment	Percentage Changes							
			Total Employment	Change at Existing Plants	Plant Openings	Plant Closings	Plant Acquisitions	Plant Divestitures	Plant Movers	Opened/ Acquired then Closed/ Divested
New England										
Connecticut	171,021	168,112	(1.7)	(.4)	1.1	3.1	5.8	5.4	1.5	.5
Maine	19,688	31,935	62.2	14.0	10.5	1.4	42.9	4.9	1.6	.6
Massachusetts	188,827	220,479	16.8	10.0	4.0	5.6	13.4	4.7	1.7	.7
New Hampshire	15,473	24,389	57.6	2.0	17.6	2.3	41.1	1.4	5.0	1.4
Rhode Island	18,797	27,310	45.3	1.0	35.8	6.7	16.6	1.2	10.2	4.9
Vermont	13,538	18,731	38.4	23.9	2.8	3.3	15.8	.7	0	1.3
Mid-Atlantic										
New Jersey	228,193	221,605	(2.9)	(2.6)	3.0	10.2	10.7	4.2	1.0	1.7
New York	411,332	433,084	5.3	.5	1.9	2.8	8.1	2.4	1.0	.9
Pennsylvania	469,827	468,352	(.3)	(4.7)	2.3	3.0	8.6	3.0	.8	1.1
East North Central										
Illinois	442,780	452,222	2.1	.2	2.5	3.2	10.3	6.3	1.2	2.0
Indiana	322,282	354,761	10.1	.2	2.3	2.0	10.9	1.6	.3	.8
Michigan	525,977	547,794	4.1	1.7	2.0	3.6	4.8	1.0	1.0	.4
Ohio	592,688	652,028	10.0	1.5	3.7	3.0	11.3	3.8	.9	.6
Wisconsin	132,669	158,271	19.3	4.5	6.0	2.7	17.1	5.0	1.5	1.3
West North Central										
Iowa	83,803	121,748	45.3	20.5	10.4	3.4	20.6	1.1	.9	2.2
Kansas	59,448	83,317	40.2	27.3	3.4	1.1	10.2	2.3	5.2	.5
Minnesota	80,017	96,895	21.1	3.7	5.0	1.4	16.4	2.9	4.2	1.1
Missouri	159,262	175,815	10.4	4.7	4.0	2.3	6.2	1.8	.9	.8
Nebraska	29,621	36,703	23.9	3.2	7.2	1.1	20.0	2.1	3.0	2.5
North Dakota	1,434	2,700	88.3	17.2	58.4	.3	13.1	0	0	1.5
South Dakota	4,158	6,122	47.2	1.2	32.7	6.7	20.4	0	0	.8

Table 4-8 (cont'd.)

State By Region and Division	Earlier Year Employment	Later Year Employment	Total Employment	Percentage Changes						
				Change at Existing Plants	Plant Openings	Plant Closings	Plant Acquisitions	Plant Divestitures	Plant Movers	Opened/Acquired Then Closed/Divested
South Atlantic										
Delaware	24,743	27,532	11.3	1.3	3.9	3.2	12.8	3.5	0	1.2
District of Columbia	812	878	8.1	6.2	0	1.5	3.4	0	0	0
Florida	75,031	118,384	57.8	30.1	14.2	5.0	21.4	5.7	9.6	2.7
Georgia	129,825	144,236	11.1	(2.4)	11.5	3.2	10.0	4.4	1.3	2.2
Maryland	113,275	115,917	2.3	(1.0)	2.6	2.4	5.0	2.0	1.3	1.5
North Carolina	212,110	261,026	23.1	6.4	14.1	3.9	12.2	5.2	.9	1.1
South Carolina	97,289	125,932	29.4	4.4	15.1	1.1	14.8	3.3	3.1	.9
Virginia	150,477	165,574	10.0	(2.4)	8.5	1.3	8.1	3.3	.8	1.2
W. Virginia	55,639	56,140	.9	(.3)	1.3	3.9	8.8	5.6	0	1.5
East South Central										
Alabama	86,475	113,664	31.4	10.3	14.1	3.1	12.9	2.2	.9	1.1
Kentucky	106,994	129,503	21.0	10.1	8.3	5.5	9.5	.9	1.3	1.2
Mississippi	56,812	80,398	41.5	17.7	14.8	1.8	19.4	5.7	1.4	4.4
Tennessee	130,928	197,705	35.7	6.0	15.6	1.2	22.4	5.5	.5	3.2

Table 4-8 (cont'd.)

State By Region and Division	Earlier Year Employment	Later Year Employment	Percentage Changes							
			Total Employment	Change at Existing Plants	Plant Openings	Plant Closings	Plant Acquisitions	Plant Divestitures	Plant Movers	Opened/Acquired Then Closed/Divested
West South Central										
Arkansas	47,432	71,035	49.8	17.4	20.3	1.4	18.0	5.8	2.9	.8
Louisiana	56,162	77,253	37.6	18.9	11.2	3.9	16.2	4.6	.3	.7
Oklahoma	35,740	55,009	53.9	12.4	31.0	1.5	14.2	2.9	1.8	3.2
Texas	242,493	350,793	44.7	14.8	15.8	1.6	17.6	2.2	2.0	1.8
Mountain										
Arizona	40,731	58,840	44.5	13.0	10.2	0	24.8	3.5	.5	.3
Colorado	48,699	73,584	51.1	18.7	12.5	1.8	23.0	1.9	2.1	.3
Idaho	9,063	14,171	56.4	15.0	35.1	.8	17.1	6.3	2.2	3.7
Montana	11,470	8,942	(22.0)	(39.7)	4.6	0	16.3	3.2	0	.3
Nevada	2,930	3,576	22.0	(24.0)	12.4	0	35.7	0	4.1	2.0
New Mexico	5,919	9,120	54.1	4.8	43.5	1.0	8.4	5.1	8.8	0
Utah	15,173	20,316	93.2	51.2	12.4	2.4	32.8	1.7	2.2	0
Wyoming	2,127	3,686	73.3	55.6	23.7	0	12.0	12.0	0	6.1

Table 4-8 (cont'd.)

				Percentage Changes						
State By Region and Division	Earlier Year Employment	Later Year Employment	Total Employment	Change at Existing Plants	Plant Openings	Plant Closings	Plant Acquisitions	Plant Divestitures	Plant Movers	Opened/Acquired Then Closed/Divested
Pacific										
Alaska	1,082	1,792	65.6	16.5	.2	13.9	62.8	0	0	0
California	480,697	588,824	22.5	10.2	4.9	5.5	16.1	4.0	3.9	1.9
Hawaii	4,505	3,531	(21.6)	(5.4)	0	28.3	14.1	0	0	2.0
Oregon	43,023	65,503	52.3	20.2	11.5	.7	22.4	2.0	2.7	3.1
Washington	93,693	119,803	27.9	21.4	5.9	3.4	5.1	1.0	.1	.1

Table 4-9

Region-To-Region Movement by Relocating Plants

Region to

Region From	New England	Mid-Atlantic	South Atlantic	East North Central	East South Central	West North Central	West South Central	Mountain	Pacific	Totals
New England	33			1	1	1				36
Mid-Atlantic	1	45	13	1	1	1				62
South Atlantic	1		55							56
East North Central		1	7	77	8	1	4	2		100
East South Central				1	14					15
West North Central						33	1			34
West South Central						1	41			42
Mountain								16		16
Pacific			1	1			1	1	80	84
Totals	35	46	76	81	24	37	47	19	80	445

Table 4-10

Employment Movement Between Regions by Relocating Plants

Region to

Region From	New England	Mid-Atlantic	South Atlantic	East North Central	East South Central	West North Central	West South Central	Mountain	Pacific	Totals
New England	8,378			50	480	700				9,608
Mid-Atlantic	250	10,286	2,587	226	75	512				13,936
South Atlantic	200		12,160							12,360
East North Central		12	1,390	18,328	1,400	21	1,575	240		22,966
East South Central				75	1,676					1,751
West North Central						8,320	240			8,560
West South Central						8	5,056			5,064
Mountain								2,097		2,097
Pacific			30	70			66	80	19,603	19,849
Totals	8,828	10,298	16,167	18,749	3,631	9,561	6,937	2,417	19,603	96,191

185

Comparing this study's plant census to the U.S. census of manufactures

A word is in order about how the private plant census of 410 major manufacturers compares to the broader Census of Manufactures. A comparison of the private census's late 1970s employment data by region against the 1977 Census of Manufactures reveals an average coverage of 37% of total U.S. manufacturing employment, with a range of 30% coverage in the Mid-Atlantic and 34% in the Pacific to 43% in the Mountain states and in the East North Central.

The industry-by-industry coverage is considerably more variable. The large, capital-intensive industries are dominated by major manufacturing companies; the data base coverage in those industries reflects this fact: 79% coverage for transportation equipment, 78% for petroleum, 69% for tobacco, and 63% for chemicals. At the other extreme are the labor intensive industries where major manufacturers are less likely to be significant presences: 8% coverage only for apparel and printing, 12% for furniture and leather goods, 16% for lumber and miscellaneous manufacturing. These industries then are generally under-represented in our regional data by industry, whereas the former set of industries are over-represented.[1]

That the regional coverage is less variable than the industry coverage hints that the industries covered most poorly are apt to be evenly spread across the U.S. For the most part, this is true, although there are some industrial concentrations in particular regions which are missed by the private plant census data. Of note are apparel in the Mid-Atlantic and furniture in the South Atlantic, industries in which there are no dominant companies.

It has been alleged that most of the growth in private sector employment over the past decade was due to small rather than large companies.[2] Judging from a comparison of the Census of Manufactures with this private study plant census, this allegation is certainly unfounded for the manufacturing sector. During the 10-year period from 1967 to 1977, total manufacturing employment in the U.S., as measured by the Census of Manufactures, rose from 19,323,200 to 19,588,700, an increase of 265,500 or 1.4%. Over an overlapping, although not identical, span of time,

[1]It has been suggested that under-representation of industries such as apparel, textiles, and shoes has biased this plant census toward the conclusion that plant relocations (so-called runaway plants) are fewer in number than they really are. While the study of major manufacturers did not address small company plants nationwide, it is nevertheless significant that, at least for the major companies in industries like apparel, textiles, and shoes, the *incidence* of plant relocations is actually *lower* than average, all less than 2%, as compared to other industries. Among major manufacturers, plant relocations are relatively most prevalent in instruments, printing, and miscellaneous manufacturing (toys, jewelry, sporting goods). Moreover, the number of inter-state relocations in any industry remains insignificant.

[2]David L. Birch, "The Job Generation Process," MIT Program on Neighborhood and Regional Change, Cambridge, MA, 1979. The basis for Birch's allegations is Dun and Bradstreet's market identifiers file which, unfortunately, is notoriously deficient for such research purposes. See Appendix A for a more thorough explanation of the Dun and Bradstreet data and its limitations for this kind of research.

1970–1980, the 410 major manufacturers investigated increased their employment from 6,352,184 (33% of the total U.S.) to 7,354,040 (37% of the total). If one ignores the acquisitions and divestitures of these companies, and deals strictly with the changes in employment at their plants due solely to on-site expansions or contractions and plant openings or closings, the increase over the decade was 513,250. This figure is larger than the gain for all manufacturing during the 1967–77 period, suggesting that the employment in smaller company plants actually shrank on balance during the past decade while the employment of major company plants grew.

Industrial Gains and Losses During the 1970s

The impressive growth during the 1970s of the major companies comprising this study is reflected in the industry-specific data reported here. The specially defined groups reported are each collections of 3-digit level Standard Industrial Classification (SIC) codes. They are assembled as they are to reflect some of the controlling considerations on location choice mentioned in chapter 1 and other special constraints on plant location specific to particular industries. These nine groupings represent collections of industry which can, more or less, be expected to locate their plants according to many of the same influences. The following is a list of the component industries making up each group:

Industry Group	SIC Code	Industry
Agriculture-Tied	201	Meat products
	203	Canned/preserved fruits and vegetables
	204	Grain mill products
	206	Sugar and confectionery products
	207	Fats and oils
	21X	Tobacco
Market-Sensitive	202	Dairy products
	205	Bakery products
	208	Beverages
	209	Miscellaneous food preparations
	264	Converted paper and paperboard
	265	Paperboard containers and boxes
	266	Building paper and building board mills
	27X	Printing
	295	Paving and roofing materials
	307	Plastics products
	341	Metal cans and shipping containers
	39X	Miscellaneous manufacturing (jewelry, silverware, musical instruments, toys, pens and pencils, brooms and brushes, sporting goods, signs, notions, caskets)
Forest-Tied	24X	Lumber and wood products
	261	Pulp mills

	262	Paper mills
	263	Paperboard mills
Labor Rate-Sensitive	22X	Textile mill products
	23X	Apparel and other fabrics products
	25X	Furniture
	31X	Leather goods
	363	Household appliances
	364	Electric lighting and wiring
	365	Radio and TV receivers
Heavy Chemicals/Oil/ Rubber/Glass	281	Industrial inorganic chemicals
	282	Plastics materials and resins
	286	Industrial organic chemicals
	287	Agricultural chemicals
	291	Petroleum refining
	299	Miscellaneous petroleum and coal products
	301	Tires and inner tubes
	302	Rubber and plastics footwear
	303	Reclaimed rubber
	304	Rubber and plastics hose and belting
	306	Other fabricated rubber products
	32X	Stone, clay, glass, and concrete products
Specialty Chemicals/Metals	283	Drugs
	284	Soap, detergents, cosmetics, etc.
	285	
	289	Miscellaneous chemicals products (adhesives, inks, etc.)
	342	Cutlery, hand tools, and hardware
	347	Coating, engraving
	348	Ordnance
	349	Miscellaneous fabricated metals (springs, pipe fittings, foil)
Heavy Metals	33X	Primary metals
	343	Heating equipment and plumbing fixtures
	344	Fabricated structural metal products
	345	Screw machine products, bolts, nuts, etc.
	346	Metal forgings and stampings
Industrial Machinery/ Transportation Equipment	351	Engines and turbines
	352	Farm and garden machinery
	353	Construction, mining, and materials handling machinery
	354	Metalworking machinery
	355	Special industry machines (food, textile, lumber, paper, printing, etc.)
	356	General industrial machinery (pumps, bearings, compressors, etc.)

	358	Refrigeration and service industry machinery
	359	Miscellaneous machinery
	361	Electric transmission and distribution equipment
	362	Electrical industrial apparatus (motors, welding)
	369	Miscellaneous electrical machinery (batteries, etc.)
	371	Motor vehicles
	372	Aircraft
	373	Shipbuilding
	374	Railroad equipment
	375	Motorcycles and bicycles
	379	Miscellaneous transport equipment (trailers, tanks)
High Technology	357	Computers and office equipment
	366	Communication equipment
	367	Electronic components
	376	Guided missiles and space vehicles
	38X	Instruments (measuring, analyzing, controlling, photographic, medical, clocks)

Tables 4-11 and 4-12 examine these industry groups by region, exactly paralleling what Tables 4-2 and 4-3 did with census of manufactures data. The importance of various industry groups to particular regions, as well as the importance of various regions to particular industry groups are readily seen in these tables.

Table 4-13 displays the changes during the past decade in plants and employment by these industry groups. The fastest growing industry groups are High Technology and Specialty Chemicals/Metals; the lowest are Heavy Metals and the foreign competition-plagued Labor Rate-Sensitive group. Table 4-14 looks into the composition of the growth in these various industry groups. This table reveals that the slow growth in the Labor Rate-Sensitive and Heavy Metals groups is associated with actual shrinkage in the size of existing plants. Conversely, the high growth in High Technology, Specialty Chemicals/Metals, and Industrial Machinery/Transportation Equipment is associated with significant growth at plants that stayed put during the 1970s. Plant opening employment overshadowed plant closing employment in all industries, but particularly so in the Market-Sensitive and Forest-Tied groups. Acquisitions outnumbered divestitures with significant net employment increases resulting for all groups except Heavy Chemicals/Oil/Rubber/Glass, Heavy Metals, and Industrial Machinery/Transportation Equipment. Relocations show less effect on employment rates. Openings/acquisitions followed by closings/divestitures in the same decade were of even less consequence than relocations.

Table 4-11

Percentage Distribution of Late 1970s Employment by Industry Group for Each Region

Industry Group	New England	Mid-Atlantic	South Atlantic	East North Central	East South Central	West North Central	West South Central	Mountain	Pacific	Nation
Agriculture Tied	0.7	3.2	6.2	3.6	4.0	14.6	5.2	5.6	6.4	5.0
Market Sensitive	10.5	9.9	10.1	8.3	9.2	12.4	9.6	10.5	11.0	9.8
Forest Tied	4.0	1.8	4.7	1.7	6.1	1.2	6.2	5.6	7.9	3.6
Labor Rate Sensitive	6.0	3.8	22.8	6.0	18.7	3.5	6.1	3.4	2.4	8.2
Heavy Chemicals/ Oil/Rubber/Glass	7.2	11.6	15.9	7.0	15.1	6.4	25.1	9.9	6.2	10.8
Specialty Chemicals/Metals	7.7	8.1	3.2	5.0	3.5	5.7	3.6	2.4	2.4	4.9
Heavy Metals	5.3	15.7	5.9	19.0	19.6	3.9	7.5	16.6	5.9	12.4
Industrial Machinery/ Transportation Equipment	34.7	25.8	19.6	44.0	16.9	39.8	22.3	15.0	35.2	31.7
High Technology	23.9	20.2	11.5	5.5	7.0	12.5	14.5	31.1	22.6	13.6
Total Employment	490,956	1,123,041	1,015,619	2,165,076	501,270	523,300	554,090	201,235	779,453	7,354,040

Table 4-12

Percentage Distribution of Late 1970s Employment by Region
for Each Industry Group

Industry Type	New England	Middle Atlantic	South Atlantic	East North Central	East South Central	West North Central	West South Central	Mountain	Pacific	Total Employment
Agriculture Tied	1.0	9.8	17.2	21.2	5.4	20.9	7.8	3.1	13.5	365,672
Market Sensitive	7.2	15.5	14.4	25.2	6.4	9.0	7.4	2.9	12.0	717,910
Forest Tied	7.3	7.5	17.9	13.5	11.5	2.3	12.8	4.2	22.9	266,829
Labor Rate Sensitive	4.8	7.1	38.4	21.4	15.5	3.1	5.6	1.1	3.1	603,709
Heavy Chemicals, Petroleum, Rubber, Stone/Clay/Glass	4.5	16.3	20.3	18.9	9.5	4.2	17.5	2.5	6.1	794,471
Specialty Chemicals and Metals	10.5	25.3	9.0	29.9	4.8	8.3	5.6	1.3	5.3	359,910
Heavy Metals Work	2.9	19.3	6.6	45.1	10.7	2.2	4.5	3.7	5.0	913,011
General Industrial Machinery and Transportation Equipment	7.3	12.4	8.5	40.8	3.6	8.9	5.3	1.3	11.7	2,333,610
High Technology	11.8	22.7	11.7	11.9	3.5	6.6	8.0	6.3	17.6	998,918
Nation	6.7	15.3	13.8	29.4	6.8	7.1	7.5	2.7	10.6	7,354,040

Table 4-13

Plants and Employment by Industry Group

Industry Group	Plants			Employment		
	Early 1970s	Late 1970s	Percent% Change	Early 1970s	Late 1970s	Percent% Change
Agriculture Tied	1077	1238	14.9	318,811	365,672	14.7
Market Sensitive	3023	3410	12.8	608,070	717,910	18.1
Forest Tied	626	780	24.6	225,625	266,829	18.3
Labor Rate Sensitive	1152	1287	11.7	557,137	603,709	8.4
Heavy Chemicals/Oil Rubber/Glass	2110	2280	8.1	709,491	794,471	12.0
Specialty Chemicals/ Metals	973	1164	19.6	290,187	359,910	24.0
Heavy Metals	1106	1243	12.4	883,865	913,011	3.3
Industrial Machinery/Transportation Equipment	1847	2368	28.2	1,957,013	2,333,610	19.2
High Technology	864	1160	34.3	801,985	998,918	24.6

The elements of growth and decline in regions, by industry group

The tables in the previous section present snapshots in time of where industries of various kinds are located within the United States. What they do not present is any information on *how* the regional locations of industry have changed over the course of the past decade. The tables in this section are devoted to that task.

Analyzing how a region has grown or declined in its industrial make-up requires some care. Merely indicating what share a region enjoys of an industry's growth in employment ignores the fact that some regions are very much larger than others. The East North Central region, representing as it does about a quarter of the nation's manufacturing employment, would have to garner a quarter of all employment increases just to stay even, in a relative sense, with the national average. Table 4-15 presents

Table 4-14

Composition of Employment Changes During the 1970s by Industry Group

Industry Group	Stay-Put Plants Early 1970s Employment	Change at Stay-Put Plants	Change as a Percent of Early 1970s Stay-Put Plants Employment					
			Openings	Closings	Acquisitions	Divestitures	Relocations	Opens/Closes
Agriculture Tied	277,934	3.8	7.7	6.6	18.3	5.0	1.5	2.2
Market Sensitive	507,671	3.6	11.4	6.3	21.5	8.4	4.9	2.9
Forest Tied	206,179	2.8	6.7	2.2	18.7	5.3	0.8	3.2
Labor Rate Sensitive	467,987	-1.7	9.3	6.3	20.3	9.4	1.1	4.0
Heavy Chemicals/Oil/ Rubber/Glass	660,728	5.6	5.2	2.9	8.8	3.6	0.6	0.8
Specialty Chemicals/ Metals	257,844	7.4	6.8	3.1	21.4	5.8	4.1	1.5
Heavy Metals	830,285	-1.1	3.2	2.9	7.5	2.9	0.3	0.7
Industrial Machinery/ Transportation Equipment	1,866,316	9.0	5.8	1.8	9.2	1.8	1.0	0.7
High Technology	738,211	8.6	8.6	4.7	14.8	1.6	3.4	0.6
Nation	5,813,155	5.3	6.7	3.5	12.9	3.8	1.7	1.4

Table 4-15

Index of Percentage Growth in an Industry Relative to the Size of that Industry in Each Region

Panel A. Changes at Existing Plants

Industry Group	New England	Middle Atlantic	South Atlantic	East North Central	East South Central	West North Central	West South Central	Mountain	Pacific
Agriculture Tied	-.40	.03	.22	.09	.72	.47	.45	.77	-.33
Market Sensitive	-.46	-.34	.28	.09	.22	.44	.62	1.55	.27
Forest Tied	.18	.24	-.44	.03	.56	-.26	.54	.55	.08
Labor Rate Sensitive	-.96	-.38	-.03	-.41	.11	-1.45	.88	-.45	-.58
Heavy Chemicals/Oil/ Rubber/Glass	.40	.17	.43	-.73	.89	.98	1.19	1.76	-.13
Specialty Chemicals/Metals	.10	.19	.21	.34	.17	.51	.38	1.38	0
Heavy Metals	-.10	-2.05	-1.18	-.47	2.95	-2.77	1.02	-.73	2.24
Industrial Machinery/ Transportation Equipment	.40	.02	.16	.30	.75	.96	.40	.69	1.16
High Technology	.72	-.33	.79	-.40	.49	.14	1.21	.43	.66

Table 4-15 (cont'd.)

Index of Percentage Growth in an Industry Relative to the Size of that Industry in Each Region

Panel B. Expansions On-Site

Industry Group	New England	Middle Atlantic	South Atlantic	East North Central	East South Central	West North Central	West South Central	Mountain	Pacific
Agriculture Tied	0	.17	.37	.27	.24	.50	.24	.77	.23
Market Sensitive	.23	.13	.26	.31	.20	.41	.44	1.51	.25
Forest Tied	.37	0	.17	.01	.28	-.26	.54	.57	.22
Labor Rate Sensitive	.02	.15	.39	.49	.27	.19	.82	0	.54
Heavy Chemicals/ Petroleum/Rubber/Glass	.88	.47	.50	.29	.82	1.07	.99	1.56	.32
Specialty Chemicals and Metals	.30	.15	.43	.53	.37	.60	.41	1.38	.11
Heavy Metals	.96	-.11	.13	.81	2.50	1.09	1.66	2.37	1.20
General Industrial Machinery & Transportation Equipment	.56	.15	.23	.35	.52	.76	.39	.61	.31
High Technology	.86	.22	.73	.41	.62	.24	1.08	.55	.69

Table 4-15 (cont'd.)

Index of Percentage Growth in an Industry Relative to the Size of that Industry in Each Region

Panel C. Openings

Industry Group	New England	Middle Atlantic	South Atlantic	East North Central	East South Central	West North Central	West South Central	Mountain	Pacific
Agriculture Tied	0	.32	.96	.27	.46	.41	.94	.39	.06
Market Sensitive	.33	.51	.88	.37	.98	.33	.68	.48	.38
Forest Tied	.15	.12	.26	.39	.75	.30	.55	.48	.15
Labor Rate Sensitive	.60	.18	.90	.20	1.27	1.13	4.07	2.64	.32
Heavy Chemicals/Oil/ Rubber/Glass	.31	.21	.59	.16	.45	.40	.63	.56	.43
Specialty Chemicals/Metals	.19	.03	1.04	.11	.73	.17	.55	.15	.28
Heavy Metals	1.17	.24	1.50	.81	1.27	1.50	2.42	2.19	.40
Industrial Machinery/ Transporation Equipment	.16	.11	.62	.16	1.25	.33	.87	.77	.15
High Technology	.38	.09	.37	.12	.31	.15	.68	.60	.47

Table 4-15 (cont'd.)

Index of Percentage Growth in an Industry Relative to the Size of that Industry in Each Region

Panel D. Acquisitions

Industry Group	New England	Middle Atlantic	South Atlantic	East North Central	East South Central	West North Central	West South Central	Mountain	Pacific
Agriculture Tied	4.80	.82	.71	.81	.80	1.40	2.04	1.29	.98
Market Sensitive	.72	.89	.71	1.21	1.11	.86	-.93	1.17	1.22
Forest Tied	1.16	.89	.99	.65	1.09	1.74	.92	1.36	.77
Labor Rate Sensitive	4.46	4.13	1.60	1.85	1.76	1.23	.21	8.09	3.71
Heavy Chemicals/ Petroleum/Rubber/Glass	1.07	.72	.62	.68	.53	1.02	.62	.48	.90
Specialty Chemicals and Metals	.19	.79	.58	.87	1.6	.45	1.64	.48	.63
Heavy Metals	5.14	1.58	1.64	2.33	1.88	5.31	1.62	.02	2.30
General Industrial Machinery/Transportation Equipment	.45	.35	.44	.40	1.03	.21	1.00	1.46	.40
High Technology	.49	.30	.49	.46	.65	.83	.68	.74	.77

some relative comparisons of industry growth of different types in each region. The entries are constructed as the ratios of the absolute percentage share of an industry's employment growth nationally due to a particular component of change (that is, on-site expansion, plant openings, acquisitions) in a particular region to the percentage of that industry's total national employment residing in that region. This procedure thus scales the growth, or decline, of employment in particular industry groups for each region. The higher the ratio (or index), the better the region has done in increasing employment in an industry group by a certain means such as plant openings.

Table 4-15's results lead to a multitude of comparisons and thus merit careful study. Here are some region-by-region highlights:

West South Central and Mountain

- Strong relative gains in almost all industries due to plant expansions on-site and new plant openings
- Rapid gains in several industries (e.g., agriculture-tied, labor rate-sensitive, machinery) due to acquisitions

Mid-Atlantic and East North Central

- Weak relative showings in all industries and by every component of change

New England

- Generally weak showings in most industries and by most components of change
- Exceptions include a strong showing in high technology, particularly through on-site expansions and new plant openings
- Acquisition gains in agriculture-tied, labor rate-sensitive, and heavy metals were also strong.

South Atlantic

- Strong relative gains in most industry groups due to plant openings, but not due to expansions on-site
- However, strong gains in high technology by all means. Rapid gains in labor rate-sensitive industries via acquisition

East South Central

- Strong relative gains in agriculture-tied, forest-tied, heavy metals, and machinery industries due to expansions on-site
- Relative gains due to plant openings and acquisitions in market-sensitive, labor rate-sensitive, and machinery concerns.

West North Central

- Relative gains due to on-site expansion in all industry groups except forest-tied, labor rate-sensitive, heavy metals, and high technology
- Weaker showing, however, in plant openings across all industries

- Gains in forest-tied, heavy chemicals and metals, and high technology from acquisition

Pacific

- Relative gains due to plant openings in high technology but not in other industries
- Gains in employment at existing plants in heavy metals and machinery, but not because of on-site, "bricks and mortar" expansion
- Strong gains via acquisition in market-sensitive, heavy chemicals, and high technology industries

DECLINES AND RELOCATIONS

Tables 4-16 through 4-18 look at the employment change nationally for all industry that is attributable respectively to plant closings, divestitures, and relocations. Those tables point out where the greatest impacts from closings, divestitures, and relocation have been.

Plant closings in the following industry group/region pairs have been most influential to total national employment lost to closings:

High Technology in the Mid-Atlantic
Industrial Machinery/Transportation Equipment in the East North Central
Market-Sensitive and Heavy Chemicals/Oil/Rubber/Glass in the East North Central
Market-Sensitive in the Pacific

Plant closings have been fairly well spread out across regions and industry. This appears even more to be the case with divestitures. The highest levels pertain to the East North Central region in the Industrial Machinery/Transportation Equipment, Heavy Metals, Labor Rate-Sensitive, and Market-Sensitive industry groups. Another high level exists in Labor Rate-Sensitive industries in the South Atlantic.

As established earlier, relocations are local phenomena primarily and involve fundamentally footloose industries. It is not surprising to find the High Technology, Market-Sensitive, and Industrial Machinery/Transportation Equipment industry groups dominating the national action and specifically in the South Atlantic, Pacific, and East North Central regions.

City, Suburb, and Rural Area Statistics

Urban, suburban, and rural breakdowns for major manufacturers

Tables 4-19 to 4-24 deal with plant and employment changes by region partitioned into central city, suburban, and rural area jurisdictions. As anticipated, central cities, in general, have not performed as well as suburbs or rural areas, but their performance varies markedly from one

Table 4-16

Percentage Distribution of Total Plant Closing Employment Among Regions and Industry Groups

Industry Type	New England	Middle Atlantic	South Atlantic	East North Central	East South Central	West North Central	West South Central	Mountain	Pacific	Total
Agriculture Tied	.3	.8	1.1	1.8	1.8	.6	.6	.3	1.7	9.1
Market Sensitive	1.7	2.8	1.2	4.1	.4	.8	.7	.1	4.0	15.7
Forest Tied	0	.7	.5	.5	.1	.2	0	0	.2	2.3
Labor Rate Sensitive	.9	3.4	3.6	2.1	1.4	1.8	.5	.1	.8	14.5
Heavy Chemicals, Petroleum, Rubber, Stone, Clay, Glass	.3	1.1	1.7	4.1	.1	.6	.3	.1	1.2	9.5
Specialty Chemicals and Metals	.3	.4	.1	2.6	0	.1	.3	0	.3	4.0
Heavy Metals	.8	3.8	2.2	3.3	.4	.1	.4	0	.8	11.8
General Industrial Machinery and Transporation Equipment	1.3	1.4	.5	8.8	0	.2	.8	.2	3.0	16.3
High Technology	2.4	8.0	1.5	.8	.5	.2	.1	0	3.5	16.9
Total	8.0	22.5	12.4	28.0	4.7	4.6	3.5	.8	15.6	

Table 4-17

Percentage Distribution of Total Divestiture Employment Among Regions and Industry Groups

Industry Type	New England	Middle Atlantic	South Atlantic	East North Central	East South Central	West North Central	West South Central	Mountain	Pacific	Total
Agriculture Tied	0	.5	1.2	1.0	.5	.4	1.2	.2	1.3	6.3
Market Sensitive	1.8	3.6	2.7	5.6	1.0	1.1	.5	.4	2.5	19.3
Forest Tied	1.5	.1	1.0	1.0	.1	.3	.3	.2	.5	5.0
Labor Rate Sensitive	2.0	1.7	6.9	5.0	2.6	.2	.7	0	.9	20.0
Heavy Chemicals, Petroleum, Rubber, Stone, Clay, Glass	.2	2.9	1.9	2.1	.7	.2	1.1	.5	1.1	10.7
Specialty Chemicals and Metals	2.2	1.4	.8	1.1	.4	.5	.1	0	.3	6.8
Heavy Metals	.3	2.1	1.7	5.3	.6	.1	.3	.1	.3	10.9
General Industrial Machinery and Transportation Equipment	.8	2.5	.9	8.0	.2	.8	1.1	.3	1.1	15.6
High Technology	.2	1.0	.1	1.0	0	.1	0	.8	2.2	5.4
Total	8.9	15.6	17.2	30.3	6.1	3.8	5.5	2.5	10.1	

Table 4-18

Percentage Distribution of Total Relocation Employment Among Regions and Industry Groups

Industry Type	New England	Middle Atlantic	South Atlantic	East North Central	East South Central	West North Central	West South Central	Mountain	Pacific	Total
Agriculture Tied	0	.2	0	1.1	.6	1.2	.4	.1	.7	4.4
Market Sensitive	2.2	2.4	3.1	5.4	.7	3.6	1.6	.7	5.7	25.5
Forest Tied	0	.2	.2	.8	C	0	.1	.3	0	1.7
Labor Rate Sensitive	0	.2	1.3	.3	1.2	0	1.1	.5	.9	5.5
Heavy Chemicals, Petroleum, Rubber, Stone, Clay, Glass	.7	.4	1.2	.3	.1	0	.4	.2	.6	4.0
Specialty Chemicals and Metals	2.3	.9	.2	3.7	0	1.6	1.4	.1	.7	10.8
Heavy Metals	.5	.1	0	.2	0	.3	.4	.4	.5	2.4
General Industrial Machinery and Transportation Equipment	2.2	2.1	5.0	4.5	.8	.8	1.0	.2	3.2	19.7
High Technology	1.2	4.0	6.0	3.2	.4	2.3	.8	0	8.1	26.1
Total	9.1	10.6	17.0	19.5	3.7	9.9	7.2	2.5	20.4	

Table 4-19

Plants and Employment in Cities, Suburbs, and Rural Areas, by Region

Region	CENTRAL CITIES				SUBURBS				RURAL AREAS			
	Plants		Employment		Plants		Employment		Plants		Employment	
	Early 1970's	Late 1970's	Early 1970's	Late 1970's	Early 1970's	Late 1970's	Early 1970's	Late 1970's	Early 1970's	Late 1970's	Early 1970's	Late 1970's
New England	255	240	129,841	126,397	355	400	218,145	260,408	210	251	79,358	104,151
Mid Atlantic	490	462	384,744	365,016	1,004	1,095	522,506	569,898	376	425	171,629	187,777
South Atlantic	576	622	284,132	305,411	589	735	242,532	302,645	852	1,024	327,037	400,720
East North Central	1,019	1,045	930,893	921,801	1,152	1,322	757,960	846,830	785	967	327,543	396,175
East South Central	307	359	156,164	184,020	175	256	91,929	122,154	426	585	133,116	195,096
West North Central	376	407	243,338	283,026	185	238	71,815	90,874	423	545	102,590	149,400
West South Central	557	712	192,892	286,602	271	380	98,862	139,995	320	421	90,073	127,493
Mountain	155	212	62,502	91,754	101	144	35,735	56,036	146	178	37,875	53,445
Pacific	538	579	213,874	229,906	907	1,047	351,210	475,630	224	273	57,916	73,917
Totals	4,273	4,638	2,598,380	2,793,933	4,739	5,617	2,390,694	2,864,470	3,762	4,669	1,327,137	1,688,174

region of the country to another. Central city employment by these large companies actually dropped in absolute terms over the 1970s in the three traditionally industrial regions of the Northeast. Table 4-20 breaks down this employment drop into components. For the most part, as this table shows, the Northeast central city lost some employment at its stay-put plants, had significantly fewer plant openings than closings, and did not have enough acquisition employment in excess of divestiture employment to make up the difference. Nevertheless, the employment performance of major corporations in central cities appears to be better than that of all companies in central cities, as judged by various city-specific studies.[3] These studies indicate that employment from plant "deaths" exceeding that of plant "births" is the single most important explanation for the employment decline in older cities and that this difference is relatively greater for all industry than it is for major corporations taken by themselves.

Apart from the traditionally industrial Northeast, the central city's major corporation manufacturing employment is growing, in some cases (the West South Central and Mountain states) spectacularly so. The spectacular growth of cities in these regions is due to sizable on-site growth at stay-put plants, widespread acquisitions in excess of divestitures and, most prominently, to significant numbers of plant openings and few plant closings.

In five of the nine regions, plant closings in central cities and the employment lost thereby overshadow the plant openings and their employment. This is particularly true of the East North Central, Mid-Atlantic, and New England regions, but it is also true of the Pacific, and East South Central regions. Even in the South Atlantic and West North Central regions, plant opening employment in central cities is not that much larger than plant closing employment.

The suburbs continue to grow at a more rapid pace than the central cities. However, all is not well with suburban employment by major manufacturers in the Mid-Atlantic states. There, employment actually declined at suburban stay-put plants, and plant closing employment exceeded that of plant openings. Only the sizable employment at acquisitions salvaged a net growth in employment in the mid-Atlantic's suburbs. In all other regions, suburban stay-put plant expansions and the difference between openings and closings had net employment gains. Suburban opening plant employments greater than closed plant employments were especially impressive in the South Atlantic, East North Central, East South Central, and West South Central regions' suburbs.

[3]For example, Roger W. Schmenner, *The Manufacturing Location Decision: Evidence from Cincinnati and New England*, report to the Economic Development Administration of the U.S. Department of Commerce 1978; Robert A. Leone, "Location of Economic Activity in the New York Metropolitan Area", unpublished Ph.D. dissertation, Yale University, 1971; and Raymond J. Struyk and Franklin J. James, *Intrametropolitan Industrial Location*, Lexington Books, D.C. Heath (Lexington, MA), 1975.

Table 4-20

Plants and Employment in Cities, by Region for Each Class of Plant

Region	Stay-Put Plants			Openings		Closings		Acquisitions		Divestitures		Relocations	
	Plants	Employment Early 1970's	Employment Late 1970's	Plants	Employment	Plants	Employment	Plants	Employment	Plants	Employment	Plants	Employment
New England	173	108,364	110,078	13	2,231	39	7,239	47	13,144	26	12,062	7	944
Mid Atlantic	334	352,200	330,565	16	2,394	59	17,407	104	29,117	63	11,687	8	2,940
South Atlantic	449	263,180	272,560	50	12,032	40	10,284	99	14,466	39	5,156	24	6,353
East North Central	760	855,627	837,608	44	8,046	104	30,250	218	69,765	85	29,943	23	6,382
East South Central	247	143,255	158,909	29	5,930	22	6,126	74	17,861	21	2,560	9	1,320
West North Central	276	227,223	247,624	23	8,528	32	5,614	90	21,519	34	5,130	17	5,080
West South Central	419	178,287	217,669	107	31,089	43	5,099	158	32,696	34	4,497	28	5,148
Mountain	114	59,361	68,258	32	7,245	10	639	56	15,428	13	2,818	10	823
Pacific	365	184,128	190,379	47	7,767	56	9,635	142	24,092	62	13,814	22	7,518
Totals	3,137	2,371,625	2,433,650	361	85,262	403	92,293	988	238,088	377	87,667	148	36,508

Table 4-21

Plants and Employment in Suburbs, by Region for Each Class of Plant

Region	Stay-Put Plants			Openings		Closings		Acquisitions		Divestitures		Relocations	
	Plants	Employment Early 1970's	Employment Late 1970's	Plants	Employment	Plants	Employment	Plants	Employment	Plant	Employment	Plants	Employment
New England	249	202,007	221,466	41	13,631	37	5,424	93	19,986	30	6,102	17	5,325
Mid Atlantic	711	502,085	496,384	91	17,185	93	24,025	265	51,665	108	17,012	28	4,664
South Atlantic	456	225,710	239,827	104	31,857	35	4,224	145	25,104	40	8,197	30	5,857
East North Central	852	709,391	733,568	113	33,493	84	15,565	307	70,154	96	23,735	49	9,440
East South Central	132	85,977	93,174	50	16,558	12	1,012	69	11,486	20	3,099	5	936
West North Central	139	67,755	75,108	21	1,939	11	1,316	66	11,525	13	935	12	2,302
West South Central	218	95,224	103,275	72	17,849	14	492	75	17,535	16	2,405	15	1,336
Mountain	77	33,229	40,194	24	3,317	7	720	36	11,441	9	1,313	6	969
Pacific	630	317,211	387,443	91	22,263	78	19,455	270	55,237	81	6,594	55	10,609
Totals	3,464	2,238,589	2,390,439	607	158,092	371	72,233	1,326	274,133	413	69,392	217	41,438

Table 4-22

Plants and Employment in Rural Areas, by Region for Each Class of Plant

Region	Stay-Put Plants			Openings		Closings		Acquisitions		Divestitures		Relocations	
	Plants	Employment Early 1970's	Employment Late 1970's	Plants	Employment	Plants	Employment	Plants	Employment	Plants	Employment	Plants	Employment
New England	155	70,383	74,022	23	5,489	13	3,601	62	22,081	17	1,486	11	2,559
Mid Atlantic	296	157,726	162,034	30	5,764	27	4,259	89	17,285	26	5,749	10	2,694
South Atlantic	632	287,697	296,455	156	43,744	54	10,595	210	55,678	91	24,499	23	4,257
East North Central	619	297,744	319,771	94	17,835	61	11,129	244	55,452	58	13,050	10	3,117
East South Central	319	118,945	133,836	120	27,427	25	2,478	135	32,343	31	7,841	10	1,375
West North Central	339	94,520	112,032	81	15,035	27	2,336	117	20,154	26	2,206	8	2,179
West South Central	256	82,643	95,596	83	16,304	16	1,544	78	15,140	31	5,120	4	453
Mountain	116	35,588	39,471	27	8,701	6	169	32	4,648	15	1,383	3	625
Pacific	162	51,722	54,471	28	3,834	18	2,526	77	13,934	21	1,903	6	1,678
Totals	2,894	1,196,968	1,287,688	642	144,133	247	38,637	1,044	236,715	316	63,237	85	18,937

Rural areas gained everywhere and in every way, even in the Mid-Atlantic states. Particularly impressive are the scores of plant openings and their sizable employments in the rural areas of the South Atlantic and East South Central States. The level of rural acquisition remains high in every region.

Table 4-23 approaches the issue of urban/suburban/rural growth from a slightly different direction. Displayed there is the percentage of each region's major company manufacturing employment which is to be found in central cities, suburbs, and rural areas. The relative growth of suburbs and rural areas, at the expense of central cities, can be seen clearly there. Only for the West South Central region does the percentage of employment in cities actually grow during the decade. Nationally, we can see that central cities no longer hold most metropolitan area major company employment; the suburbs surpassed them during the 1970s.

It is interesting to note as well where major company manufacturing is concentrated. In the New England, Mid-Atlantic, and Pacific regions, most manufacturing employment is found in the suburbs. In the West North Central and West South Central regions, most of it rests in central cities. Elsewhere, neither city nor suburb nor rural area holds more than half of all manufacturing employment but certain trends are evident. For example, nearly 40% of the major company employment in the South Atlantic and East South Central regions lies outside metropolitan areas, in rural locales. Central cities are relatively preferred in the East North Central and Mountain states.

It was observed above that plant relocations constitute a small fraction of the facilities and employment involved in the geographic shifts of manufacturing and that comparatively few relocations involve moves of greater than 20 miles. Most plant relocations, then, are around local areas, particularly metropolitan areas. To what degree are these relocations decentralizing? Table 4-24 addresses that question.

First observed is that most relocations from a city, suburb, or rural area are destined to the same type area. Even for central cities, 114 of the 203 relocations starting from a central city (56%) ended up in a central city. Corresponding percentages for suburbs and rural areas are even higher, 75% and 73% respectively. Nevertheless, a net decentralization is occurring; more plants and employment shift out of central cities than move into them from elsewhere. Suburbs are the largest beneficiaries of this decentralization. Rural areas do only moderately better than break even.

The extent of the employment decentralization out of central cities due expressly to the relocation of major manufacturers should be kept in mind. Nationally, central cities lost about 3800 jobs (pre-move employment) over the course of the 1970s due to relocations. That is only about 0.15% of all central city employment and about 10% of all central city relocating employment. Of course, relocations are more important to some cities (say,

Table 4-23

Percentage of Each Region's Major Company Manufacturing
Employment in Cities, Suburbs, and Rural Areas

Region	Percentage in Central Cities		Percentage in Suburbs		Percentage in Rural Areas	
	Early 70s	Late 70s	Early 70s	Late 70s	Early 70s	Late 70s
New England	30.4	25.7	51.0	53.0	18.6	21.2
Mid-Atlantic	35.7	32.5	48.4	50.8	15.9	16.7
South Atlantic	33.3	30.3	28.4	30.0	38.3	39.7
East North Central	46.2	42.6	37.6	39.1	16.2	18.3
East South Central	41.0	36.7	24.1	24.4	34.9	38.9
West North Central	58.3	54.1	17.2	17.4	24.6	28.5
West South Central	50.5	51.7	25.9	25.3	23.6	23.0
Mountain	45.9	45.6	26.3	27.8	27.8	26.6
Pacific	34.3	29.5	56.4	61.0	9.3	9.5
Nation	41.1	38.0	37.9	39.0	21.0	23.0

Table 4-24

The Urban, Suburban, and Rural Movement of Plant Relocations

Panel A. Number of Plants, Nationally, Moving From One Type Area to Another

		To			
		City	Suburb	Rural Area	Totals
From	City	114	75	14	203
	Suburb	26	126	16	168
	Rural Area	7	13	54	74
	Totals	147	214	84	445

Panel B. Post-Move Employment Nationally, Moving From One Type Area to Another

		To			
		City	Suburb	Rural Area	Totals
From	City	25,413	12,335	1,775	39,523
	Suburb	9,199	25,936	3,510	38,645
	Rural Area	1,856	2,914	13,352	18,122
	Totals	36,468	41,185	18,637	96,290

Panel C. Pre-Move Employment, Nationally, Moving From One Type Area to Another

		To			
		City	Suburb	Rural Area	Totals
From	City	21,316	10,807	1,374	33,497
	Suburb	6,722	17,105	3,573	27,400
	Rural Area	1,596	1,369	9,342	12,307
	Totals	29,634	29,281	14,289	73,204

older Northeast cities) than to others, and the trend is against central cities. But relocations are not the chief bogey of urban areas nationally, plant closings in excess of plant openings are.

City, suburb, and rural area industry statistics

Tables 4-25 through 4-29 investigate the industrial concentration and its changing composition within central cities, suburbs, and rural areas. Certain types of industry, as discussed earlier, require city or metropolitan area plant sites. The metropolitan area-concentrated industries include those classed as Market-Sensitive, Specialty Chemicals/Metals, Heavy Metals, Industrial Machinery/Transportation Equipment, and High Technology. The latter two are especially prevalent in and around metropolitan areas. The heavily rural industries are those classed as Forest-Tied or Labor Rate-Sensitive, an expected combination. Two other industry groups, Agriculture-Tied and Heavy Chemicals/Oil/Rubber/Glass are more evenly distributed across the landscape, with the former understandably showing greater preference for rural areas than the latter.

Over the decade, the central city's share of employment in all of these industry groups declined, while the share held by rural areas gained in every case. The suburban share of these industry groups stayed about the same. In three groups central city employment declined in absolute terms: Forest-Tied, Labor Rate-Sensitive, and Heavy Metals. Employment increases were registered in every other industry and in the suburbs and rural areas for all industry groups.

The composition of the declines in central cities is examined in Table 4-27. For three industries: Forest-Tied, Labor Rate-Sensitive, and perhaps most disturbing, Market-Sensitive, employment at stay-put plants dropped. In even more industry groups did the employment at plant closings exceed that of plant openings: Agriculture-Tied, Market-Sensitive, Labor Rate-Sensitive, Specialty Chemicals/Metals, and Heavy Metals. Only a significant number of acquisitions kept the Market-Sensitive industry group from registering an absolute decline in central cities.

Employment at the stay-put plants in the Forest-Tied, Labor Rate-Sensitive, and Heavy Metals industries dipped at suburban locations. For other industry groups in the suburbs and for all groups in rural areas, employment gains were made in every way: expansions at stay-put plants, openings greater than closings, and acquisitions greater than divestitures.

The pattern of industry location around Cincinnati, 1971–1975/6

This section presents a detailed investigation of the pattern of manufacturing locations in the Cincinnati metropolitan area during the 1971–75/6 time period. Before examining the data, it is useful to pause briefly for a discussion of the area and its industrial history.

Table 4-25

Plants and Employment in Cities, Suburbs, and Rural Areas, by Industry Group

Industry Group	Central Cities				Suburbs				Rural Areas			
	Plants		Employment		Plants		Employment		Plants		Employment	
	Early 1970s	Late 1970s	Early 1970s	Late 1970s	Early 1970s	Late 1970s	Early 1970s	Late 1970s	Early 1970s	Late 1970s	Early 1970s	Late 1970s
Agriculture Tied	383	430	141,500	151,441	274	312	77,807	93,152	420	496	99,504	121,079
Market Sensitive	1,268	1,311	278,133	297,330	1,117	1,319	226,970	273,150	638	779	102,967	147,370
Forest Tied	105	108	47,477	46,353	133	161	45,912	49,804	388	511	132,236	170,672
Labor Rate Sensitive	281	270	160,920	152,016	286	337	141,166	161,055	584	679	253,851	288,855
Heavy Chemicals/Oil/ Rubber/Glass	587	607	257,037	268,014	849	936	246,796	285,985	672	735	201,308	235,422
Specialty Chemicals/ Metals	340	393	101,803	113,945	455	535	136,395	169,226	177	235	51,566	76,439
Heavy Metals	385	383	381,353	379,500	432	493	355,840	363,641	289	367	146,672	169,870
Industrial Machinery/Transportation Equipment	648	799	882,129	987,808	738	905	821,614	983,557	461	663	253,270	361,975
High Technology	276	337	348,028	397,526	455	619	368,194	484,900	133	204	85,763	116,492

Table 4-26

Percentage of Each Industry Group's Employment in Cities, Suburbs, and Rural Areas

Industry Group	Central Cities		Suburbs		Rural Areas	
	Early 1970s	Late 1970s	Early 1970s	Late 1970s	Early 1970s	Late 1970s
Agriculture Tied	44.4	41.4	24.4	25.5	31.2	33.1
Market Sensitive	45.7	41.4	37.3	38.1	16.9	20.5
Forest Tied	21.0	17.4	20.3	18.7	58.6	64.0
Labor Rate Sensitive	28.9	25.3	25.4	26.8	45.7	48.0
Heavy Chemicals/Oil/ Rubber/Glass	36.5	34.0	35.0	36.2	28.5	29.8
Specialty Chemicals/ Metals	35.1	31.7	47.1	47.1	17.8	21.3
Heavy Metals	43.1	41.6	40.3	39.8	16.6	18.6
Industrial Machinery/ Transportation Equipment	45.1	42.3	42.0	42.2	12.9	15.5
High Technology	43.4	39.8	45.9	48.5	10.7	11.7

Table 4-27

Plants and Employment in Cities, by Class for Each Industry Group

Industry Group	Stay-Put Plants			Openings		Closings		Acquisitions		Divestitures		Relocations	
	Plants	Employment Early 1970's	Employment Late 1970's	Plants	Employment	Plants	Employment	Plants	Employment	Plants	Employment	Plants	Employment
Agriculture Tied	238	124,482	126,536	23	5,730	41	7,870	104	15,927	25	3,444	18	2,876
Market Sensitive	918	232,160	228,647	85	11,319	125	14,111	256	44,047	125	17,713	51	13,277
Forest Tied	67	40,530	37,263	10	1,458	14	1,326	29	7,015	13	5,003	2	617
Labor Rate Sensitive	160	130,969	116,620	30	10,625	44	12,062	71	22,509	40	14,590	9	2,262
Heavy Chemicals, Petroleum, Rubber, Stone/Clay/Glass	481	240,787	244,335	33	8,000	39	7,007	95	14,782	44	9,235	8	897
Specialty Chemicals/Metals	255	87,321	90,067	27	1,786	21	3,903	96	19,499	30	7,816	15	2,593
Heavy Metals	285	359,092	359,147	19	3,351	36	10,921	73	16,413	36	9,011	6	589
General Industrial Machine, Transportation	502	838,785	899,729	81	22,339	47	17,347	193	60,873	43	13,664	22	4,827
High Technology	186	317,499	331,279	53	20,654	36	17,746	81	37,023	21	7,191	17	8,570
Totals	3,137	2,371,625	2,433,623	361	85,262	403	92,293	988	238,088	377	87,667	148	36,508

Table 4-28

Plants and Employment in Suburbs by Class for Each Industry Group

Industry Group	Stay-Put Plants			Openings		Closings		Acquisitions		Divestitures		Relocations	
	Plants	Employment Early 1970's	Employment Late 1970's	Plants	Employment	Plants	Employment	Plants	Employment	Plants	Employment	Plants	Employment
Agriculture Tied	196	68,923	71,504	32	6,933	32	3,894	78	13,545	27	3,192	5	1,055
Market Sensitive	818	185,773	199,387	153	23,327	81	14,240	285	41,145	90	16,759	63	9,291
Forest Tied	92	42,091	41,861	19	3,012	11	1,572	44	4,103	7	1,266	4	575
Labor Rate Sensitive	175	121,003	120,649	35	11,083	35	8,518	117	27,853	43	8,010	10	1,470
Heavy Chemicals, Petroleum, Rubber, Stone/Clay/Glass	675	228,537	244,742	76	15,056	58	6,948	169	24,355	70	7,345	16	1,832
Specialty Chemicals/Metals	326	125,141	135,119	45	4,739	31	2,164	139	24,141	48	4,262	25	5,227
Heavy Metals	324	335,019	323,295	37	13,812	30	8,983	117	24,832	43	9,761	15	1,702
General Industrial Machine/Transporation	540	789,629	865,147	112	48,864	56	12,389	208	60,061	58	14,247	45	9,485
High Technology	318	342,473	388,735	98	31,266	31	13,525	169	54,098	27	4,550	34	10,801
Totals	3,464	2,238,599	2,390,439	607	158,092	371	72,233	1,326	274,133	413	69,392	217	41,438

Table 4-29

Plants and Employment in Rural Areas by Class for Each Industry Group

Industry Group	Stay-Put Plants			Openings		Closings		Acquisitions		Divestitures		Relocations	
	Plants	Employment Early 1970's	Employment Late 1970's	Plants	Employment	Plants	Employment	Plants	Employment	Plants	Employment	Plants	Employment
Agriculture Tied	315	84,529	90,520	56	8,838	40	6,638	118	21,427	42	7,145	7	294
Market Sensitive	467	89,738	98,134	121	22,944	41	3,493	174	24,161	77	8,050	17	2,131
Forest Tied	293	123,558	132,855	66	9,418	23	1,691	144	27,377	30	4,674	5	436
Labor Rate Sensitive	432	214,815	220,883	87	21,618	43	8,864	152	44,804	54	21,536	8	1,550
Heavy Chemicals, Petroleum, Rubber, Stone/Clay/Glass	542	187,054	203,359	74	11,597	44	5,393	111	19,217	53	6,968	7	1,134
Specialty Chemicals/Metals	138	44,959	51,381	36	10,957	15	2,050	55	11,425	13	2,849	6	2,676
Heavy Metals	240	136,174	139,102	40	9,775	14	4,083	86	20,913	21	5,239	1	80
General Industrial Machine, Transportation	362	237,902	269,901	127	37,751	21	3,284	155	49,582	22	6,555	19	4,741
High Technology	105	78,239	81,553	35	11,235	6	3,141	49	17,809	4	221	15	5,895
Totals	2,894	1,196,968	1,287,688	642	144,133	247	38,637	1,044	236,985	316	63,237	85	18,937

215

An Introduction to the Cincinnati Area

First settled in 1788, Cincinnati is one of the oldest manufacturing centers in America. Throughout much of the middle of the 19th century, Cincinnati's industrial output was surpassed only by New York and Philadelphia. Its influence across a wide spectrum of industry waned only as the tide of westward expansion moved to cities like Chicago and St. Louis.

The Cincinnati area has always enjoyed a great diversity in its manufacturing. It has never been a one company or one industry town. In 1972, for instance, the area had considerably more than its share of food processing, pulp and papermaking, printing, chemicals, fabricated metals, machinery, transportation equipment, and miscellaneous manufacturing. Moreover, this mix of key industries is pretty much what one would have expected considering Cincinnati's early history.

Cincinnati's eminent position in metal-working, for example, has its roots in the early decades of the 19th century when steamboat travel along the Ohio River demanded not only boat-building but steam engine manufacture and repair. These tasks required foundries, machine shops, and machine tool shops. As a result, Cincinnati has long dominated the machine tool industry, not only with Cincinnati Milacron but also with Le Blond, G. H. Gray, Cincinnati, Inc., Lodge and Shipley, and others. Other metalworking companies, especially in transportation equipment, are located within the area, including General Electric (jet engines), Ford Motor (automotive transmissions), General Motors (auto assembly), Interlake (steel), William Powell Co. (valves), Lunkenheimer (valves), Siemens-Allis (electric motors), and others.

While Cincinnati's location was first chosen because it was a relatively flat basin along the river, suitable for the docking of flatboats and opposite a river highway into already populated Kentucky (the Licking River), Cincinnati was bounded by some fertile river valleys and substantial forests. The valleys, especially those to the west of the town, produced grain which made Cincinnati both a milling town and a brewing and distilling center. The latter industries persist to this day. More important agriculturally, the forests were ideal for raising hogs. By the 1840s, Cincinnati was known as "Porkopolis" because of its extensive meat packing industry, which persists to this day. With meat-packing came the derivative industries of soap and candle manufacture. In 1837 William Procter and James Gamble formed a company that still bears their names. At the time they were just one of many such companies however.

The forests surrounding Cincinnati supplied a lumber and then a paper-making industry. Further, with the growth and importance of Cincinnati—then the "Queen City of the West"—printing, especially of school books, became important. The city's size and location also fostered an apparel industry which was among the largest in the country for years. The shoe industry became important in the late 19th century.

Given this history, it is not surprising to discover which industries are the dominant ones in Cincinnati today. With these insights as background, let us examine Cincinnati's recent patterns of industrial location.

Cincinnati's recent pattern of location—size by category

The first fact of industry location around any metropolitan area is that relatively few plants account for the great bulk of employment. The 25 largest plants in the Cincinnati area account for more than 54,000 jobs, fully 36% of the area's manufacturing employment. The 50 largest plants, only 2.4% of the total number, account for more than 70,250 jobs or 46.3% of the total. Consistent with this size distribution of plants are the branch or subsidiary status facilities, those generally associated with the nation's leading industrial concerns; these are typically much larger than those of single plant companies, as Table 4-30 documents. While branch plants account for only 31.3% of 1975 plant totals, they account for 79.9% of all manufacturing employment in that year. Those multiplant company establishments that remained at the same location during this period tend to be older and presumably more settled than the twice as numerous single plant companies.

Table 4-30 also provides information on the extent of plants and employment involved in location decisions. Consider plant relocations first. During the 1971–1975 time period, between 10% and 11% of all Cincinnati-based plants relocated within the metropolitan area, although these plants involved only a little more than 3% of all industrial employment. One finds that 28.7% of the relocating plants are branch plants that account for about 50% of relocating employment. The relative incidence of plant relocation is about the same for single plant companies and branches, slightly less than 11% and 10% respectively, but the fraction of employment involved by category differs sharply. Whereas 6%–8% of single-plant employment involved within-area relocation, less than 2% of the branch plant employment relocated. Thus, while mover plants of both kinds are smaller than average for their catagories, branch plant movers are very much smaller than the average size branch plant.

Similar dramatic differences are evident for plant openings and closings. Such changes occur to roughly 17% of all plants, although they only employ between 2.4% (openings) and 6.0% (closings) of all manufacturing employment. Here, as with the plant relocations, branch plants account for proportionately more employment than their numbers would indicate; 17% of the closings and 23% of the openings involved branch plants, but the respective employment percentages were much higher, 50% and 56%. The single plant company is much more likely to open or close a plant, about 20% do so, as compared with branch plants, where only between 9.5% (closings) and 12.3% (openings) do so. The employment share for the single plant company either opening or closing is also greater. About 15% of all single plant company employees were put out of work by plant closings during 1971–1975 and only slightly more than 5% were made up by plant openings. For branch plants, these relative incidence figures were much less; 3.7% of branch employment was involved in closings and 1.7% was involved with branch plant openings.

Table 4-30

Plants and Employment by Single Plant-Multiplant Status
Cincinnati Metropolitan Area

Panel A. 1971 Figures

Status	Items	Stay-Put Plants	Local Mover Plants	Plant Clos- ings	Total
Single Plant Companies	Plants	979	154	288	1,421
	Average Employment	25	12	16	
	Total Employment	24,475	1848	4608	30,931
	Average Date of Founding			1956.9	
	Median Date of Founding			1961.5	
Headquarters, Subsidiary or Branch Plants	Plants	499	62	59	620
	Average Employment	237	32	78	
	Total Employment	118,263	1984	4602	124,849
	Average Date of Founding			1958.8	
	Median Date of Founding			1962	

Panel B. 1975 Figures

Status	Items	Stay-Put Plants	Local Mover Plants	Plant Open- ings	Total
Single Plant Companies	Plants	979	154	272	1,405
	Average Employment	27	16	6	
	Total Employment	26,433	2464	1632	30,529
	Average Date of Founding	1954.2	1961.0	1971.2	
	Median Date of Founding	1958	1965	1972	
Headquarters, Subsidiary or Branch Plants	Plants	499	62	79	640
	Average Employment	234	36	26	
	Total Employment	116,766	2232	2054	121,052
	Average Date of Founding	1949.4	1959.8	1971.1	
	Median Date of Founding	1957	1966.5	1972	

Cincinnati's recent pattern of location—
differences by industry

A decomposition of Cincinnati data by major industry group is displayed in Tables 4-31 and 4-32. Certain categories of industry have more economic importance to the area than others—the most important being transportation equipment, machinery, food processing, and fabricated metals.

Certain industries also play a greater role in shifting the geographic pattern of the metropolitan area over time as Table 4-32 documents. For example, lumber, furniture, rubber/plastics, and miscellaneous manufacturing, such as jewelry, toys, sporting goods, are industries that have high rates of opening, closing, and within-area movement.[4] That this tumult exists is not so surprising, however, because these industries are characterized by free and vigorous competition and relatively low levels of fixed investment. Table 4-33 provides some helpful cross-industry comparisons of capital-labor and concentration ratios. (The concentration ratio measures the market share held by the largest four companies in the industry.) The data confirm that the four industries experiencing considerable location tumult are, in fact, among those with low capital-labor and low concentration ratios.

By the same token, one would expect that industries with more sedate patterns of competition and high levels of fixed investment would generate fewer plant openings, closings, or within-area relocations. Indeed, this is the case. Food, paper, petroleum, and transportation equipment generate lower than average numbers of plant and employment location changes, and are all industries with high capital-labor and concentration ratios as Table 4-33 documents.

These four industries are not the only ones with both high capital-labor and high concentration ratios. Four others, textiles, chemicals, primary metals, and electrical equipment, have opening and/or closing rates that are higher, rather than lower, than average. One plausible characteristic which may explain this reversal is technological change. The first group of four "low tumult" industries (food, paper, petroleum, and transportation equipment) are, generally speaking, slow to innovate with either new products or new production processes. However, the second group (textiles, chemicals, primary metals, and electrical equipment) are among the most innovative and technologically sensitive industries in the nation. Technological change, coupled with competitive vigor and levels of investment, seems to be a key factor in explaining industry patterns of location tumult.

[4]To be precise, the reference should be to plant "births" and "deaths" rather than "openings" and "closings" since it was not known from the Cincinnati data whether the new plant had relocated into the area from elsewhere or whether the plant closing represented a relocation out of the area. However, as other data show, such long-distance moves are rare.

Table 4-31

The Composition of Employment by Major Industry Group, Cincinnati Metropolitan Area

Industry	Stay-Put Plants			Plant Openings and Closings				Plant Movement Within the Area			
	1975 Number*	1971 Employment	1975 Employment	Number of Births	1975 Birth Employment	Number of Deaths	1971 Death Employment	Number of Moves To	Employment Moves To	Number of Moves From	Employment Moves From
20 Food	128 (127)	15,240	16,000	10	50	23	368	6	90	6	144
21 Tobacco	1	50	3	0	0	1	10	0	0	0	0
22 Textiles	12	1,452	1,548	2	160	6	132	1	20	1	25
23 Apparel	49	4,508	4,263	7	21	8	184	6	198	6	186
24 Lumber	50 (47)	658	1,100	21	105	25	375	10	70	10	60
25 Furniture	47 (50)	2,050	1,880	12	216	15	135	9	108	9	117
26 Paper	62	6,448	6,386	12	192	10	350	4	100	4	92
27 Printing	219	12,264	12,702	62	310	48	432	50	900	50	650
28 Chemicals	89	9,968	10,591	15	405	22	440	11	231	10	140
29 Petroleum	16	736	736	3	12	3	12	3	15	3	24
30 Rubber, Plastics	34	3,196	3,434	19	247	21	315	7	238	8	144
31 Leather	11	2,629	1,947	0	0	1	3	1	1	1	1
32 Stone, Clay, Glass	63	2,772	2,835	26	338	28	504	10	90	10	100
33 Primary Metals	39 (41)	4,059	3,939	5	120	8	328	1	7	1	12
34 Fabricated Metals	185 (186)	15,066	14,985	27	261	31	1,274	28	980	27	378
35 Machinery	255	20,655	21,420	73	657	48	672	35	563	35	1,067
36 Electrical Equipment	55 (57)	8,949	9,405	17	221	14	1,582	6	102	7	126
37 Transportation Equipment	27	27,864	23,598	3	18	6	150	3	285	3	168
38 Instruments	40 (37)	1,887	2,120	7	210	6	330	11	517	10	210
39 Miscellaneous	94	3,290	3,666	30	150	22	1,012	14	224	15	210
Total	1,476	143,741	142,558	351	3,693	346	8,608	216	4,739	216	3,854

*Numbers in parentheses indicate plant counts according to the 1971 data. Differences reflect changes in SIC classification.

Table 4-32

Incidence of Openings, Closings, and Within Area Relocations
By Major Industry Group, 1971-75
Cincinnati Metropolitan Area
(Items as Percent of Industry's Total Plants and Employment at That Time)

	Openings		Closings		Relocations	
					1975	
	Number	1975	Number	1971	Number	1975
	of	Employ-	of	Employ-	of	Employ-
Major Industry	Plants	ment	Plants	ment	Plants	ment
20 Food	6.9%	0.3%	14.7%	2.3%	4.2%	0.6%
22 Textiles	13.3	9.3	31.6	8.2	6.7	1.2
23 Apparel	11.3	0.5	12.5	3.8	9.7	4.4
24 Lumber	25.9	8.1	30.1	34.3	12.3	5.4
25 Furniture	17.6	9.6	20.3	5.9	13.2	4.8
26 Paper	15.0	2.9	12.8	5.1	5.0	1.5
27 Printing	18.6	2.2	15.1	3.2	15.0	6.5
28 Chemicals	12.8	3.6	17.9	4.2	9.4	2.0
29 Petroleum	13.6	1.6	13.6	1.6	13.6	1.9
30 Rubber, Plastics	31.1	6.3	32.3	8.6	11.5	6.1
31 Leather	0	0	7.7	0.1	8.3	0.1
32 Stone, Clay, Glass	26.0	10.3	27.5	14.9	10.0	2.8
33 Primary Metals	11.1	3.0	16.0	7.5	2.2	0.2
34 Fabricated Metals	11.1	1.5	12.7	7.6	11.5	6.0
35 Machinery	19.9	2.9	14.3	3.3	9.5	2.4
36 Electrical Equip.	21.3	2.3	16.5	14.9	7.5	1.0
37 Transport Equip.	9.1	0.1	16.7	0.6	9.1	1.2
38 Instruments	12.1	7.4	11.3	13.6	19.0	18.2
39 Miscellaneous	21.6	3.7	16.7	22.4	10.1	5.6
Overall Industry	17.3	2.4	17.0	5.6	10.7	3.1

There are some puzzles, however. Lumber, furniture, rubber/plastics, and miscellaneous manufacturing are not the only industries with low capital-labor and low concentration ratios; apparel, leather, printing, and fabricated metals share these characteristics. Yet, both apparel and leather plant sites are very stable, while printing and fabricated metals facilities evidence an above-average frequency of relocation, only. The slow growth in the markets for apparel and leather, the substantial foreign competition, and the snail's pace of technological advance in apparel and leather may explain the below-average location churning in these two industries, but the below-average entry and exit in printing and fabricated metals is more puzzling.

Cincinnati's recent pattern of location—
differences by geography

To aid in the analysis of where location changes have occurred, the Cincinnati metropolitan area has been divided into zones, each a collection of zip codes. These zones were chosen to separate the metropolitan area, more or less, into three large "rings" surrounding the Central Business

Table 4-33

Capital-Labor and Concentration Ratios for Major Industry Groups

Major Industry	National Capital-Labor Ratio[1]	(Rank)	Cincinnati-Specific Concentration Ratio[2]	(Rank)
20 Food	5.95%	(4)	34.4	(6)
21 Tobacco	30.23	(2)	NA	-
22 Textiles	3.74	(10)	39.8	(4)
23 Apparel	1.75	(19)	24.2	(11)
24 Lumber	3.36	(12)	17.9	(15)
25 Furniture	1.45	(20)	17.0	(16)
26 Paper	4.23	(7)	29.4	(7)
27 Printing	2.26	(16)	14.7	(18)
28 Chemicals	7.24	(3)	35.0	(5)
29 Petroleum	73.03	(1)	28.2	(8)
30 Rubber, Plastics	2.81	(15)	6.0	(19)
31 Leather	2.03	(18)	27.4	(10)
32 Stone, Clay, Glass	3.23	(13)	24.1	(12)
33 Primary Metals	4.95	(5)	27.5	(9)
34 Fabricated Metals	2.09	(17)	16.5	(17)
35 Machinery	3.93	(9)	23.7	(13)
36 Electrical Equipment	4.21	(8)	39.8	(3)
37 Transportation Equipment	4.90	(6)	53.6	(1)
38 Instruments	3.47	(11)	45.8	(2)
39 Miscellaneous	3.18	(14)	18.8	(14)

[1]Capital-labor ratios constructed as 1973 Total Assets figure from IRS, Statistics of Income divided by 1972 Payroll figure for all employees from the Census of Manufactures.
[2]Concentration-ratio constructed as a weighted average of 1972 Census of Manufactures 4-digit SIC concentration ratios, weighted by the percentages of firms in Cincinnati classified in the particular 4-digit SIC codes.

District (CBD). The first of these, the core, is composed of those zones within the outer boundaries of the cities of Cincinnati, Covington, and Newport. About these central cities lies an "inner ring" of suburbs. Filling out the boundaries of the metropolitan area is an "Outer Ring." All the zones are named to indicate the ring to which they belong.

The numbers of plants and the total employment by zone are summarized in Table 4-34. In broad fashion this table documents the heavy concentration of industry within the core areas of the metropolitan area, especially within the long-established mid-Mill Creek Valley. The north and northeast inner ring suburbs, which are extensions of Mill Creek Valley, also host large quantities of industrial activity.

Rather more complete pictures of the composition of employment and employment change by zone are found in Tables 4-35 and 4-36. The first of these tables clearly suggests a good deal of "churning" of plants and employment within the metropolitan area. Even the zones that attract considerable new development surely cannot be characterized as hosting only new plant openings or relocations from other zones in the area; plant closings and movers out are evident as well. Even zones like the Central Business District, which is a net loser of employment, show a sizable number of plant openings and relocations settling within their boundaries.

Table 4-34

Plant Numbers and Employment Summaries by Zone
Cincinnati Metropolitan Area

	1971		1975	
Zone	Number of Plants	Employ- ment	Number of Plants	Employ- ment
1. Central Business District	252	9,448	208	7,836
2. Inner Core North of CBD	137	6,666	116	6,254
3. City Mid-Millcreek Core	140	12,098	131	12,447
4. Non-Cincinnati: Mid-Millcreek Core	90	15,377	89	14,982
5. West Core	332	18,285	316	16,067
6. East Core	151	20,902	151	19,080
7. West Inner Ring	137	3,060	149	2,999
8. North Inner Ring	178	28,464	200	26,635
9. Northeast Inner Ring	173	17,167	183	18,397
10. East Inner Ring	72	3,953	69	4,053
11. West County Outer Ring	41	1,571	49	3,108
12. West Indiana Ring	22	3,887	26	3,566
13. E. Outer Ring (Clermont & Warren)	132	4,702	155	5,513
14. Covington	54	2,036	52	1,743
15. Newport	30	2,878	30	2,468
16. West Inner Kentucky Ring	39	1,049	44	1,560
17. East Inner Kentucky Ring	22	357	23	531
18. West Outer Kentucky Ring	26	2,820	44	3,907
19. South Outer Kentucky Ring	4	55	4	18
20. East Outer Kentucky Ring	8	61	6	50

The second of this pair of tables, Table 4-36, breaks down the metropolitan area's loss of 3,629 manufacturing jobs during 1971–1975 into (1) those explained by changes in employment at plants that have stayed put, (2) those explained by an excess of plant closings over plant openings, and (3) those explained by plant relocations within the area. For the entire Cincinnati area, stay-put plant employment registered a tiny gain of 490 jobs. Within-area mover plants increased their employment by 883. What accounted for the area's overall job loss is the greater number of jobs associated with plant closings as compared to plant openings.

The impact of employment changes attributable to these three effects varies enormously within individual zones. Some zones, notably those on the fringes of the area, have gained employment in all three ways. Other areas, notably the innermost portions of the area, have lost employment in all three ways. In general, all but four areas have lost employment due to closures exceeding openings, and most of the central and core areas have lost employment due to net plant relocations to the inner and outer suburban rings. The change attributable to fluctuations in stay-put plant employment is rather more erratic.

It is frequently lamented that the central portions of cities have declined in economic vigor because they have been abandoned by firms fleeing to the suburbs. While Tables 4-35 and 4-36 support the fact that firms have been decentralizing, only one-quarter of the job loss in Cincinnati's CBD can be assigned to "firms fleeing to the suburbs." More than half of the employment loss in the CBD occurred in plants that remained

Table 4-35

The Composition of Employment by Zone, Cincinnati Metropolitan Area

Zone	Stay-Put Plants 1975 Number	1971 Employment	1975 Employment	Plant Openings and Closings Number Opened	1975 Opening Employment	Number Closed	1971 Closing Employment	Plant Movement Within the Area Moves to Zone	1975 Employment to Zone	Moves from Zone	1971 Employment From Zone
1. Central Business District	172	8,251	7,386	16	128	41	467	20	322	39	730
2. Inner Core North of CBD	92	5,869	6,051	15	84	26	437	9	119	19	360
3. City Mid-Millcreek Core	105	11,251	12,218	16	150	20	376	9	79	14	471
4. Non-Cincinnati: Mid-Millcreek Core	71	15,043	14,836	7	54	13	295	11	92	6	39
5. West Core	258	15,185	15,496	27	223	44	1,032	31	348	30	1,068
6. East Core	111	18,098	18,301	25	400	22	2,559	15	379	18	245
7. West Inner Ring	85	2,377	2,644	50	206	31	559	14	149	21	124
8. North Inner Ring	128	27,126	24,957	41	340	29	1,059	31	1,338	21	279
9. Northeast Inner Ring	125	16,068	16,907	30	572	32	907	28	918	16	192
10. East Inner Ring	50	3,833	3,702	12	60	14	85	6	291	7	35
11. West County Outer Ring	35	1,506	2,964	8	85	5	55	6	59	1	10
12. West Indiana Ring	16	3,838	3,495	7	31	4	40	3	40	2	9
13. East Outer Ring (Clermont & Warren)	88	4,160	4,480	56	887	34	442	10	146	9	100
14. Covington	38	1,737	1,660	8	26	10	154	6	57	6	145
15. Newport	21	2,819	2,410	5	12	5	32	4	46	4	27
16. West Inner Kentucky Ring	32	1,009	1,320	8	176	6	34	4	64	1	6
17. East Inner Kentucky Ring	17	296	452	1	1	5	61	5	78	0	0
18. West Outer Kentucky Ring	24	2,780	3,452	15	243	1	35	5	212	1	5
19. South Outer Kentucky Ring	2	4	9	2	9	1	50	0	0	1	1
20. East Outer Kentucky Ring	4	47	47	2	3	3	13	0	0	1	1
Totals	1,474	142,297	142,787	351	3,690	346	8,692	217	4,737	217	3,847

Table 4-36

Employment Change Composition By Zone

Zone	1971-1975 Employment Change	Employment Change Attributable To:		
		Stay-Put Plants	Opened-Closed	1971-1975 Within Area Movers
1. Central Business District	-1612	-865	-339	-408
2. Inner Core North of CBD	-412	+182	-353	-241
3. City Mid-Millcreek Core	+349	+967	-226	-392
4. Non-Cincinnati: Mid-Millcreek Core	-395	-207	-241	+53
5. West Core	-2218	-689	-809	-720
6. East Core	-1822	+203	-2159	+134
7. West Inner Ring	-61	+267	-353	+25
8. North Inner Ring	-1829	-2169	-719	+1059
9. Northeast Inner Ring	+1230	+839	-335	+726
10. East Inner Ring	+100	-131	-25	+256
11. West County Outer Ring	+1537	+1458	+30	+49
12. West Indiana Ring	-321	-343	-9	+31
13. East Outer Ring (Clermont & Warren)	+811	+320	+445	+46
14. Covington	-293	-77	-128	-88
15. Newport	-410	-409	-20	+19
16. West Inner Kentucky Ring	+511	+311	+142	+58
17. East Inner Kentucky Ring	+174	+156	-60	+78
18. West Outer Kentucky Ring	+1087	+672	+208	+207
19. South Outer Kentucky Ring	-37	+5	-41	-1
20. East Outer Kentucky Ring	-11	0	-10	-1
Total Metropolitan Area	-3629	+490	-5002	+883

there; the remainder, slightly less than one-quarter, came as a result of plant deaths exceeding births. In Covington, in the central core portion of the Kentucky side of the Ohio river, "fleeing" firms accounted for 30% of its net job loss.

For the City of Cincinnati, roughly defined for our purposes by zones 1–3, 5, and 6, industrial flight accounted for 28.5% of the city's net job loss of 5,715 between 1971 and 1975. The change in employment at stay-put plants accounted for a scant 3.5% drop in net job loss, with the remaining 68% explained by plant deaths exceeding plant births.

Table 4-35's data also speaks to the incidence of plant openings, closings, and relocations by zone. City zones, for example, are more likely to display a higher than average incidence of relocations originating there, while suburban zones are more apt to show an above average incidence of relocations destined there. This is consistent, of course, with the observed suburbanization of manufacturing.

The incidence of plant closings by zone is less variable, more likely a random occurrence. No trends are evident. The incidence of plant openings, however, appears to be not so random geographically. The incidence of openings is below average in all CBD and core zones, including Covington and Newport. Above-average values are found in many of the suburbs, particularly those in more outlying areas.

These facts support the decentralization of employment as a more complex phenomenon than simply the relocation of central city firms to the suburbs. While it is true that employment does decentralize for that reason, two other effects need to be considered. For stay-put plants, employment growth appears more likely in suburban than in central city sites. This is a modest effect and is probably keyed to space availability. A much stronger effect centers on plant openings and closings. Since closures exceed openings dramatically in central locations, one suspects that the decentralization of employment may owe more to the failure of central cities to spawn new manufacturers than their failure to hold on to plants already located there. Put another way, it may be that the relocation of growing plants to the suburbs has always occurred but that the spawning of new industry in the city had previously reduced the net decentralization of industry to a trickle. The substantial industrial decentralization may be caused more by a falling off in the capacity of the city to spawn new plants rather than a sharp increase in the incidence of plant relocations to the suburbs. One factor may be a supply effect; suburbs now provide vacant space as well as a substantial amount of low-cost industrial space put up on speculation. With the population decentralized already, and many business services available in the suburbs, new companies need not search for downtown locations as they were once obliged to do. Because this study deals strictly with the 1970s, it cannot support this hypothesis with data, but the composition of change observed for Cincinnati in the 1970s suggests it.

General trends in industrial relocation around Cincinnati, 1971–1975

The data available from Cincinnati permit some broad-brush characterizations of mover plants, particularly as compared to plants which have remained at the same location. According to these data, during 1971–1975 slightly less than 11% of the total number of plants then located in the metropolitan area relocated elsewhere in the area.

Some general comparisons of local mover and stationary plants, found in Table 4-30, have already been discussed. As can be seen there, the local mover plant is much smaller than the stationary plant, and their companies are quite a bit younger as well. These facts and the observation that mover plants are less likely to lose employment over time (from data not shown here), suggest a picture of the mover plant as a young, growing concern. As other evidence attests, this characterization is not far off the mark.

For 216 mover plants identified within the Cincinnati area, knowledge of each plant's zone of origin, zone of destination, and employment has permitted the construction of two matrices which describe the number of plants and the employment that have moved from one zone to another during the period 1971–1975. These matrices are reproduced as Tables 4-37 and 4-38. The main diagonal elements of each matrix refer to plants that have relocated to a different site within the same zone. For most zones, the same-zone movers represent the largest single bloc of either origins or destinations. Many other moves are made to adjacent or nearby zones.

Because of the ordering of the zones, entries lying above the main diagonal generally reflect decentralization while entries lying below the diagonal generally reflect centralization. Note that more entries fall above the diagonal, signifying the predominance of the decentralization trend in intrametropolitan industry location.

A close examination of the evidence underscores the prevalence of short moves and some of the character of longer moves. More than 40% of local moves—23% of all moving employment—account for moves within the same zone. Another 30% of moves—almost 48% of the moving employment—represent moves to an adjacent zone. The remainder, about 30% of the moves and 29% of the employment is accounted for by moves to more distant zones. Of the destinations to more distant zones almost half are moves from the two most central zones in the area. These moves also represent more than two-thirds of the longer distance moving employment.

More information about the general character of intrametropolitan moves can be gleaned from the 219 moves for which sufficient data exist.

For example, net decentralization is true only for 23% of total moves made. Nevertheless, 23% can be a big number, depending on one's outlook. For example, the City of Cincinnati lost 51 plants to the suburbs but gained 16 for a net loss of 35 plants—3.6% of Cincinnati's 1972 Census total of 960 plants. These 35 plants that were lost employed 1,627 people at 1971 employment levels—2.4% of Cincinnati's 1972 Census total of 68,200 workers. This is a net loss of 0.9% of the city's plants per year and a net loss of 0.6% of the city's manufacturing jobs per year. This is a steady and very definite loss of jobs for the city due solely to the suburbanization of existing companies, but as mentioned before, it is not the main source of job loss for the City of Cincinnati.

It is also true that the longer the move, the higher the plant's average employment and its average gain in employment during the period 1971–1975. These various facts and trends are not very startling if one accepts the view that plants seeking new locations for reasons such as increased space requirements, worn-out plant or equipment, decreased space requirements, expired leases, or similar reasons first seek locations close to their existing plants. Close by, a mover plant risks less, is more certain of keeping its labor force intact, and is likely to make the move quickly and efficiently. It is more probable, however, that suitable new sites will be found for small concerns that have few or no demands for specialized production space but not for larger concerns. In fact, the larger the plant the more apt it will need specialized and difficult to locate space. It is no

Table 4-37

Matrix of Relocations Within the Cincinnati Metropolitan Area
Employment Moving From Zone to Zone, Using 1975 Employment Figures

Zone of Destination (columns correspond to left-hand margin)

Zone or Origin	1	2	3	4	5	6	7	8	9	10	11	12	13	14	15	16	17	18	19	20	Totals
1. Central Business District	288	24	42		27	246	84	14	3		6		7	12		30	10	110			903
2. Inner Core North of CBD	16	45	1		66	5		72	297	200											702
3. City Mid-Millcreek Core		15	25	20	48		2	272	70												452
4. Non-Cincinnati: Mid-Millcreek Core			4	9																	25
5. West Core	5			25	119	12	4	760	42				42								1074
6. East Core	5			6	26	13		4	268	60			1		2	7	60				440
7. West Inner Ring	3	18	2	14	64	70	54	8													182
8. North Inner Ring		12	3	16	1		3	132	80		39	2						100			361
9. Northeast Inner Ring					3	25		58	144		11		9								239
10. East Inner Ring				1		6		4		27			4								42
11. West County Outer Ring											2										2
12. West Indiana Ring												38									38
13. East Outer Ring (Clermont & Warren)								10	18	6			84	11							129
14. Covington														27	18	20	7				72
15. Newport															26	6	2				34
16. West Inner Kentucky Ring														4							4
17. East Inner Kentucky Ring																					0
18. West Outer Kentucky Ring																		2			2
19. South Outer Kentucky Ring																		1			1
20. East Outer Kentucky Ring		7																			7
Totals	317	121	77	91	354	377	147	1334	922	293	58	40	147	54	46	63	79	213			4721

Table 4-38

Matrix of Relocations Within the Cincinnati Metropolitan Area
Number of Plants Moving from Zone to Zone

Zone of Destination
(columns correspond to left-hand margin)

Zone of Origin	1	2	3	4	5	6	7	8	9	10	11	12	13	14	15	16	17	18	19	20	Totals
1. Central Business District	16	1	3		3	2	4	1	1		1		1	1		1	2	2			39
2. Inner Core North of CBD	1	3	1	2	6			3	3												19
3. City Mid-Millcreek Core		1	2	2	2		1	4	2												14
4. Non-Cincinnati: Mid-Millcreek Core			1	3	1			1													6
5. West Core	1			1	12	1	2	7	2				2		1	1					30
6. East Core				1	3	7		1	4				1		1						18
7. West Inner Ring	1	3	1	1	2	3	5	1			3										20
8. North Inner Ring	1	1	1	1	1	1	1	11	1	1	1										21
9. Northeast Inner Ring								1	12			1	1					1			16
10. East Inner Ring					1	1		1		3			1								7
11. West County Outer Ring											1										1
12. West Indiana Ring												2									2
13. East Outer Ring (Clermont & Warren)									1	1			4	1		1	1				9
14. Covington									2	1				3							6
15. Newport														1	2	1					4
16. West Inner Kentucky Ring																	1				1
17. East Inner Kentucky Ring																					0
18. West Outer Kentucky Ring																	1				1
19. South Outer Kentucky Ring																		1			1
20. East Outer Kentucky Ring																		1			1
Totals	20	9	9	11	31	15	13	31	28	6	6	3	10	6	4	4	5	5	0	0	216

229

wonder then that the largest plants and the ones changing most rapidly are most likely to locate at a considerable distance from their old sites and at new sites that represent decentralization.

Issues in Corporate Behavior Concerning Location

The plant census of major manufacturers has also lent itself to use in investigating several general questions about corporate actions with regard to location. Each of the following subsections treats a specific issue.

Capacity change around headquarters

Is a corporation more likely to open a new plant close to its headquarters? Is it less likely to close an old plant near its headquarters? Are communities or states with an abundance of headquarters operations doubly blessed in this sense, or not? The plant census data provides a means by which this notion can be tested.

From the company documents and discussions, the headquarters—corporate or divisional—to which each plant directly reports was ascertained. Codes were developed for each plant to indicate whether the plant was located in the same state or metropolitan area of both the corporate headquarters and any divisional headquarters. Also known was whether the plant was classed as a stay-put, an opening, or a closing, and whether it had expanded or contracted on-site. The major results are shown in Table 4-39.

In evaluating these results we can, as a basis for comparison, look to the frequency with which stay-put plants and their employment fall within the same state or metropolitan area as a company's various headquarters operations. For example, are plant openings relatively more numerous around headquarters locations than company plants already in place? Or are they less numerous? The hypotheses in question are tested by making this comparison. It is clear from the results that more plants and employment of all types are found around divisional as opposed to corporate headquarters. More than that, the plants located near headquarters are larger, on balance, than plants located at a distance. This is not surprising, of course, in that many large plants double as division headquarters anyway.

Table 4-39's findings are intriguing in that neither plant openings nor closings are as likely to be found near a headquarters operation as are the existing set of stay-put plants. Moreover, plant openings are no more probable near headquarters than are plant closings; their values are very close together, and in fact are not significantly different statistically. In fact, judging from the employment figures, plant closings of substantial size are

Table 4-39

Plant Locations vis-à-vis Headquarters Locations: Percent Locating in Same Area as Headquarters

Location of Plant	Category of Plant					
	All Stay-Put Plants	On-Site Expansions	On-Site Contractions	Plant Openings	Plant Closings	Relocations
Same State as Corporate Headquarters						
Plants	15.4	17.1	18.7	12.0	12.0	13.8
Employment	27.3	28.9	26.2	15.0	23.6	19.2
Same Metropolitan Area as Corporate Headquarters						
Plants	10.2	12.0	14.2	8.4	9.6	11.6
Employment	21.8	24.6	20.1	10.2	22.3	15.5
Same State as Division Headquarters to Which It Reports						
Plants	27.6	30.3	32.4	19.8	19.3	28.0
Employment	40.5	43.5	36.4	23.4	32.6	40.4
Same Metropolitan Area as Division Headquarters to Which It Reports						
Plants	21.5	24.2	28.9	15.3	15.2	25.3
Employment	34.8	38.3	30.2	18.1	26.7	38.4

more likely near headquarters locations than are plant openings. This result runs counter to the conventional intuition on the matter which would have relatively more openings near headquarters. The trend is not strong, but it does appear that, relative to plants already in place, both openings and closings are more likely to occur at a distance from headquarters.

What is relatively more likely to occur near a corporate or division headquarters is the physical, "bricks and mortar" expansion or contraction of stay-put plants. More on-site expansions and more, especially smaller, on-site contractions occur in the vicinity of headquarters locations than would be expected merely from the distribution of stay-put plants and employment.

While plant openings are less likely than expected to be in the same area or state, plant relocations are as likely, if not more so, to locate near a headquarters operation, particularly a divisional headquarters. In part, this is due to the independent character of relocations, many of which, although smaller than many plants, are reasonably autonomous, frequently being their own division headquarters.

In sum, these data do not support the hypothesis that a corporation is more likely to increase capacity close to a headquarters operation and, similarly, less likely to decrease capacity near a headquarters. While there is reason to believe that on-site expansions are more likely to be close to a headquarters than could be expected, it appears that plant openings are, in fact, less likely to locate near headquarters. Although plant closings are relatively more probable at a distance from a headquarters operation, on-site contractions are more probable in the vicinity of a headquarters. Instead of supporting the hypothesis that a corporation cares better for the communities around its headquarters, the data suggest that major changes (openings and closings) occur, more often than anticipated, at a distance from headquarters and that more minor changes (on-site expansion or contraction) are accomplished nearby.

The capacity change behavior of conglomerates

Conglomerates are criticized for many things. Among them is the assertion that conglomerates are more ruthless in closing plants than are companies which are more single-product in orientation; conglomerates allegedly do not care as much for communities as do other companies. How true is this? The plant census data provide us with the opportunity to test this assertion, since conglomerate companies can be isolated from the others. Table 4-40 lists 30 companies which most observers would classify as conglomerates since they each operate several very diverse product divisions. These 30 companies are contrasted against the remaining 380 in the plant census data base in Table 4-41. That table breaks out by class the plants and employment of both the conglomerate and non-conglomerate groups.

Table 4-40

Companies Considered Conglomerates
for Purpose of Analysis

American Standard	Northwest Industries
Bangor Punta	Norton Simon
Chromalloy	NVF
Consolidated Foods	Olin
Dart Industries	Pepsico
Esmark	Phillip Morris
General Mills	Rockwell International
Greyhound	SCM
Gulf and Western	Talley Industries
Indian Head	Teledyne
ITT	Tenneco
Walter Kidde	Textron
Litton	TRW
LTV	United Technologies
Martin-Marietta	Whittaker

What is most striking about Table 4-41's results is that conglomerates are simply more active than other companies in changing their capacity. Most salient, naturally, is the high level of acquisitions by conglomerates. Not only are plant acquisitions relatively more numerous, but they involve larger plants (more established businesses?). Divestitures are less numerous, but conglomerates divest companies at about twice the rate of non-conglomerates.

As for the issue of plant closings, it is true that conglomerates are involved in relatively more plant closings than other companies, although these tend to be smaller in size. The difference is not all that large, however, and is balanced somewhat by the observation that the new plant openings of conglomerates also involve a larger fraction of their base employment than is true of non-conglomerates. Conglomerates are also involved in a greater relative share of relocations and of plants opened or acquired in the 1970s and then closed or divested later in the decade.

In sum, it seems reasonable to observe that conglomerates are simply more active in their capacity decisions and that this activity implies a relatively higher rate of plant closings. However, conglomerates do not appear to be especially "ruthless" in their actions, taking into account their high level of activity in all phases of capacity change.

Table 4-41

The Capacity Change Behavior of Conglomerates

Class of Plant	Conglomerates				Non-Conglomerates			
	Plants		Employment		Plants		Employment	
	Number	As Percent of Stay-Puts	Number	As Percent of Stay-Puts	Number	As Percent of Stay-Puts	Number	As Percent of Stay-Puts
Stay-Put	1399	100%	658,398	100%	8100	100%	5,460,512	100%
Opening	187	13%	51,005	8%	1424	18%	336,542	6%
Closing	195	14%	33,274	5%	826	10%	169,889	3%
Acquisition	651	47%	179,144	27%	2708	33%	570,062	10%
Divestiture	247	18%	40,171	6%	859	11%	180,125	3%
Relocation	87	6%	18,932	3%	363	4%	77,951	1%
Open/Close	157	11%	23,392	4%	545	7%	55,828	1%
Close/Open	2	1%	315	1%	9	1%	1,179	1%

5

Plant Closings: the
toughest decisions

During the course of interviewing companies about their location decision-making, the subject of plant closings as well as openings was broached.
Since most companies interviewed were growing, plant closings were discussed much less frequently than openings. Only 13 of 60 company interviews specifically addressed plant closings. Although this is a relatively
small sample, some suggestive comments can be made that may be representative of manufacturers more generally.

Plant Closings: Interview Evidence

The clearest implication from the interview responses is that a plant closing
is approached strictly as an economic decision. In most cases, the plant that
is closed is one that has already lost money by the company's accounting
practices. That it was even considered for closing is due in every case to
recognized poor performance over a number of years. The reasons for
poor performance vary but can be grouped into two major categories:

    (1) Unfavorable industry economics

- Sales drop due to national recession
- Sales drop due to intense foreign competition (for example, shoe and
  apparel industries)
- Product's sales never got off the ground
- Product has become obsolete (for example, RCA's vacuum tube
  business)

- Consumer tastes changed (for example, less Pet Evaporated milk purchased today versus years ago)
- Production process has become obsolete (for example, Diamond Shamrock's Solvay process soda ash plant in Painesville, Ohio closing due to the discovery of lower cost natural soda ash (trona ore) in Wyoming)
- Level or lower sales coupled with technological advances and increases in the size of production equipment making plant consolidations attractive
- Declines over time in the quantity and quality of raw materials (for example, Del Monte's tomato packing in Indiana).

(2) Severe production problems due to poor layout and materials flow, cramped space, outmoded equipment, and aging plant (for example, Cities Service's inability to make unleaded gasoline at its Chicago refinery).

Of the plant closings discussed, roughly ¾ were caused by unfavorable industry economics and ¼ by severe production problems. None of the closings in this admittedly small sample of 13 companies were triggered by poor labor relations. In fact, one company (not of these 13) specifically mentioned that it viewed as its social responsibility to keep its plants operating and its concern that any closing of northern, unionized plants to transfer operations to new southern, non-union plants might trigger labor problems company-wide.

Many companies recognize that there are costs incurred as well as costs saved by closing a plant. Labor expenses persist in the form of retirement benefits to workers who choose to retire early and unemployment compensation to those laid off. Other costs of maintaining the property until it can be sold may persist as well.

With both costs and with social responsibility in mind, some companies have modified their decisions regarding plant closings from what might be termed a rigid financial accounting approach. The most common modification—one that is seen as the most equitable one amid a distasteful situation—is to close the least senior plant. The least senior plant usually employs workers who have been with the company the shortest period of time; it resides in a community that is considered best able to cope without the plant, much as it had before the plant opened. This strategy, for example, is followed by Texas Instruments, Incorporated and it guided their only plant closing in the United States, that in Ft. Walton Beach, Florida during the depths of the 1974–75 recession.

In most cases, closing a facility is a painful process: admitting that the company failed in the marketplace is tough, putting people out of work is even tougher. And, there are generally fond memories attached to the older facilities by senior managers who worked in those facilities earlier in their careers. It is understandable then that plant closings are supported by rigorous, objective financial data.

The Character of Plant Closings: Survey Results

That a plant closing decision is not made lightly and is as objective an economic decision as a corporation makes is supported by the findings on 175 plant closings in a host of companies surveyed. As Table 5-1 documents, about a quarter of these closings can be accounted for by business decisions to cease manufacturing the product(s) altogether. In a majority of closings, however, the company maintains the product but shuts down the particular plant and absorbs its operation into another existing facility. That this practice is common is reinforced by other data which indicates that 23% of the plants in the survey sample absorbed operations from other plants which were then closed or divested.

The specific reasons for plant closures are numerous, as is plain from Table 5-2. The economics of the industry, reflected in the figures on competitive pressure and product economics, are certainly major factors; observe that only 30% of the sample fails to list one of these. Even more impressive is the importance of plant-specific considerations in driving up costs (only 22% of the sample fails to list one of these reasons). The dominant influence on plant economics is neither labor, materials, nor transportation costs, but inefficient and outmoded production technology, exacerbated in many instances by poor factory layout and materials handling.

Table 5-1

The Disposition of the Plant's Former Operations

Disposition	Percentage Affected
The operations were absorbed by one or more then-existing company plants	61%
The company got out of the business	24%
The operations were relocated to a new plant	12%
The operations were subcontracted	2%
The operations were transferred out of the USA	0%
Government contract was completed	1%

Note: These figures are based on 175 completed surveys, each representing a closed facility.

Table 5-2

The Reasons Behind Plant Closings: Frequency of Mention

	Percentage Acknowledging
A. Competitive Pressure	
From foreign operations:	
• Price competition	10
• Competition on performance and features	5
From other American operations:	
• Price competition due to better production technology	25
• Price competition due to lower cost labor, etc.	17
• Competition on performance and features	16
B. Plant Economics	
• Inefficient/outdated production technology, layout, materials handling	46
• High labor rates	21
• Crippling union work rules	10
• Compliance with environmental, OSHA regulations too expensive	7
• Transportation costs made competition too expensive	13
• Raw materials shortage, price, transportation	5
• Space too small, economics of scale with consolidation	3
• Maintenance, energy costs	2
• High taxes, utility rates	1
• Inconsistent with corporate strategy	1
• Miscellaneous (poor neighborhood, high labor turnover, not near enough to other company plants, government contract completed, management change, product specification too variable)	< 1 each
C. Product Economics	
• Fall off in sales, lack of sales volume	27
• Product obsolete	2
• Sales too cyclical	5

NOTE: The figures are based on 175 completed surveys, each representing a closed facility.

A greater than average percentage of closures involved multistory plants, and more than half of these factories were closed partly because of inefficient production technology. Plants older than the median age of 13 are also likely to suffer from inefficient/outmoded production technology; 52% of the plants cited this as opposed to only 36% of those below the median.

The median age of plants closed is 13 years; 33% of these were operated only 6 years or less when they were closed. In contrast, the median age of plants enjoying on-site expansion is 20 years. Of course, many of the facilities closed were creaky rattletraps, but that stereotype does not prevail as often as commonly believed. That a third of those closed are recently-opened facilities highlights the dependence and vulnerability of young plants. When adversity strikes, these plants are often closed because they are not typically home to the support functions of the operation (for example, new product engineering, marketing, purchasing, industrial engineering). In many cases they "just make the product" and so, for managerial reasons, they are the first candidates for closing.

A minority of plant closings are attributable to labor situations that got out of hand. Whereas an above average fraction of the plant closings surveyed were unionized (66% vs. 52% of the stay-put plants surveyed and 20% of the newly opened plants), union-management relations were, generally, good. Twenty-nine percent of the plants characterized their unions as "constructive, responsible" while only 16% termed their unions "militant, uncompromising" or noted a history of work stoppages. And, as Table 5-2 shows, only 10% of the plant closings surveyed indicated that "crippling union work rules" contributed to the closure. Of course, high labor rates were a contributing factor in 21% of the surveyed plant closings, and of these 81% were union, a figure somewhat higher than the corresponding 66% figure for all closings. These data suggest that poor labor relations is a minor, yet observable, reason for plant closures. While a considerable number of new plants were located with union avoidance in mind, facilities are closed infrequently because of sour union relationships or excessive labor costs.

This evidence that plant-specific economics, rather than simple drops in sales volumes, has greater importance in the closing decision is supported by corporate headquarters survey data gleaned from companies operating in Cincinnati and New England. This information suggests that sales volume declines are a major reason for closing about a third of the plants surveyed, and phase-out of a product line is important in about a third of the cases also. However, the single most important consideration—that of plant inefficiency—is cited in half or more of the plant closings surveyed.

Appendix A:

comments on the study design

The study reported in these pages grew in scope over time, and is best viewed as three separable research projects which systematically built on one another. The issues addressed and many of the techniques of analysis employed were the same, but the focus of the data-gathering shifted with each one. Thus, the three research projects comprising this study highlight particular aspects of the manufacturing location decision, complementing one another in the process.

The first research effort was confined to the Cincinnati's metropolitan area during 1971 to 1975/76. Both large and small company decisions were investigated there. Research on the Cincinnati area was supplemented by the second research project, which followed shortly thereafter. This effort concentrated on plants in New England, during the same time frame, particularly new or relocated facilities. The third, far broader, research project focused on large manufacturing corporations, almost all of which were drawn from the Fortune 500 list. This effort examined plant location decisions in the United States from 1970–1979.

While these target populations differed, the issues addressed and the data sought from each were much the same. Interviews with companies in Cincinnati, in New England, and on Fortune's 500 list were conducted, examining the location decision process itself and what influences seemed to guide it. In the case of both Cincinnati and the large manufacturers, a plant "census" was accomplished, which breaks down the geographic shift of plants and employment into its components. And, in each of the three research efforts, detailed surveys of individual plant operations were completed.

Each of these sources of data, culled from the three target populations identified, merits more description.

Interviews

For each of the research projects, interviews with companies actively engaged in location decision-making were deemed essential. With a business decision of such complexity, infrequency, and individuality, only personal interviews could reveal the subtleties and nuances of the decision process. The results of the interviews were critical to the development of the plant survey forms, as well.

In Cincinnati, 18 companies were interviewed; in New England, 7 were interviewed; of the Fortune 500, 60 were interviewed. The companies visited were selected deliberately from widely divergent industries and organizational structures. Included were some strongly centralized companies, some highly diversified, and some usually labelled conglomerates. The 18 interviews in Cincinnati included smaller companies, many of which had recently relocated. The New England interviews concentrated on larger, regionally important manufacturers. The Fortune 500 company interviews, although restricted by definition to large companies, were scattered among all regions of the country and among broadly different industries.

In most cases, I approached the companies through their main switchboards, identifying myself, and asking to speak with a manager who was a key player in the manufacturing location decision process. In most cases, my call was transferred between two or more individuals before I was able to speak with a manager who felt qualified to talk about the location decision process in his company. As might be expected, the titles and functions of the managers I interviewed varied quite a bit. In 18 of the companies, I spoke with two or more managers. Table A-1 lists the titles of the most senior managers with whom I spoke at each company. The variety of titles indicates that these plant location decisions cut across many of the corporate functions.

For the most part, the interviews ranged in length from 1-½ to 2-½ hours. The managers with whom I spoke were assured of confidentiality and the right to review and change any paragraphs in the text of the research which mention their companies. The managers were free to discuss any aspect of industry location and, frequently, the interview followed a fairly open-ended agenda. There was a checklist, however, that I followed to assure myself that all of the major points I wanted to cover were in fact discussed. That checklist is reproduced as Table A-2.

Titles of Senior Manager Interviewed

Members of the Corporate Staff	Number Interviewed with That Title		
Title	Cincinnati	New England	Fortune 500
Chief Executive Officer	8	2	-
Vice President/Director— Corporate Real Estate	2	3	17
Vice President/Director— Corporate Planning/Development	2	2	7
Vice President/Director— Facilities Planning	1	-	6
Vice President/Director— Manufacturing	2	-	5
Vice President— Engineering	-	-	2
Vice President/Director— Industrial Engineering	-	-	2
Manager—Corporate Financial Planning/Capital Appropriations	-	-	2
Manager—Industry Economics/ Operations Analysis	-	-	2
Corporate Manufacturing Staff	-	-	2
Vice President—Human Resources	-	-	1
Vice President—Community Affairs	-	-	1
Totals	15	7	47

Members of Division Management Title			
Vice President/Director— Manufacturing	-	-	5
Director of Planning	-	-	4
General Manager	-	-	3
Plant Manager	3	-	-
Director of Plant Expansion and Special Projects	-	-	1
Totals	3	-	13
Grand Totals	18	7	60

Plant Censuses

Many of the statistics reported in this book derive from a kind of "census" performed on the manufacturing establishments of the Cincinnati area and on 410 large companies, almost all drawn from the Fortune 500 (see Appendix B). The data items investigated by these two censuses included the following:

Identification Code: Each manufacturing plant located within the Cincinnati area or associated with a major manufacturer was assigned a unique identification code.

Table A-2

Checklist of Company Interview Questions

1. <u>Decision Process</u>

Stages in Decision:

- o What initiates review of capacity needs? Formal planning process, ad hoc procedures, etc.?

- o What argues for a new plant vs. on-site expansion vs. relocation?

    - o Place of employment ceilings?
    - o Place of technological or market considerations or other?

- o Procedures for uncovering new suitable sites.

- o Evaluation of potential sites.

- o Lengths of time spent on various stages of decision.

Characters in Decision:

- o Who initiates, makes new plant vs. on-site expansion vs. relocation decision, tracks down sites and evaluates them?

- o Nature of division - corporate staff interaction.

- o Who prepares capital appropriations request?

Factors in Decision:

- o What molds or constrains decision early - and thus limits region choice, for example?

- o What affects decision later on?

- o What makes an area or town appealing?

Costs - Which higher or lower than anticipated?

II. <u>Multiplant Manufacturing Strategy</u>

- o How are plant "charters" assigned to individual plants, and why?

- o Does this have an impact on the geographic spread or clustering of plants?

244

For our purposes a plant is defined as one or more manufacturing operations (whose major Standard Industrial Classification codes to 4 digits fall between 2000 and 3999) which occupy the same plot of land. Many operations, for example in the chemicals industry, consist of several facilities scattered over large expanses of acreage. These facilities may have separate addresses, may be controlled by separate plant or division managements, and in all other ways may be strictly autonomous units, but if these facilities rest on property that is contiguous to properties of other manufacturing facilities of the company, all the facilities are treated as a single plant or "works" for the purposes of this census. Only if the plots of land on which these manufacturing operations sit are not contiguous, are separate plants identified.

Company Name: The name of the parent company.

The major manufacturers included in this study are, in all cases, listed in the 1978 Fortune 500 Directory. Companies of this group which have merged since that time (Olinkraft and Johns-Manville, Gardner-Denver and Cooper Industries, Carrier Corporation and United Technologies) are treated separately.

Division Name: The division or divisions under whose management the plant operates.

Address: Street addresses where available, post office mailing addresses otherwise.

City: Actual political jurisdiction, not merely the closest city.

Employment: Two estimates of employment are included. For the Cincinnati data, the years included are 1971 and 1975/76. For the Fortune 500 group, the employment estimates included one for a year early in the decade of the 1970s and one for a year late in the decade. To the extent possible, these employment figures reflect counts of all manufacturing personnel who worked at the plant site. Significant numbers of sales, R&D, or distribution personnel who could be identified as employed at the plant site were excluded.

Industry Classification Codes: Three different Standard Industrial Classification codes, to three digits in all cases (and to four digits in most cases) were included. The first three or four digit SIC code indicates the main manufacturing classification; the second code indicates the second most important manufacturing classification; and the third code indicates any major manufacturing that was performed in the early years of the decade which is not now being performed. Major product shifts that have sometimes been discovered are identified with this code.

Plant Status Category: Various categories that depict a plant's status during the 1970s have been established, and each census has classed them into one or the other. These categories and their descriptions follow.

Stay-Put Plant—one in existence since 1970 or before, which has remained at the same site during the time period examined. This plant may have absorbed operations from another plant or it may have spun off some operations to another, possibly new, plant.

Plant Opening—a new facility built for the company, purchased, or leased since about 1970, usually hiring new personnel and acquiring new equipment.

Acquisition—an on-going business's facility which merged with or was purchased by the corporation since about 1970, usually operated within a separate division or subsidiary.

Divestiture—the sale of the production plant of an existing business of the corporation to an outside company. The plant is expected to continue operations, as before, but under new management.

Plant Closing—the shut-down of a facility of the corporation since about 1970. The building may have been sold to another company subsequently, but the former operation is *not* continued as it was under the old management.

Mover—a plant closing since about 1970, followed by the simultaneous or near-simultaneous opening of a new plant to perform essentially the same tasks, and which often employs some of the same people and equipment.

Opened/Closed—a plant opening or acquisition during the 1970s followed by the closing or divestiture of that plant, within that decade.

Closed/Opened—A plant closing, usually the result of the 1974–5 recession, followed by its re-opening later in the decade. (Note: in the Cincinnati plant census, acquisitions, divestitures, opened/closed plants, and closed/opened plants were not distinguished separately. Acquisitions and divestitures in that census were treated as stay-put plants. The plant openings classification in the Cincinnati census also includes recently founded companies as well as new plants of existing companies. By the same token, the plant closings classification there includes companies that have gone out of business as well as facilities closed by existing companies.)

Growth/Contraction Indication: (Fortune 500 plants only) The type of growth or contraction experienced by plants during the 1970s is indicated here. The categories identified follow.

Expansion on-site—an expansion of "bricks and mortar" at a plant site since about 1970. This expansion may have included a major increase in employment as well.

Contraction on-site—space once available at a plant site is no longer used for manufacturing or has been sold, leased, or torn down. This contraction may have included a major decline in employment as well.

Employment Increase Only—an indication, separate from the employment figures themselves, of a significant increase in employment during the 1970s, without the addition of space.

Employment Decrease Only—an indication, separate from the employment figures themselves, of a significant decline in employment during the 1970s without contraction of space in use.

Former Address: For all mover plants, the former address, city, state, and zip code of the closed plant are included. In some other cases—notably acquisitions which themselves had relocated prior to being acquired—the former address is also included. Existing plants which absorbed the operations of plants subsequently closed during the 1970s may also exhibit a former address.

Conduct of the plant census

The base data for the census of manufacturing plants were purchased from the Dun and Bradstreet Corporation. Their Duns Marketing Services division offers a Duns Market Identifiers file, which lists all of the known facilities of a corporation. This list is related to and triggered by Dun and Bradstreet's credit checking operations but is not the same thing. It contains among other entries:

- name of the parent corporation
- name of the division or subsidiary
- address (street or mailing address), city (often the post office city rather than the particular political jurisdiction), state, and zip code
- estimate of employment
- Standard Industrial Classification codes—Three codes to four-digit precision
- code that indicates whether manufacturing is done on-site or not.

What makes Dun's Market Identifiers data base attractive is that it is the most comprehensive source of individual plant data that is publicly available. Presumably, the Census of Manufactures is a better source of this information, but the confidentiality restrictions of the Census Bureau prohibit its use. Moreover, the Duns Market Identifiers data enjoy some advantages over the Census of Manufactures. The Dun and Bradstreet data have an identification code that is supposed to be invariant over time, even if the plant relocates. Because these data are updated periodically, this code can serve to match up plants across years, even if they have moved from one region to another. In this way, changes in a company's plant sites over a period of time can be isolated. Not only can plants be identified that have remained at the same location, but those that have been relocated, those that have been opened or acquired (no entry in the early year but an entry in the later year), and those that may have been closed or divested (an entry in the early year but no entry in the later year) can be determined.

This advantage of the Dun and Bradstreet data was exploited for the research discussed here. For the Fortune 500 study, the Corporate Family Tree of the Duns Marketing Identifiers file for 1978 (the year the research project began) was purchased for a broad selection of large manufacturing companies. Each Corporate Family Tree was backcasted, then, to 1972. Backcasting isolated each plant that was in the 1972 data file as well as all the 1978 active plants that were in existence in 1972 although they may have belonged to a different company. These two data bases—1978 and 1972—were then sorted and matched by company and plant identification numbers. This matched data base formed the raw material for the major manufacturer plant census performed.

For the Cincinnati study, all of the manufacturers on the Duns Marketing Identifiers files for 1971 and 1976/76 were pulled out and matched. This matched data base, then, provided the raw material for the Cincinnati area plant census.

The reason that such matched data could serve only as "raw material" for these plant censuses is that the Dun and Bradstreet data were seriously flawed. The data base was not as comprehensive as would be desired for research of this type nor was the quality of the data included up to the necessary standards. The kinds of errors which existed and the relative incidence of each are listed below:

Omissions:

- Of plants which stayed put through the 1970s—15%
- Of plants opened or acquired since 1970—34%
- Of plants closed or divested since 1970—42%

Incorrect time series data:

- False openings (missed early year record)—12%
- False closings (missed late year record)—9%
- False move (incorrect match of records)—3%
- Missed move (records matched when they should not have)—2%

Factual errors in records:

- Incorrect addresses—2%
- Incorrect SIC codes—2%
- Employment errors > 300 workers—2%

Four and one-half worker years of effort were expended in correcting these data for the Fortune 500 study and one worker year of effort for the Cincinnati study. The correction effort generally followed this procedure:

(1) The matched Dun and Bradstreet listings were scanned for duplicate entries, suspicious entries (that is, alleged manufacturing at locations where this would not be expected, such as downtown addresses), potential relocations, potential plant openings or acquisitions (no early year record), and potential plant closings or divestitures (no late year record).

(2) Readily available information on the Fortune 500 companies (annual reports, Form 10-K statements to the Securities and Exchange Commission, entries in Moody's Industrial Manual, a plant directory furnished by the companies themselves) were consulted. This information corrected or supplemented the matched listings of plants. In the cases of Cincinnati area companies, the Great Cincinnati Business and Industry Directory and metropolitan area telephone directories for various years were used to correct or supplement the Dun and Bradstreet data.

(3) For the Fortune 500 companies, telephone calls were placed to corporate headquarters and/or to individual plants. All potential plant openings/acquisitions and potential relocations were telephoned as well as plants whose data entries indicated a substantial increase or decrease in employment.

In those instances on-site expansions or contractions were checked out. The telephone calls sought information as well about plants that were presumably closed or divested. Any suspicious entries were investigated and inconsistencies in data beween the Corporate Family Tree listings and published data about the company were checked. Where possible, the telephone calls confirmed the locations, product responsibilities, whether manufacturing was done on-site or not, employment in the late 1970s versus the early 1970s, and whether there had been expansion or contraction on-site during the decade.

(4) The corrected information was entered into a computer file and a copy of the file mailed out to the corporations surveyed. Typically, a vice-president for facilities, manufacturing, or public relations received the print-out of information and was asked to correct any errors. The response rate to this request was good, and a significant volume of corrections resulted from the cooperation of the companies involved.

The size of each census

The plant census of 410 major manufacturers uncovered a total of 17,759 plants, all classified according to the stay-put plant, plant opening, plant closing, and other categories described above. On average, 36.4 domestic manufacturing plants were associated with these major firms in the late 1970s versus an average of 31.2 plants early in the decade. The employment associated with these plants, as measured for late in the 1970s, totalled 7,354,040, or 37% of the manufacturing employment accounted for by the 1977 Census of Manufactures.

The census of Cincinnati area plants was intended to be a 100% sample of that area's manufacturing establishments and has been contrasted against the Census of Manufacture's 1972 results. This comparison argues persuasively that the plant census accurately portrays the pattern of industry location around Cincinnati and the change to that pattern.

Surveying particular plants

The plant census, while useful in its own right, served also as a mailing list from which the addresses of plants of various kinds could be drawn.

For the Fortune 500 company study, surveys for each of the following categories of plant were developed and sent using the plant census data:

- Existing plants that had expanded on-site
- Acquisitions that had expanded on-site
- Plant openings
- Relocations
- Plant closings

For the Cincinnati area study, all plants then open for business were sent surveys. For the New England study, companies with 20 or more employees, which were identified through the 1970 and 1976 editions of the Directory of New England Manufacturers and mostly inhabited eastern New England, were sent surveys. Table A-3 lists the particular data sought from plants of various types, and indicates which data are common to more than one survey.

Response rates for the surveys are shown in the following small table:

	Stay-Put Plants	On-Site Expansions	Plant Open- ings	Plant Closings	Relocations
Fortune 500 Study	NA	11%	10%	17%	8%
Cincinnati Area Study	28%	NA	16%	NA	30%

The response rate for the New England study's surveys is not known with any precision.

The Study Designs

The major sections of each study's design are straightforward, flowing from the perspective taken on the location decision and the data gathered. The data sources (interviews, censuses, surveys) were meant to complement one another as well as to spotlight particular aspects of the location decision process. The major uses to which each data base was put deserve separate comment which follows.

INTERVIEWS:

    (i) These provided the source for this book's comparison of management styles and techniques in dealing with so complex and multifaceted a decision. This use of the interview data demanded that a relatively large number of companies, in a wide variety of industries, be interviewed.

    (ii) They also served as a source of hypotheses to be tested by both the plant census and plant surveys and

    (iii) As a source of questions, possible responses, and organization for the plant surveys.

(iv) They further provided a rough, admittedly anecdotal, data base of their own for confirming conjectures about the organization, forces, and factors that drive the location decision process through various management levels and at different phases of time.

Table A-3

Information Sought by Surveys of Plant Expansions, Plant Openings, and Plant Relocations Since 1970

Information Sought By All Three Surveys

I. Company Identity

Person Completing Survey
Position Within Company
Company Name
Company Division(s) at Site
Address
*Chief executive officer of parent company (if applicable)
*Year of company founding
*Whether plant's founder lived in Cincinnati or New England prior to founding plant there
*How true it is that plant was located to offer the chief executive officer(s) a short commute

II. Nature of This Plant

Major product lines manufactured
Number of product lines manufactured
Products made to customer specifications?
How production is triggered (order, forecast, inventory levels)
Process type (batch, line flow, continuous flow)
How plant is controlled (profit center, cost center)
Management functions performed at the plant (e.g., industrial engineering)
Where warehousing and distribution for the plant is done
Year division first occupied plant
Area of plant site in acres
Square feet of plant
Number of manufacturing structures on-site
Type of major structure (single story, multistory)
Character of space required (e.g., special construction, almost any type of structure, etc.)
Is division sole occupant of site?
How structure and site were acquired (e.g., built, purchased, leased)
Nature of site's previous use
Room for expansion on-site? (substantial, modest, none)
Average employment over the past year (full and part-time)
Maximum employment since 1970
Predominant skill level of the workforce
Are most workers unionized?
Characterization of union attitude
Number of shifts typically run at the plant
*Plant's use of water
*Plant's use of various public utilities
*Any disappointment with present site

III. This Plant Relative to Other Company Plants (Questions in this
     section were asked only of plants in the Fortune 500 study)

Plant Charters:

The "charter" for the plant (e.g., a particular product line shipped over
  the division's entire domestic market area, a feeder plant to an
  assembly and test plant, etc.)
This plant's charter relative to others in the company
This plant's profitability/efficiency relative to others in the division

Dependence on Other Company Facilities
    Distance to division's headquarters
    This plant "spun off" from another company plant?
    How far away is that "mother" plant?
    Comparison with that "mother" or "base" plant
        What fraction of the employment
        Product line: (broader, narrower, same)
        Products: (more mature, newer, same)
        Growth: (faster, slower, same)
        Production process: (more capital intensive, more labor intensive, same)
        Production runs: (longer, shorter, same)
        Labor: (more skilled, less skilled, same)
        New product introduction: (more, less, same)
        Labor productivity: (better, worse, same)
        Labor unionization at mother plant
        Labor situation at mother plant

IV. Markets, Supplies, and Transportation

Plant's Market Area
    Within how many miles is 50% of output shipped?
    Within how many miles is 75% of output shipped?
    Any geographic shifts in the market during last decade?
    Percent of output value shipped to other company plants

(Note: In the Cincinnati and New England surveys, the market area was
 determined by asking what percentages of the plant's output was shipped
 to various areas: e.g., Midwest or New England, nationally)

Supplies
    From within how many miles are 50% of supplies shipped?
    From within how many miles are 75% of supplies shipped?
    Any geographic shifts in the supply pattern during last decade
    Percent of supplies value shipped to other company plants
  **Percent of supplies classed as subassemblies? As really "raw" materials?

(Note: In the Cincinnati and New England surveys, the area from which
 supplies were drawn was determined by asking what percentages of the
 plant's supplies were shipped from various geographic areas)

Rail use: Siding? Percent of output shipped by rail? Percent of supplies
  received by rail?
Important transport modes other than truck
Relative importance of transportation costs

V. Changes Since 1970

Average growth rate in value of output over the past decade
Pattern of trend: (e.g., cyclical, seasonal, erratic, steady)
Nature of product change: (e.g., technological innovation, different
    product mix, increasing product standardization or customization,
    no change, etc.)
Breadth of product line: (broader now, narrower now, little change)
Change in production technology: (e.g., increased capital investment,
    equipment more sophisticated, more rigid process flow, less rigid
    process flow)
Change in vertical integration: (more integration, less integration, same)
**Labor changes at the plant
    Absenteeism: (higher, lower, same)
    Worker turnover: (higher, lower, same)
    Labor availability: (better, higher, same)
    Union attitudes: (e.g., more constructive, more militant, same)
    Weeks lost to work stoppages since 1970
Cost changes since 1970, as a percent of sales
    Direct labor costs plus fringes (higher, lower, same)
    Materials costs (higher, lower, same)
    Transport costs (higher, lower, same)
    **Overhead costs (higher, lower, same)
    Profit (higher, lower, same)

VI. Some Statistics

Approximate sales from this plant
Wage and salary costs plus fringes as a percent of sales
Materials costs as a percent of sales
Value of land and structures if owner (in $), if renter (in $/sq.ft.)
Value of equipment and inventories

Information Sought Only for Plant Expansion on Site Since 1970

VII. Plant Capacity Considerations

Years in past decade when plant was expanded
Total square feet added
Operations this plant absorbed from other plants
Operations this plant spun off to new plants
As an alternative to on-site expansion, did company consider opening a new
    branch plant or relocating this plant?
**What factors argued most persuasively for on-site expansion?
**What problems at the plant did on-site expansion cause or aggravate?

Information Sought Only for Plant Openings Since 1970

VII. Capacity and Location Consideration for This Plant

Has plant expanded since it was first occupied?
When was the expansion?
Total square feet added
**Since its opening, has plant absorbed operations which were then closed or sold?
**As an alternative to opening, did company seriously consider expanding
   on-site elsewhere?
As alternative to opening, did company seriously consider relocating
   another plant?
**What factors argued most persuasively for opening a new plant?
**What states were seriously considered for this plant's location?
**What factors were perceived as "musts" in selection of region and state?
   Of site itself?
**What factors were perceived as "desirable, if available" and helped to
   tip scales in favor of this site?
**Means by which labor climate was assessed
How town was first identified as possible site
State/local government aid taken advantage of (e.g., industrial revenue bonds;
   help with environmental permits; tax concessions; new roads, sewerage
   treatment, etc.; zoning changes; training programs)
**Relative to expectations, how plant fared on: Costs of construction/staffing,
   speed of construction/staffing, government regulatory delay, speed/
   effectiveness of start-up, labor costs, labor productivity, absenteeism/
   turnover/attitudes
Who first proposed a new plant? Division or corporate management
**Was joint division/corporate staff team formed?
**Who lead site selection process? Division or corporate management
How many months was need for new plant debated?
How long did site search take?
Once site selected, how long was start-up for plant?
*How many managers became involved in the decision to locate?
   In planning the start-up?
*Over how large an area was the search conducted? (locally, state, etc.)
*How many sites were considered?
*Were these sites explicitly costed out?
*How did sites get identified?
*What kinds of outside consultation were engaged in for the search itself?
*How is investment financed?
*Characterize dealings with state and local officials
*How did transition to new site occur? (e.g., warehousing first)

Information Sought Only for Plant Relocations Since 1970

VII. Plant Capacity and Relocation Considerations

Has plant been expanded since it was first occupied?
When was the expansion?
Total square feet added
Since its opening, has plant absorbed operations which were then closed
    or sold?
**As alternative to relocating, did company seriously consider expanding at
    plant's former location?
As alternative to relocating, did company seriously consider expanding
    on-site at another location?
As alternative to relocating, did company seriously consider opening this
    plant while maintaining operations at this plant's former location?
How many operations at former plant sites were consolidated into this
    new location?
**What factors argued most persuasively for relocating this plant?
**What states were seriously considered for this plant's location?
**What factors were perceived as "musts" in selection of region and
    state? Of site itself?
**What factors were perceived as "desirable, if available" and helped tip
    scales in favor of this site?
**Means by which labor climate was assessed
How town was first identified as possible site
State/local government aid taken advantage of
**Relative to expectations, how plant fared on: costs of construction/staffing,
    speed of construction/staffing, government regulatory delay, speed/
    effectiveness of start-up, labor costs, labor productivity, absenteeism/
    turnover/attitudes, transportation costs, attractiveness to manager/engineers

Based solely on the change of location and not on time, what qualitative
    differences exist, if any, between the plant's new site and its
    former one along these categories:

        Breadth of product line
        Production technology
        Scope of functions and responsibilities
        Wage rate
      **Labor productivity
        Labor/union attitudes
        Labor availability
        Labor unionization
        Energy availability/rates
        Same suppliers?
        Same customers?
        Loading dock operations
        Expressway access
        Railroad service
        Rent or property value per square foot
        Government attitude toward industry
        Location in industrial park
        Property tax rates
        Income tax rates
        Unemployment, workmen's compensation rates

Distance between new plant location and former one
Area of former plant site
Square footage of former plant site
Employment prior to relocation
Condition of former plant
Was former plant in multistory facility?
How former plant was acquired
Had company division been sole occupant of former site?
**Who occupies former plant now?
Who first proposed the relocation? Division or corporate management?
Was joint division/corporate staff team formed?
Who led site selection process? Division or corporate management?
How many months was need for plant relocation debated?
How long did site search take?
Once site selected, how long was start-up for plant?
*How many shifts were run before move?
*Rent or land and structure value prior to move
*Percent of labor force that moved along with plant
*Impact of crime (vandalism) on decision to move
*If relocation was forced, to what was it due? (e.g., highway construction)
*How many managers become involved in the decision to locate? In planning
the start-up?
*Over how large an area was the search conducted? (locally, state, etc.)
*How many sites were considered?
*Were these sites explicitly costed out?
*How did sites get identified?
*What kinds of outside consultation were engaged in for the search itself?
*How was investment financed?
*Characterize dealings with state and local officials
*How did transition to new site occur? (e.g., warehousing first)

NOTES:

*Was asked in the Cincinnati/New England questionnaires but not in the Fortune
500 questionnaires
**Was asked in the Fortune 500 questionnaires but not in the Cincinnati/New
England questionnaires

PLANT CENSUS:

(i) This documented the location/capacity changes of major US manufacturers nationally during the 1970s as well as the location/capacity changes
in the Cincinnati metropolitan area in the early 1970s. While not as
widely drawn a sample as the total sample represented by the Census of
Manufactures, these data bases have some distinct built-in advantages:

(a) These have enabled us to separate an area's employment (and plant)
gains or losses into component parts. The plant "census" data have
indicated how much of an area's employment growth is due to existing plant expansion, how much to new plants opening and their
prevalence over plant closings, and how much to relocations from
elsewhere. This is not possible with Census Bureau data.

(b) The census enabled us to investigate the degree of stability or turmoil
in the location decisions of various industries. Which industries are
locating many new plants, closing many, acquiring or divesting many
existing operations, or doing little or nothing about new plant construction? This, too, is not possible with Census Bureau data.

(c) It focused attention on trends in plant size, plant expansion/
contraction, and plant clustering around division headquarters, and

(d) enabled us to trace trends pertaining to central cities, suburbs, and
rural areas separately.

(ii) The plant census served as the mailing list for the surveys as well as a
test for possible biases in the survey returns.

PLANT SURVEYS:

(i) These provided much of the statistical confirmation of the character of
different types of plants (for example, on-site expansion versus plant opening or
relocation) and of plants situated in different places (Sunbelt versus Frostbelt).

(ii) They also provided much of the statistical confirmation of the factors
that shaped the location decisions of companies, including those internal to the
firm and those external to it, such as public policy measures.

(iii) The surveys confirmed some of the time pattern and management organization employed for the decision process suggested by the interview data.

This report is an investigation in depth into the content of these data
bases amplified by the actual criteria and procedures of some of the nation's
top manufacturing managers and what they have to say about their location
decisions as these concern both U.S. business and public policy.

Appendix B:
the 410 companies
comprising this study's
major manufacturer plant census

ABBOTT LABORATORIES
AFC INDUSTRIES
AGWAY
ALLIED CHEMICAL
ALLIS-CHALMERS
ALCOA
AMAX
AMERADA HESS
AMERICAN BAKERIES
AMERICAN BRANDS
AMERICAN CAN
AMERICAN CYANAMID
AMERICAN GREETINGS
AMERICAN HOIST
AMERICAN HOME PDTS
AMERICAN HOSPITAL SUPPLY
AMERICAN MOTORS
AMERICAN PETROFINA
AMERICAN STANDARD
AT&T
AMF
AMPEX
AMSTAR
AMSTED INDUSTRIES
AMTEL
ANCHOR HOCKING
ANDERSON CLAYTON

ANHEUSER-BUSCH
ARCATA
ARCHER DANIELS MIDLAND
ARMCO
ARMSTRONG CORK
ARMSTRONG RUBBER
ASARCO
ASHLAND OIL
ASSOCIATED MILK PRODUCERS
ATLANTIC RICHFIELD
AVERY INTERNATIONAL
AVNET
AVON PRODUCTS
BABCOCK & WILCOX
BAKER INTERNATIONAL
BALL
BANGOR PUNTA
BAUSCH & LOMB
BAXTER TRAVENOL
BEATRICE FOODS
BECTON DICKINSON
BEECH AIRCRAFT
BEMIS
BENDIX
BETHLEHEM STEEL
BLACK & DECKER
BLUE BELL

BOEING
BOISE CASCADE
BORDEN
BORG-WARNER
BRISTOL-MYERS
BROCKWAY GLASS
BROWN GROUP
BROWN & WILLIAMSON
BUCYRUS-ERIE
BUDD
BURLINGTON INDUSTRIES
BURROUGHS
BUTLER
C F INDUSTRIES
CABOT
CAMERON IRON WORKS
CAMPBELL SOUP
CAMPBELL TAGGART
CANNON MILLS
CARNATION
CARRIER
CASTLE & COOKE
CATERPILLAR TRACTOR
CELANESE
CENTRAL SOYA
CESSNA AIRCRAFT
CHAMPION INTERNATIONAL
CHAMPION SPARK PLUG
CHARTER
CHESEBROUGH-PONDS
CHICAGO BRIDGE & IRON
CHROMALLOY AMERICAN
CHRYSLER
CIBA-GEIGY
CINCINNATI MILACRON
CITIES SERVICE
CLARK EQUIPMENT
CLARK OIL & REFINING
CLOROX
COCA-COLA
COLGATE-PALMOLIVE
COLLINS & AIKMAN
COLT INDUSTRIES
COMBUSTION ENGINEERING
CONE MILLS
CONGOLEUM
CONSOLIDATED ALUMINUM
CONSOLIDATED FOODS

CONTINENTAL GROUP
CONTINENTAL OIL
COOPER INDUSTRIES
ADOLPH COORS
CORNING GLASS WORKS
CPC INTERNATIONAL
CRANE
CROWN CENTRAL PETROLEUM
CROWN CORK & SEAL
CROWN ZELLERBACH
CUMMINS ENGINE
CYCLOPS
DAIRYLEA COOPERATIVE
DAN RIVER
DART INDUSTRIES
JOHN DEERE
DEL MONTE
DENNISON
DIAMOND INTERNATIONAL
DIAMOND SHAMROCK
DIGITAL EQUIPMENT
RR DONNELLEY & SONS
DOW CHEMICAL
DOW-CORNING CORPORATION
DRESSER INDUSTRIES
DUPONT
EASTERN ASSOC. COAL
EASTMAN KODAK
EATON
EG&G
EMHART
ESMARK
EVANS PRODUCTS
EXXON
FAIRCHILD INDUSTRIES
FAIRMONT FOODS
FARMLAND INDUSTRIES
THE FEDERAL COMPANY
FEDERAL PAPER BOARD
FERRO
FIELDCRESTS MILLS
FIRESTONE TIRE & RUBBER
FLINTKOTE
FORD MOTOR
FOSTER WHEELER
FOXBORO
FRUEHAUF
GANNETT

GARDNER-DENVER
GATES RUBBER
GATX
GK TECHNOLOGIES
GENERAL DYNAMICS
GENERAL ELECTRIC
GENERAL FOODS
GENERAL HOST
GENERAL MILLS
GENERAL MOTORS
GENERAL SIGNAL
GTE
GEORGIA-PACIFIC
GERBER PRODUCTS
GETTY OIL
GILLETTE
GLOBE-UNION
GOODYEAR TIRE & RUBBER
GOULD
WR GRACE
GREAT NORTHERN NEKOOSA
GREAT WESTERN UNITED
GREEN GIANT
GREYHOUND
GULF & WESTERN
GULF OIL
HALLMARK CARDS
HAMMERMILL PAPER
HANDY & HARMAN
HARCOURT BRACE JOVANOVICH
HARNISCHFEGER
HARRIS
HJ HEINZ
HERCULES
HEUBLEIN
HEWLETT-PACKARD
HOBART CORPORATION
HONEYWELL
HOOD
HOOVER UNIVERSAL
GEO A HORMEL
HOUDAILLE INDUSTRIES
HOWARD D JOHNSON
HUGHES TOOL
HYSTER
IC INDUSTRIES
IDLE WILD FOODS
INDIAN HEAD

INGERSOLL-RAND
INLAND CONTAINER
INLAND STEEL
INSILCO
INTERLAKE
IBM
INTERNATIONAL HARVESTER
IMC
INTERNATIONAL MULTIFOODS
INTERNATIONAL PAPER
ITT
INTERPACE
IOWA BEEF PROCESSORS
JOHNS-MANVILLE
JOHNSON & JOHNSON
JOHNSON CONTROLS
JOY
KAISER STEEL
KELLOGG
KENNECOTT
KERR-MCGEE
WALTER KIDDE
KIMBERLY-CLARK
KOEHRING
KRAFT
LAND O'LAKES
LEVER BROTHERS
LIGGETT GROUP
ELI LILLY
THOMAS J. LIPTON
LITTON INDUSTRIES
LOCKHEED
LOEWS
LONE STAR INDUSTRIES
M LOWENSTEIN & SONS
LTV
LUBRIZOL
LYKES
MACMILLAN
P.R. MALLORY
MARATHON OIL
MARTIN MARIETTA
MARYLAND CUP
MASONITE
MATTEL
OSCAR MAYER
MCCORMICK
MCDONNELL DOUGLAS

MCLOUTH STEEL
MEAD
MELVILLE
MEMOREX
MERCK
MILES LABORATORIES
MINNESOTA MINING AND
  MANUFACTURING
MOBIL OIL
MONFORT
MORTON-NORWICH
MOTOROLA
MURPHY OIL
NABISCO
NALCO CHEMICAL
NASHUA
NATIONAL CAN
NATIONAL DISTILLERS &
  CHEMICAL
NATIONAL SEMICONDUCTOR
NATIONAL STARCH &
  CHEMICAL
NATIONAL STEEL
NCR
NEW YORK TIMES
NEWMONT MINING
N L INDUSTRIES
NORTHROP
NORTHWEST INDUSTRIES
NORTON
NORTON SIMON
NVF
OCCIDENTAL PETROL
OLIN
OLINKRAFT
OUTBOARD MARINE
OWENS-CORNING FIBERGLAS
OWENS-ILLINOIS
OXFORD INDUSTRIES
PACCAR
PACIFIC RESOURCES
PEABODY INTERNATIONAL
PENNZOIL
PEPSICO
PERKIN ELMER
PET
PFIZER
PHELPS DODGE

PHILIP MORRIS
PHILLIPS PETROLEUM
PILLSBURY
PITNEY-BOWES
POLAROID
HK PORTER
POTLATCH
PPG INDUSTRIES
PROCTER & GAMBLE
PULLMAN
PUROLATOR
QUAKER OATS
QUAKER STATE
QUESTOR
RALSTON PURINA
RATH PACKING
RAYTHEON
RCA
REICHHOLD CHEMICALS
RELIANCE ELECTRIC
REPUBLIC STEEL
REVERE COPPER & BRASS
REVLON
REYNOLDS METALS
REYNOLDS INDUSTRIES
RICHARDSON-MERRELL
ROCKWELL INTERNATIONAL
ROHM & HAAS
ROPER
SAFEWAY
SAXON INDUSTRIES
SCHERING PLOUGH
JOS. SCHLITZ BREWING
SCM CORP
SCOTT & FETZER
SCOTT PAPER
SCOVILL MFG
JOSEPH E. SEAGRAM
G.D. SEARLE
SHELL OIL
SHELLER-GLOBE
SHERWIN-WILLIAMS
SIGNAL
SIGNODE
SIMMONS
SINGER
SMITHKLINE
SOUTHWEST FOREST INDUSTRIES

SPERRY & HUTCHINSON
SPERRY RAND
SQUARE D
SQUIBB
ST JOE MINERALS
AE STANLEY
STANDARD BRANDS
STANDARD OIL OF CALIFORNIA
STANDARD OIL OF INDIANA
STANDARD OIL OF OHIO
STANLEY WORKS
STAUFFER CHEMICAL
STERLING DRUG
STOKELY-VAN CAMP
LEVI STRAUSS
STUDEBAKER WORTHINGTON
SUN
SUNBEAM
SUNDSTRAND
SYBRON
TALLEY INDUSTRIES
TECUMSEH
TEKTRONIX
TELEDYNE
TENNECO
TESORO PETROLEUM
TEXACO
TEXAS INSTRUMENTS
TEXASGULF
TEXTRON
THIOKOL
TIMKEN
TOSCO
TRANE
TRW

TYLER
UNION CAMP
UNION CARBIDE
UNION OIL OF CALIFORNIA
UNIROYAL
UNITED BRANDS
UNITED MERCHANTS &
  MANUFACTURERS
U S FILTER
UNITED STATES STEEL
UNITED TECHNOLOGIES
UPJOHN
UV INDUSTRIES
VARIAN ASSOCIATES
WALLACE-MURRAY
JIM WALTER
WARD FOODS
WARNACO
WARNER COMMUNICATIONS
WARNER LAMBERT
WESTINGHOUSE ELECTRIC
WESTMORELAND COAL
WESTVACO
WEYERHAEUSER
WHEELABRATOR-FRYE
WHEELING-PITTSBURGH
WHIRLPOOL
WHITE CONSOLIDATED
WHITE MOTOR
WHITTAKER
WILLAMETTE INDUSTRIES
WILLIAMS COMPANIES
WITCO CHEMICAL
XEROX
ZENITH

Selected Bibliography

BIRCH, David L., "The Job Generation Process", MIT Program on Neighborhood and Regional Change, 1979.

BROWNING, Jon E., *How to Select a Business Site* (New York: McGraw-Hill), 1980, 225 pages.

CAMERON, Helen A., "Property Taxation as a Location Factor", *Bulletin of Business Research,* Ohio State University, April 1969.

CARLTON, Dennis W., "Models of New Business Location", Report 7756 (November 1977) of the Center for Mathematical Studies in Business and Economics, University of Chicago, 48 pages.

——, "Why New Firms Located Where They Do: An Econometric Model", Working Paper 1978, Department of Economics, University of Chicago, 45 pages.

COLLINS, Lyndhurst and David F. WALKER, (eds.), *Locational Dynamics of Manufacturing Activity* (John Wiley and Sons; London), 1975, 402 pages.

DUE, John F., "Studies of State-Local Tax Influences on Location of Industry", *National Tax Journal*, XIV, no. 2, 1961, pp. 163–173.

EICHNER, Alfred S., *State Development Agencies and Employment Expansion,* Institute of Labor and Industrial Relations, The University of Michigan–Wayne State University, 1970.

FAGG, J. J., "A Re-examination of the Incubator Hypothesis: A Case Study of Greater Leicester", Urban Studies, vol. 17, no. 1 (February 1980), pp. 35–44.

The Fantus Company, Inc., "Industrial Location: Processes, Factors, Trends", Presentation at The White House, April 8, 1980.

GENETSKI, Robert J. and Young D. CHIN, "The Impact of State and Local Taxes on Economic Growth", Harris Economic Research Office Service, November 1978.

GRIESON, Ronald E., et al., "The Effect of Business Taxation on the Location of Industry", Journal of Urban Economics 4, no. (April, 1977), pp. 170–85.

GUDGIN, Graham, *Industrial Location Processes and Regional Employment Growth*, (Saxon House, Tekfield, Ltd.; Farnborough, England), 1979, 344 pages.

HAMER, Andrew, *Industrial Exodus from Central City*, (Lexington Books, D.C. Heath; Lexington, MA), 1973, 107 pages.

HAMILTON, F. E. Ian, *Spatial Perspectives on Industrial Organization and Decision-Making*, (John Wiley and Sons; London), 1974, 533 pages.

HAMILTON, F. E. Ian and G. J. R. LINGE, (eds.), *Spatial Analysis, Industry and the Industrial Environment, Vol. 1 Industrial Systems*, (John Wiley and Sons, Chichester, UK), 1979, 289 pages.

HEKMAN, John, "The Product Cycle and New England Textiles" *Quarterly Journal of Economics*, June 1980, pp. 697–717.

—, "What Attracts Industry to New England?", Working Paper, July 1978 (Boston College), 8 pages.

HUNKER, Henry L., *Industrial Development*, (Lexington Books, D. C. Heath; Lexington, MA), 1974, 322 pages.

JACOBS, Jerry, "Bidding for Business", Public Interest Research Group, Washington, August 1979.

KEEBLE, David, *Industrial Location and Planning in the United Kingdom* (Methuen, London, UK), 1976, 317 pages.

LEONE, Robert A., *Location of Economic Activity in the New York Metropolitan Area*, unpublished Ph.D. dissertation, Yale University, 1971, 232 pages.

LEONE, Robert A. and Raymond J. STRUYK, "The Incubator Hypothesis: Evidence from Five SMS's", *Urban Studies*, vol. 13, no. 3 (October 1976), pp. 325–331.

MANDELL, Lewis, *Industrial Location Decision: Detroit Compared with Atlanta and Chicago* (New York: Praeger, 1975).

McMILLAN, T. E., Jr., "Why Manufacturers Chose Plant Locations vs. Determinants of Plant Locations", *Land Economics*, 1965, pp. 239–246.

MILLER, E. Willard, *Manufacturing: A Study of Industrial Location*, (Pennsylvania State University Press: University Park, PA), 1977, 286 pages.

MUELLER, Eva and James M. MORGEN, "Location Decisions of Manufacturers", *American Economic Review*, May 1962, pp. 204–217.

SANT, Morgan, *Industrial Movement and Regional Development: The British Case*, (Pergamon Press; Oxford, England), 1975, 253 pages.

SCHERER, F. M., et al., *The Economics of Multiplant Operations*, (Cambridge, MA: Harvard University Press), 1975, 448 pages.

SCHMENNER, Roger W., "The Manufacturing Location Decision: Evidence from Cincinnati and New England", Report of the Office of Economic Research, Economic Development Administration, U. S. Department of Commerce, March 1978, 394 pages.

—, "The Location Decisions of Large Multiplant Companies", Report to U. S. Department of Housing and Urban Development, September 1980, 368 pages.

Site Selection Handbook and *Industrial Development Magazine*, Conway Publications, 1954 Airport Road, Peachtree Air Terminal, Atlanta, GA 30341

STRASMA, J. D., *State and Location Taxation of Industry* (Boston: Federal Reserve Bank of Boston, 1959).

STRUYK, Raymond J. and Franklin J. JAMES, *Intrametropolitan Industrial Location*, (Lexington Books, D. C. Heath; Lexington, MA), 1975, 190 pages.

THOMPSON, Wilbur and John MATTILA, *An Econometric Model of Postwar State Industrial Development* (Detroit: Wayne State University Press, 1959).

THOMSON, Ralph J., "An Examination of the Location Factors Governing Corporate Choice of New Industrial Sites", Control Data Corporation, January 1980.

TOWNROE, Peter M., *Industrial Location Decisions: A Study in Management Behavior*, Occasional Paper No. 15, Centre for Urban and Regional Studies, University of Birmingham (England), 1971, 128 pages.

—, *Planning Industrial Location* (London: Leonard Hill Books), 1976, 216 pages.

—, *Industrial Movement* (Farnborough, England: Saxon House), 1979, 250 pages.

VAUGHAN, Roger J., *The Urban Impacts of Federal Policies; Vol. 2,* Economic Development, (Rand Corporation; Santa Monica, CA), R-2028-KF/RC, June 1977, 159 pages.

Index